Praise for *RISK*

"Author Susan Norman offers readers ⟶ ⟶ ⟶ ows with the same intensity and grace as the rivers she once conquered professionally. The memoir is filled with sharp insights into her personal strength and vulnerability that readers from all backgrounds will appreciate. . . . Her descriptions bring the adrenaline rush of whitewater racing and the delicate moments of parenting to life with remarkable clarity. . . . Her treatment of her child is particularly moving, revealing both her struggles and triumphs with a raw authenticity that is sure to touch readers' hearts."

—*Readers' Favorite*, 5-star review

"Norman parallels the risks and rewards of parenting with her passion for whitewater paddling in this insightful debut. . . . The book's honesty is endearing and relatable, and readers from any background will connect with Norman's moments of doubt. . . . Insightful memoir of parenting, sacrifice, and giving yourself grace."

—BookLife Reviews, Editor's Pick

"Norman's muscular prose confidently pulls the reader through the author's voyage of self-discovery. . . . Vulnerable and often wise, this is a truly memorable parenting story. A fascinating and heartfelt chronicle of athleticism and family."

—*Kirkus Reviews*

"*Risk* explores the surprising lessons learned during Susan Norman's most challenging ventures: navigating dangerous currents as a competitive whitewater rafter and traveling an unconventional path to motherhood. Candid and compelling, *Risk* illustrates the beauty and power that can be found in embracing the unexpected."

—JEN BRYANT, Editor, *MUTHA Magazine*

"In this deeply thoughtful, often funny, and resonant memoir, Norman deftly explores not just the landscapes and adventures that made her who she is, but also the terrain of the human heart."

—CAROLINE PAUL, *New York Times* best-selling author of *Gutsy Girl* and *Tough Broad*

RISK

RISK

A Memoir of
a Life Saved
by the River

SUSAN NORMAN

SHE WRITES PRESS

Copyright © 2025, Susan Norman

All rights reserved. No part of this publication may be reproduced, distributed, or transmitted in any form or by any means, including photocopying, recording, digital scanning, or other electronic or mechanical methods, without the prior written permission of the publisher, except in the case of brief quotations embodied in critical reviews and certain other noncommercial uses permitted by copyright law. For permission requests, please address She Writes Press.

Published 2025

Printed in the United States of America

Print ISBN: 978-1-64742-924-9
E-ISBN: 978-1-64742-925-6
Library of Congress Control Number: 2025900948

For information, address:
She Writes Press
1569 Solano Ave #546
Berkeley, CA 94707

Interior design and typeset by Katherine Lloyd, The DESK

She Writes Press is a division of SparkPoint Studio, LLC.

Company and/or product names that are trade names, logos, trademarks, and/or registered trademarks of third parties are the property of their respective owners and are used in this book for purposes of identification and information only under the Fair Use Doctrine.

NO AI TRAINING: Without in any way limiting the author's [and publisher's] exclusive rights under copyright, any use of this publication to "train" generative artificial intelligence (AI) technologies to generate text is expressly prohibited. The author reserves all rights to license uses of this work for generative AI training and development of machine learning language models.

Names and identifying characteristics have been changed to protect the privacy of certain individuals.

This memoir is dedicated to
my mother, Bette Norman;
my river sister, Kelley Kalafatich;
my father, Dean Norman;
and my son, Seth.

"Joy is the holy fire that keeps our purpose warm and our intelligence aglow. Resolve to keep happy, and your joy and you shall form an invincible host against difficulty."

—Helen Keller

Contents

1 Seth 1
2 The Great Missouri River Wreck 11
3 Pot Candy 24
4 Whitewater Pioneers 33
5 A Quality Partner 55
6 Living Alone 62
7 Class V Therapy 68
8 Paddling through Puberty 78
9 Motherhood after Menopause 87
10 Passion 98
11 The Abduction 110
12 You're in the Army Now 117
13 Day in Court 132
14 What It Takes to Be a Champion 137
15 The Aging Athlete 155
16 Dirtbag 164
17 Isolation 176
18 Risk 183
19 Broken 197
20 US Women's Whitewater Team 206

21	Finding the Gifts	221
22	Strength through Vulnerability	231
23	Building Resiliency	242
24	Fragility	253
25	Bad Risk and Good Risk	265
	Epilogue	273

Helpful Resources 277

Acknowledgements 279

Author Biography 281

Chapter 1
Seth (2014)

The blue line on the MapQuest app indicates my destination is the squat, dark building coming up on the left. I squint at the phone again to make sure. It seems an unlikely edifice for the Paradise Preschool. Tiny windows located high on one side of the building are covered in black metal bars. There are no windows on the sooty red brick wall facing the road. However, a small sign with whimsical lettering in bright primary colors confirms this is indeed the place.

I pull into the parking lot, next to which sits a basketball court–size compound enclosed in a chain-link fence with a locked gate. Inside the compound, a toddler playground set constructed of green, blue, red, and yellow plastic sits on the hot black asphalt, next to a square of artificial turf.

Apparently, this is the exercise yard.

I park and make my way to the front entrance. A sign on the solid steel door instructs me to press the button on the adjacent intercom to seek entry. I wonder, perhaps unfairly, just how many pervs reside in the surrounding seedy neighborhood. Is the prison-like security to keep the little animals in or the big animals out? Maybe both.

Feeling like I'm on a first date, I nervously push the button.

RISK

I flew to Cleveland from my home in Lake Tahoe, California, yesterday. In my suitcase, I brought with me a one-way ticket for my four-year-old nephew to fly back with me in six days.

This is day one of less than one full week of me getting to know Seth before whisking him away from everything he has known in his short life.

A cheerful, plump Black woman brings Seth up out of the clamoring horde of toddlers inside, the only white face among dozens of children.

He looks so unhealthy compared to his schoolmates. His light brown hair is greasy and unkempt. His pasty complexion only highlights the purplish-blue shadows under his eyes. Bright pink welts splotch his face, neck, and arms.

My brother, David, warned me about the welts. Bed bugs.

I quickly sign the check-out sheet and crouch down to meet Seth at eye level.

"Hey buddy, are you ready to go have some fun today?"

With wide, solemn eyes, he slowly nods his head. Is he scared? From our brief encounter yesterday evening, I know he does not remember me from previous visits. But when I reach out my hand, he slips his impossibly tiny fingers into mine.

"So, buddy, here is our plan. The first thing we're going to do is go to Grandpa's house to get a bath and breakfast. They will have a lot of yummy things to choose from, so I hope you are hungry. After that, you and I are going to a really fun playground by the lake for a couple of hours. Then we're going to come back to Grandpa's house for lunch."

I glance in the rearview mirror to see if Seth is expressing any reaction. He is still looking out the window with his wide-eyed stare. I keep talking.

"Now, after lunch, we'll go to the park to take Sasha for a walk with Grandpa and Grandma. Sasha's a cool dog, don't you think?

Seth (2014)

It's going to be fun to play with her. Then later, your dad will come over to Grandpa's, and we're all going to have dinner together. After dinner, your dad will take you home, and tomorrow I will pick you up at the preschool again so we can have more fun!"

Again, I look in the mirror. This time I catch Seth staring back. He's still not smiling, but he doesn't seem upset. I take that as a positive sign.

For the rest of the fifteen-minute trip to my dad's house, I talk about things I see on the drive: a pretty tree in bloom, a cool-looking car, a cat scurrying across the road. I hope it is comforting in some way to hear me prattling on about innocuous things. That I'm assuring him, on a gut level at least, he is safe with this total stranger he is stuck with for the day.

After a brief greeting to Dad and his wife, Maureen, I lead Seth straight to the bathroom. Once the tub is full, I have him strip out of his clothes and shoes, which I secure tightly in a garbage bag Maureen surreptitiously slipped to me in the hallway.

"Go ahead and get in," I tell him, ushering him into the warm water, and handing him the ducky and shark bathtub toys Maureen has thoughtfully provided. "I'll be right back."

As quickly as I can, I carry the bag outside. I bring it all the way to the far end of the driveway, far enough away, I hope, to deter any errant bed bugs from making a run for Dad's house—just one of the many fears I have about the next few days—and then return inside.

Back in the bathroom, I help Seth wash his hair. The dime-size pink welts are everywhere. Not a single part of his body has been spared. I make a note to myself to buy aloe vera gel.

After the bath, I help him get dressed in the clothes Maureen purchased for him last week. The new wardrobe is part of our prearranged plan to ward off infestation.

Silently but willingly, Seth follows me everywhere for the rest of the day. He plays, he runs, he eats like a horse. He is curious and engaged. At the playground, he actively seeks out other kids to play with. He just doesn't talk.

Today, day two, we go through a similar routine, except I start telling Seth how exciting it will be to leave for California at the end of the week. This is not a surprise to him. Ever since David and I made this plan about four months ago, he's been talking to Seth about their move to California and all the wonderful things that are going to happen there.

Seth knows he's going to California with his dad's sister on an airplane, and then his dad will drive out in his car to join us. The extended details around those two facts are not yet clear to me, so I do not try to elaborate. When exactly will David get to California? How long will he and Seth live with me? Where will they eventually end up?

Who knows? We are all stepping into the void.

Before Seth entered my life, I had enjoyed a prolonged period of comfortable stability. I was proud of the fact I was a self-made woman who'd successfully taken on all major life hurdles. I had overcome my own broken childhood and poverty to obtain an advanced degree, leading to a rewarding career and financial stability. I was in a relationship with a compatible life partner, Lisa. With the defeat of the Defense of Marriage Act (DOMA) in the Supreme Court, we'd even been able to get married, making it possible for me to add Lisa to my sweet federal employee health insurance plan. I owned a home, almost paid off, in the outdoor wonderland of Lake Tahoe.

My leisure time was filled with adult cultural and outdoor adventures in both my beautiful backyard and exotic locations around the world. When catastrophic events had happened to some of those I was close to, I'd had the emotional strength and capacity to provide support rather than shy away from my friends' hard times.

Seth (2014)

I had foolishly lulled myself into believing that whatever future difficulties fate might throw my way, my accumulated skill set and accomplishments had created a solid foundation for navigating all challenges.

And then Seth happened.

It began before he was even born. I was on one of my typical water sport–based outdoor escapes—in this case, an outrigger canoe training camp in Hawaii with a dozen other friends from our club in Lake Tahoe. We'd planned this spring getaway to jump-start our paddling season, which was too cold to enjoy for another month or two in our High Sierra mountain town.

One evening, after enjoying a post-workout feast of fresh fish tacos, sweet papayas with lime, and potent margaritas, I was annoyed to see my brother's name pop up on my cell phone. David typically only called when he needed money, and I had recently decided I'd reached my limit in providing financial support; in fact, I'd intended to send him a letter after this trip explaining my tough-love decision.

I decided to take the call. I got up from the lanai and moved into the house, preparing myself to be vague in response to whatever financial crisis he was currently in and defer follow-up until I had time to prepare my sibling version of a "Dear John" letter.

"Hey David, what's up?" I asked, bracing myself.

"Well, I have some great news," he announced cheerfully. "I'm going to be a daddy!"

This concept did not immediately penetrate my brain. For a variety of reasons, my fifty-two-year-old twin brother had never been in a romantic relationship for more than a few short periods in his life. But here he was on the phone, with a twenty-year-old woman named Gesicyah, both of them giddily exclaiming how excited they were to have found each other and to be producing progeny together.

Somehow, I verbalized tepid responses of congratulations and fake joy at their news. On the inside, my brain screamed: *This must be a mistake—dear God, let it be a mistake!*

After the paternity test (which I paid for) provided proof that David was indeed the father, I knew I would no longer be able to send him that "Dear John" letter.

I was about to be an aunt; my allegiance now belonged to my unborn niece or nephew.

I made my first visit to Cleveland to meet Seth when he was about fourteen months old. When I first laid eyes on him, I immediately and viscerally fell head over heels in love. When he sat on my lap for the first time, a warm, aching glow emanated from my chest and spread throughout my body. I struggled to hold back tears. I stared at his face, in awe of this perfection created by two exceedingly imperfect people. His wide-set, almond-shaped brown eyes were framed with lush black lashes. His features were delicate and perfectly proportioned in the smooth, symmetrical oval of his face, which created an aura of impossible innocence.

Before this moment, I had never found children to be particularly cute or engaging and had experienced nary a twinge of maternal instincts. With Seth, I certainly could not have experienced the complex chemical stimuli new mothers are flooded with after childbirth, which biologically predispose most women to form an intense bond with their newborns. So how to explain the feelings that this little human produced in me?

Maureen thinks the phenomenon I experienced could be explained by subliminal primal recognition. Seth looked a lot like David, my twin, did when he was little. Twins begin bonding while they are still in the womb. Although I no longer felt close to my brother in many ways, it did not change the powerful attachment we'd had when we were toddlers. Maybe when I saw Seth that first time some unconscious part of my brain said, "Well, hello again! Where have you been? I've missed you."

Seth (2014)

Gesicyah parted ways with David before Seth was born. During my twice-a-year visits to Cleveland, I helped each of them clean their filthy homes and took Seth and his half-brother, Dale, to the park to play. I quietly listened to David and Gesi as they both recounted their delusional plans for finally getting their lives in order. I sent modest amounts of money to both to help with various financial crises, knowing I would not get paid back. I desperately wanted them to succeed, but none of the signs pointed in that direction.

The shit hit the fan when Seth was three years old: Gesi went to jail, and there was a real possibility she was going to be incarcerated for a long time.

From prison, Gesi prepared a one-year power of attorney for a couple who had become pseudo grandparents to Seth. This family was kind and well-meaning, but they also planned to move out of state in two months for a job prospect. David was beside himself. We both knew child custody laws became very difficult to navigate once parents and children resided in different states.

I spent many sleepless nights fretting over what was the best option for Seth. I knew the family taking care of him was doing a better job of parenting than either David or Gesi were ever likely to manage. But I also knew if Seth went to Wisconsin with his current caregivers, the likelihood of his ever returning to Ohio was very slim.

So, in a decision I still sometimes question was the right one, I committed myself to helping David keep Seth.

After the court decision awarding David temporary custody in 2013, I immediately got on a plane to Cleveland to help him prepare his home for long-term habitation with a toddler. David was a hoarder. It had been troubling enough to imagine Seth visiting him on the weekends; the idea of permanent residence was downright horrifying.

RISK

When I arrived, David's 700-square-foot house was filled with a variety of incomplete electronic fix-up projects and items he compulsively acquired from yard sales and thrift stores. Partially dismembered television sets, stereo components, VCRs, and old laptops were stacked in teetering towers atop unstable tables and shelves along the walls. Most of the floor and the few rickety chairs he owned were covered in dirty clothes and stacks of old papers and magazines; piles of dirty dishes covered every surface in the kitchen. A large cardboard box next to a murky fish tank appeared to contain only unopened bills. There was so much stuff crammed inside the sunroom that the door into it could not be opened wide enough to step through. David wouldn't let me open the door to his bedroom, so I could only imagine the horror hidden within.

Overflowing cans of cigarette butts were scattered throughout the house. Every surface was covered in a patina of dust, cigarette ashes, and birdseed with a little poop and feathers thrown in. A small cage with two softly peeping finches hung from the ceiling next to the one visible window in the living room. Two cats could be found curled up somewhere within the piles of dirty laundry.

I spent a week loading two dump truck containers with stuff to be hauled to the landfill while David was at work at his temp agency day labor jobs. In cleaning and furnishing Seth's bedroom, I strived to create a little island of relatively safe and sanitary conditions so he would not be sickened or maimed by its contents.

Two days after Seth moved in, just to keep David honest, I called Child Protective Services.

Over the next nine months, David kept his home and life in order just enough to maintain custody of Seth, but the situation was tenuous. CPS visited about twice a month, and I regularly called to get updates.

During one of my calls, the social worker spoke frankly: "Now, I'm not sayin' he is keeping his house the way you and I might like it . . . but it is safe."

Seth (2014)

David kept working at the day labor gigs his temp agency gave him—the only source of income he'd had for a decade—but the amount of financial support he required kept increasing. In addition to paying his property taxes and homeowners insurance premium, I was now paying all the utility bills.

I agonized over how involved I should get in both David and Seth's lives. I did not want to disrupt my harmonious, balanced life, but I also did not want to wait until something happened that could put Seth in foster care, or worse. I worried a few more years of bad parenting could create irreparable harm during his formative development, virtually ensuring he would follow in his parents' footsteps and become a permanent fixture in the social welfare state.

Finally in December of 2013, I called David with an offer. Knowing it would change my life but never imagining the whirlpool I was about to be sucked into, I invited him and Seth to move to California.

At the end of the week, David drives Seth and me to the airport hotel. My previously half-filled suitcase is now stuffed to capacity with Seth's new wardrobe from Grandma Maureen.

Seth clutches a small stuffed black Labrador puppy from Grandpa Dean. At this point in our one-week relationship, he still doesn't talk to me in sentences. But he will sometimes say "yes" or "no" instead of nodding or shaking his head. He also puts his arms up for me to pick him up when he is tired or has skinned his knee. And he looks into my eyes when I talk to him.

Seth hugs his dad goodbye as David tells him how much he loves him and will miss him, promising he will see him soon in California.

I am both relieved that Seth is not crying and worried by it.

What is going on in his head? How many times has this little guy had to hear these fraught goodbyes from his adult caregivers?

RISK

How often have his people just disappeared? Is he going to totally freak out on me at some point after David leaves?

Instilling confidence in my tone that I do not feel, I say, "Okay, Dave, we'll see you in a few weeks." I hope that stating a timeline aloud, however imprecise, will reinforce the imminence of David's reappearance for Seth. A four-year-old who has already experienced separation from his mother, two half-siblings, a stepfather, and one set of quasi grandparents.

I give David a hug, both fearing him leaving and wanting him to go. Then, hands shaking and stomach churning, I turn to Seth and, as cheerfully as I can, say, "Hey, let's go in so we can watch cartoons before we go to bed, okay, buddy?"

Silently, Seth slips his tiny hand into mine, and we walk through the door.

Chapter 2
The Great Missouri River Wreck (1968)

Standing in the shallow muddy water along the shore of the Missouri River and holding the bow rope of our canoe, I felt the knot in my stomach ease. We were about to head out on a two-week expedition. The soft, burbling sounds of the river were calming and familiar, and the peaceful movement of current disappearing around the first bend portended adventure.

Dad, happier than I had seen him in months, softly hummed a tune as he tightened the last straps on our gear bags. David stood on shore, handing Dad the final few small pieces of gear, which Dad expertly fit in an orderly and geometrically efficient fashion to fill every space in our seventeen-foot Alumacraft canoe.

At the start of this river trip in June of 1968, David and I were ten years old. A few weeks before our launch, my mother had permanently left our family to live with my grandparents and receive the full-time care her illness from acute multiple sclerosis required.

Dad had given away most of our belongings when we moved out of our house in Cleveland, Ohio. He'd told us we were spending the summer out West and would bring only the essentials: our canoe, a bag of clothes each, camping gear, a file cabinet full of Dad's writing and cartooning work, drawing supplies, a typewriter, and our yellow Labrador, Fawn.

RISK

Driving away from Cleveland, I'd felt both sad and relieved. At least I wouldn't have to see Mommy's empty room anymore. But it was going to be two months before we could see her again, and we had no home to return to. Dad was unclear about what was going to happen after our western adventure and had chosen to focus primarily on plans for our trip.

I had no choice but to trust he would figure it out, despite clear evidence that his ability to keep his shit together had been severely compromised.

As Fawn raced around the canoe, barking at ducks, Dad put the last piece of gear in its proper place. "Time to go!"

Fawn leapt into the canoe beside us as we pushed off into the Missouri River, ready to escape into adventure. Our recent trauma was put aside as the current carried us into the flow of the river, replacing our anxieties with anticipation.

Approaching the first bend, the river forcefully pulled us out of the past and firmly into the now, the ideal place for us to be.

Dad was clearly surprised when, a mile from our launch point at the base of the Marony Dam in Montana, we saw a small but distinct horizon line stretching all the way across the river, broken only by intermittent pulses of white spray. My pulse quickened as I recognized the telltale signs of whitewater.

None of Dad's research had informed him of any rapids of consequence on our route. This was before guidebooks or the internet; he was relying on topographic maps, the nineteenth-century journals of the explorers Lewis and Clark, and the limited word-of-mouth information he'd gleaned from modern-day paddlers to plot our canoe expedition through the Missouri River Breaks.

"Draw to the left, Susan," Dad called to me in the bow as he placed a hard rudder stroke from the stern to angle the canoe toward shore.

The Great Missouri River Wreck (1968)

Our heavily loaded canoe lumbered into the eddy, and David leapt out of his seat in the middle of the canoe onto a small sand beach to grab the bowline.

After securing the bowline to a tree, Dad said, "You guys wait here while I go scout the rapid."

I watched him boulder-hop along the shore for only about thirty feet before Fawn suddenly erupted into manic barking and began lunging wildly up and down among the rocks.

Dad yelled frantically, "Fawn, no! Fawn, stop. Come, Fawn, come!"

Even over his yelling and Fawn's barking I heard the loud, menacing buzz. *Rattlesnake!* I realized with a chill. *And it must be big.*

A few moments later, Dad snagged Fawn by the collar and dragged her back to the canoe. Urgently, he instructed, "David, you get in the canoe and hold on to Fawn; Susan, untie the bowline. We are going to paddle down along the shore to the next eddy."

Unfortunately, within seconds after pulling out of the first eddy, we encountered our first little wave—and our canoe filled with half a foot of water. With the added weight, the canoe lurched and swayed, now impossible to maneuver. The next wave swamped us completely, the following tipped the boat over, and in seconds the swift currents pulled us from shore into the middle of the river.

Clinging desperately to the gunnel of the upside-down canoe next to David, I choked and gasped for air.

"Don't let go of the canoe, kids!" Dad yelled as he swam to the back to keep the boat pointed downstream so it wouldn't breach broadside on a rock. Known as a "wrap" in river-running jargon, I knew such a breach could destroy our canoe and leave all our gear stranded in the middle of the river.

Kicking with his legs, Dad struggled to keep the canoe straight as the river swept us over barely submerged rocks and through two- to three-foot-high breaking waves.

RISK

After each wave, I blinked the water from my eyes and strained to see signs of flatwater downstream, but the end of the rapids was nowhere in sight. The shore was close enough for my father to swim to, but too far for David and me.

"Goddamn it, God, what the hell did I do to deserve this! Jesus fucking Christ get us the hell out of here! Oh, shit, not another one!" Dad exclaimed as—WHAM—another breaking wave crashed over our heads.

Hearing this barrage of profanity from our gentle and mild-mannered father, I whimpered in terror. Clearly, we were in real trouble.

The whitewater was relentless. Gasping for air as waves repeatedly crashed over my head, I struggled to maintain my tenuous grasp on the gunnel of the upside-down Grumman. It felt like I was drowning, even in my life jacket.

Dad continued to plead with and curse the Almighty.

"C'mon! This is enough, goddamn it! Fuck you, God, you asshole! This is bullshit! Aaagh! Damn it!" he yelped as his shins got bashed on another rock. Then, his voice rising to a higher octave, he cried out, "Oh Christ, hang on kids!" just before we plunged over a three-foot drop into a monstrous boil of white foam.

My fingers were ripped off the canoe as my body was sucked down toward the bottom of the river. With my eyes open underwater, I desperately clawed my way back toward the light. My head broke the surface, and as I sputtered for a breath I saw the canoe ten feet to my left. I thrashed my limbs in a frenetic dog paddle to get back to it. Despite being practically raised on canoe trips, my brother and I were terrible swimmers.

When I made it back to the canoe, I looked around until I located David and Dad. They were still several feet away from the canoe. David was choking and flailing, barely able to keep his head above the water; Dad was wrestling him into a lifesaver hold.

The Great Missouri River Wreck (1968)

Later, Dad discovered that David's life jacket had not been wholly inflated. If Dad hadn't saved him, he almost certainly would have drowned.

After Dad dragged David back to the boat and we were all clinging to the sides again, Fawn decided she was tired of swimming and tried to climb up David's back.

David screamed in terror, desperate to not get pushed under water again. Dad quickly yanked Fawn off by her collar, grabbed the back of David's pants, and yelled, "Reach for the keel and pull yourself up!" He shoved David and then me on top of the canoe, where we clung spread-eagled over its underbelly like limpets.

"Please, God, this just isn't fair, goddamn it! Just give me a fucking break!" Dad continued to plead, his voice breaking in anguish. Hearing his anger turning to what sounded like crying made me feel even more terrified.

For what seemed an eternity, David and I rode the bucking canoe over waves and hydraulics. It was uncomfortable and frightening, but at least we could breathe.

I heard barking and there was Fawn, running along the bank—followed, I was relieved to see, by two fishermen who were frantically scrambling over rocks and bushes, trying to keep up with our canoe.

Up until now I had whined quietly in my fear, not wanting to interrupt Dad's monologue with the Almighty. But now, seeing that there were able-bodied witnesses to our plight, I succumbed to an overwhelming impulse to give full voice to my terror.

"Help us, help us!" I screamed at the top of my lungs, with David soon joining in.

Finally, the waves began to diminish, and at last our canoe, with its wretched cargo, floated into a calm pool. With his last reserves of strength, Dad swam the boat close enough to shore for the two fishermen to wade in and pull us out.

RISK

David and I stepped onto the beach and plopped down on the nearest rocks. I sat mute, shivering uncontrollably. At some point, it had begun to rain.

One of the fishermen helped Dad empty the water out of the canoe and flip it back upright as the other quickly started a fire. Dad untied our clothing bags, all still securely attached inside the boat, and got me and David into dry clothes and rain gear before changing out of his own sopping clothes. Then, with his hands still shaking from the cold, he pulled out our camp stove and made hot chocolate.

I can still taste that sweet, creamy elixir. My shivering slowed with each exquisite gulp until, finally, every muscle in my body relaxed into a state of total exhaustion.

One of the fishermen, probably seeing my eyes start to droop, said worriedly, "Well, I'm not sure how to get your gear out, but the trail to our car is about three miles away."

Not getting a response from Dad, he continued, "So . . . we should probably get going if we want to get these kids out of the canyon before dark."

"Oh . . . thank you for all your help . . . but we don't need to hike out," Dad replied. He pointed to a grassy terrace on the other side of the river. "I think we will just paddle across the river over there and make camp."

The fishermen gaped at Dad in disbelief. They had just witnessed our horrific whitewater swim and had seen the condition David and I were in when they plucked us out of the river. They must have thought Dad was insane.

They spent a few more minutes trying to convince him that he should consider abandoning the trip, but he held firm.

For Dad, things were back "in control." Nobody was injured. We still had all our essential gear because of the expert job he had done tying everything in. We had only lost a couple of paddles and our cowboy hats. Why would we abort our adventure now?

The Great Missouri River Wreck (1968)

And as for David and me? Well, having been raised on the river since we were two, this was certainly not our first rodeo. It seemed scarier to leave all our stuff at the river than to continue on. After all, our canoe held almost everything we owned in the world.

We helped Dad untie our spare paddles and loaded up. As we waved goodbye to the fishermen, they tentatively waved back, their faces grim, probably wondering if they were soon going to hear some tragic story about us on the evening news.

The rain had stopped, and we set up camp in a sunlit, grassy field filled with patches of yellow and purple wildflowers.

Sitting down to dinner for our first night on the river, I felt happy. My body glowed, reveling in the warmth of our fire and hot spoonfuls of tuna and rice. In the distance, a brilliant rainbow streamed across the big Montana sky. Everything seemed so beautiful, so vivid. I felt like there was nowhere I would rather be.

Although my brother and I had experienced many whitewater swims during previous family canoe trips, this one was the worst. At ten years old, I had my first experience of a phenomenon I would come to welcome throughout my life: the euphoric endorphin release that occurs in the aftermath of surviving physically challenging and/or terrifying experiences relatively unscathed.

I would also eventually learn that this potent cocktail of chemicals which the brain produces in response to overcoming extreme challenges and fear can allow our minds to reset. It's a sort of control/alt/delete mental reboot that—for a while, anyway—pushes aside the deeper emotional terrors lurking inside our psyches.

With repeated successful outcomes, this reboot can also help prepare one to face fear and sometimes even welcome it.

That horrific swim remains one of my most vivid childhood memories, and even at ten, I knew that it meant something. I had an awareness that this day was a benchmark; we'd been tested, and we'd survived. I had gained a perspective in a way I could not yet fully understand.

It was only much later that I realized that this day, along with many other days on the river, created an intricate web of experiences that would shape my life and my ability to manage risk and uncertainty. Like the geomorphology of the river, my family and I sought a state of dynamic equilibrium, continually maintaining balance in response to the forces of nature and disturbances of man.

Curled up in my slightly damp sleeping bag that night, Fawn already snoring quietly as she pressed against my side, I listened to the river's quiet burble and babble. Surrounded by my family in our cozy A-frame tent, I felt a contentment I had not experienced for a while.

For the moment, at least, I felt safe.

We lounged around camp the following day to dry out our damp gear and allow Dad's bruised legs to heal. The next morning, before we packed up, Dad walked upstream to study the rapid in which we had taken the swim of our lives. Using his map, he calculated that the total length of our ordeal was a little over three miles of consistent Class II and III whitewater (out of a difficulty scale from Class I to VI). We all felt the capsize had lasted a long time, but until Dad did the calculation, he thought it was mostly a matter of perception. Realizing the magnitude of the length of the rapid was sobering. He must have felt we were lucky to have all survived.

However, satisfied that this rapid was an anomaly, Dad said he now understood why the few people he had talked to about this trip had launched at the town of Fort Bend, located twenty or so miles downstream of the dam. Rested and refreshed from our layover day, he was ready to launch back into the current and around the next bend in the river.

My dad was, by nature, high-strung and of a nervous dis-

The Great Missouri River Wreck (1968)

position. However, throughout his life he'd also been inexplicably drawn to push against the edges. He was drawn to wilderness exploration, often pushing beyond the boundaries of comfort—and control. Dad attempted to avoid disaster through planning and highly developed skills, but he was simultaneously attracted to the thrill of whitewater canoeing, a dynamic sport that can quickly put one entirely outside their comfort zone.

And even amid the emotional crises surrounding our escape out West, he had a plan.

For this first trip, Dad intended to follow the Lewis and Clark Expedition's route on the Missouri Breaks section of the Missouri River—a 150-mile stretch that remained pretty much in the same condition as when Lewis and Clark explored it—as research for a screenplay he wanted to write.

Dad was an experienced canoeist, and my brother and I had passable paddling and steering skills. Although many people thought he was crazy for embarking alone on a two-week canoe trip with two ten-year-olds and a dog, he felt prepared for our expedition. All our gear (food, kitchenware, clothing, tent, sleeping bags, air mattresses) was stored in waterproof army surplus rubberized bags and metal ammo cans. Everything, including spare paddles, was strapped into the canoe with a secure tie-down system. We were geared up in canvas tennis shoes and wool socks (chosen for their ability to dry faster than other materials), and lifejackets, of course. We stopped in Fort Bend the day after our swim to replace our lost cowboy hats, the last essential piece of our river gear, meant to protect us from both the hot summer sun and pounding rain during thunderstorms.

Dad's hat was a gentile gray like Ben Cartwright's on *Bonanza*. My hat was black and styled after Little Joe. David's was brown, with the crown punched out and the brim pulled down like Hoss. It irritated me that my brother had goofed out his hat like that, but almost anything my brother did annoyed me.

RISK

I was both my brother's best friend and worst enemy. Because our family moved around a lot, we were each other's most constant playmates. But we had distinctly different personalities. I was bossy, controlling, naturally athletic, and dominated my brother both physically and emotionally. David was terrible at sports and liked games of a more intellectual nature. I wanted to do things fast and had a short attention span. He wanted to take his time and immerse himself into the intricate details of any given activity. He was also extremely sensitive, sweet, and gullible, which made him a perfect victim for his controlling older-by-eleven-minutes sister.

We were both small for our age, with sharp, pixie-like features, and thin to the point of looking starved. Because of my short hair and our androgynous dress—T-shirts, denim jeans, canvas high tops, and cowboy hats—we were often mistaken initially for twin brothers. My dad also treated us equally, never assigning chores or tailoring his behavior toward us according to our gender.

Dad expected us to behave more responsibly than most parents did their ten-year-olds. He let us know that he could not be both a dad and a mom, so we would have to take care of ourselves and pitch in. We had to help cook and clean and be responsible for our personal hygiene and our belongings.

That summer, which must have been an emotionally fragile time for him, he had only my brother and me for companions.

"C'mon David, I need you to paddle a little harder," Dad called to my brother in the front of the canoe. "Susan, grab one of the spare paddles."

Usually when one of us was sitting in the middle seat we could rest, but for the last half hour we'd watched the sky behind us morph from gray to an ominous black. Now the dark sky was crisscrossed with multi-veined lightning bolts punctuated by deep, rumbling thunder. The speed at which this monster approached was terrifying.

The Great Missouri River Wreck (1968)

Dad's voice took on that panicky timbre again as he exhorted us to paddle. Since the river was not offering any grassy terraces or sandy beaches along the shore, he steered us to a mid-channel gravel bar as the first drops of rain pelted the water's surface. We set up the tent in record time and quickly clambered in with our sleeping gear and a cold supper.

After changing into dry clothes, we ate our dinner of peanuts, Spam, dried fruit, and crackers while snuggling into our sleeping bags, prepared to ride out the storm. At first, the pattering of raindrops was soothing; we felt protected in our canvas shelter. But after a deafening crack of lightning that filled the tent with bright light even through the canvas walls, Dad advised David and me to scooch away from the aluminum tent poles, worried they might act as lightning rods.

In 1969, "freestanding" tents had not yet been invented. Our tent was a conventional A-frame with aluminum poles holding up each end. The end poles were held in place by two guy ropes outside, four guy ropes on the sides pulled out the walls, and four stakes held down the tent floor. An A-frame tent requires all the stakes to be working together in dynamic tension, or the entire structure is compromised.

As the wind tore at the tent, one of the sidewall stakes came loose, causing the tent wall to shake violently. The force of the undulating wall ripped out the grommet holding one of the end poles—and the entire tent collapsed in a mess of flapping wet canvas.

David and I shrieked and flailed at the heavy, sopping canvas while Dad leapt into action with a series of moves that I still marvel at. Sort of like MacGyver meets the Incredible Hulk.

First, he grabbed one of my leather camp boots and put it over the top of the pole with the ripped-out tent grommet.

"Susan, come over here and hold up this pole," he yelled over the pounding rain drumming on the tent.

RISK

I nervously followed his command, hoping lightning would not strike while my hands were clenched on the cold metal pole that was bucking violently.

Dad ran out the tent door and returned a few moments later with two paddles.

"David, hold this paddle against the wall of the tent!"

While David held one paddle, Dad wedged the other between David's feet and the opposite tent wall and then scrambled back outside.

He came in and out twice more, each time lugging a basketball-size boulder that he dropped into respective corners of the tent.

I tried in vain to find a comfortable position as we arranged our bodies around the precarious array of boulders, paddles, and tent poles holding up our compromised tent while the storm continued to rage outside. With the beast right over us, I held my breath every time a bolt of lightning lit up the tent and thunder sounded immediately afterward.

About a half-hour later, the sounds of rolling thunder grew more distant, and I finally relaxed. Our sagging, deformed tent was crippled but still standing. I curled my sleeping bag around Fawn's warm body in the dark and fell fast asleep.

The following day, after taking our sleeping bags out of the tent to dry under another sunny bluebird sky, Dad leaned over to pick up one of the boulders.

"Ummph!" he grunted.

The boulder didn't move.

"Well, I'll be damned," he said with a laugh. "I can't pick it up!"

He got down on his knees. "Hey David, come here and help me roll it out."

They worked together to push and roll the boulder across the floor of the tent. My dad's Superman strength from the night before was gone. He had transformed back into our skinny little father.

The Great Missouri River Wreck (1968)

My camp boot, meanwhile, worked so well that Dad never did replace the grommet. The boot became an essential part of the tent kit, used long after I grew out of it.

Our two-week expedition provided restoration and healing, the building blocks for resiliency. Resiliency we would need to face the life we would be returning to at the end of the summer.

This transformation occurred incrementally, as the events of each day unfolded.

Enduring the discomforts—putting on cold, wet socks in the morning, getting by on repetitive and often unappetizing food choices, and suffering the extremes of weather—made us more appreciative of the comforts we could create, such as a warm, cozy tent at night and the fresh biscuits Dad baked by the fire in a homemade reflector oven in the morning. Finding a shady grove of cottonwoods for camp. That fresh, dry pair of socks we pulled out of our bag every fourth day.

The simple meditation of paddling and drifting, gently transported mile after mile by the steady current of the mighty Missouri River, was calming and grounding. Our canoe's passage slowly unspooled a mesmerizing and ever-changing panorama of colors and shapes formed by the spectacular cliff formations of the Missouri Breaks. Our daily journey and camp routines were filled with order, beauty, and adventure.

All this allowed us to escape the reality we would face at the end of our journey: no home to return to, and no more living as a family with my mother.

Chapter 3
Pot Candy (2014)

I wake up suddenly, eyes wide open, heart racing, my stomach tight. Gradually, I let my brain catch up to my body's visceral response and identify the cause of this nocturnal upset.

Oh yeah, right. A child is living in my house.

I pull out my iPad with a sigh, hoping it won't take too long to read myself back to sleep.

A few hours later, I get up to prepare for the day.

"Seth, where is your backpack? Why don't you have your shoes and socks on yet? I told you we had to be out of here in five minutes. Come on, Seth, try to be part of the team."

The stark reality of suddenly being the primary caregiver to a four-and-a-half-year-old. My mornings are no longer straightforward and efficient.

Four months ago, before Seth and David came to live with me, I awoke a mere half hour before work. After jumping into clothes laid out the night before and brushing my teeth, I'd grab my premade bag of breakfast, snack, and lunch food as I ran out the door. And after a ten-minute commute to the US Forest Service's Lake Tahoe Basin Management Unit, I hit the ground running. I had no trouble getting to meetings on time, fully prepped with

Pot Candy (2014)

the materials and information I needed to contribute in an efficient and meaningful way in my role as Forest Hydrologist. My mind was clear and focused, quickly forming creative management strategies and resolving obstacles to protect, restore, and maintain the watersheds of Lake Tahoe.

Now I need at least an hour and a half to get Seth fed and ready for preschool. In getting all his stuff together, I leave half of the things I need behind. At work, my fogged brain is full of worry. Is Seth going to make it through the day without hitting someone, requiring me to pick him up early? Is his lame-ass father going to make a realistic attempt at finding work, so he can move out of my house?

When I brought Seth back with me to California in June, Lisa, my spouse and partner of fifteen years, picked us up at the airport in Reno and took us to her home in Truckee, California. Although we were married, Lisa and I had a long-distance relationship—we lived about one-and-a-half hours apart—due to work and entrenchment in other aspects of the lives we'd been living when we met. It had always worked well for us, and at the time, she was entirely on board with what we both naively thought was going to be our new role as active aunties to young Seth.

Seth and I spent our first week together in California with Lisa and our two dogs, Maddie and Roscoe. Lisa and I brought him to the beach and on dog walks, introducing him to our mountain-town lifestyle. On our first walk, Lisa and I both had to take turns squatting next to a bush to convince him it really was okay for him to pee outside.

I was amazed at how stoic Seth was. He did not cry, he did not ask where his dad was, and he willingly went everywhere we took him. He was also nonverbal and utterly unresponsive to adults' attempts to engage with him, deliberately avoiding eye contact and physical touch. But what I noticed right away was how much

RISK

he liked being outside and how drawn he was to dogs. There are many dogs in Truckee and Tahoe, and Seth was enthusiastic about engaging with all of them, big and small.

His dog manners are still unrefined, and we are constantly reminding him to pet softer, to not ride them like a horse or grab their heads in a bear hug. But despite Seth's rough behavior, by the third night, my nervous little seven-year-old Chihuahua-Maltese mix, Roscoe, was sleeping on the bed with him. Roscoe, with his big brown eyes and fluffy white hair, is irresistible to children. But he has always been terrified of the "little trolls," and typically snaps at them (and most adults) viciously when approached.

Somehow, Seth tamed him within days.

David drove out from Cleveland about two months after I brought Seth here. At first, I was relieved that he had finally arrived and could theoretically actively participate in Seth's parenting. I soon realized he is more of a liability than an asset.

I expected David would find his own place to live within a few months, and we would figure out some sort of cooperative parenting arrangement for Seth. However, David has fallen into a troubling pattern of delusional thinking and downright laziness. Every day he spends hours doing two things: fiddling around on his computer and slowly and methodically eating copious amounts of sugary starch. For a guy who weighs all of 140 pounds, where he puts the multiple slices of white-bread toast and bowls of kids' cereal is a mystery to me.

In two months, he has gone to only a few job interviews, disdaining to consider the numerous service industry jobs available in our resort town. He is clearly becoming way too comfortable living rent-free in my house and requires constant reminders to help with daily parenting chores. Apparently, clean clothes, routine teeth-brushing, bedtime schedules, and nightly reading were not standard protocols in his household.

Pot Candy (2014)

How am I going to take care of a four-year-old boy-child while also getting a fifty-six-year-old man-child to cowboy up? I am beginning to realize just how far in over my head I may be.

Before sending Seth into preschool, I crouch down to make eye contact and deliver a little pep talk.

"Now, honey, if someone is mean to you today, do you think you can try using your words and asking a teacher for help?"

As opposed to slugging them in the face like you did yesterday? I refrain from adding. Hardly a day goes by without his school calling me to talk about an incident involving his rage.

Still nonverbal, Seth looks at me with his big brown eyes and nods his head slowly. And unconvincingly.

Then he smiles his angelic smile and opens his arms for a hug.

It's hard to believe this little being who can be so sweet and affectionate is a preschool thug. I give him a big hug and kiss and pray this is not one of the days I will have to pick him up early.

Continuing my race to the office for a conference call that starts in minutes, I realize I'm starving and have forgotten my food bag in the fridge. At the stoplight, I scrabble around the piles of toys, athletic wear, and trash within reach in my hopelessly cluttered car, hoping to find an uneaten portion of energy bar or maybe a Tupperware containing a partially eaten peanut butter sandwich left over from the last day or so.

I am coming up with nothing until I grasp something lodged way back in the corner of the cubby above the ashtray: a one-and-a-half-inch-long oblong item wrapped in wax paper. Inside is a yummy-looking caramel. I have no recollection of how it got there, but this might be just enough sustenance to get me through my half-hour call. I gobble the confection as the light turns green.

Although I had no time to prepare for it, the call is going well. I am reasonably focused and make several insightful contributions to the conversation. I even start pondering where I can go to get food once the call is over. Somewhere quick, I think, scanning the itemized list of the day's meetings and reporting deadlines on my desk.

Suddenly, I realize there has been an unexplainable gap in time.

"Well, I think that about wraps it up," a voice says on the other end of the phone.

"Yes," another voice chimes in, "I think we have a good plan for moving forward."

Plan? What plan? I am no longer sure where I am in the conversation or how we got there.

"Okay, I guess that's it until next month," the man's voice says again, and several other voices say goodbye, followed by a series of two-tone bleeps as they hang up.

Relieved that the call is over and apparently requires no additional response from me, I carefully place the phone headset back in its cradle.

I sit for a moment, thinking that the past week of inadequate sleep and my morning hunger have made me extraordinarily tired and spacey. Maybe I should start with a strong cup of tea.

However, in the next moment, I am overwhelmed by a weird numbness at the base of my skull and my arms cease to feel connected to my body. Dear God, am I having a brain aneurysm? It happened to my drill sergeant during Army basic training. One second, she was giving a lecture to our platoon on barracks hygiene; the next, she was collapsing on the floor, totally unconscious. She was dead on arrival at the hospital.

Holding on to the edge of my desk to make sure I am tethered to a solid object before trying to move, I slowly turn my chair around and open my mouth to ask my colleague in the cubicle across the aisle to call 911 . . . when suddenly, I remember.

OH SHIT, THE POT CANDY!

Pot Candy (2014)

In a rush, the origin of the caramel comes flooding back to me. Several months before I got Seth, I delivered some samples from a friend of mine who works in the medical marijuana business to a mutual friend who suffers from chronic nerve pain. I passed along the chocolate chip cookie and honey sticks long ago, but the caramel got lost and forgotten in the car.

I sit frozen in my chair. Is it possible to OD on marijuana? Because that's the way I feel. Like my brain might freeze and I'd just stop breathing.

I spend a few moments making sure that I'm still inhaling and exhaling and could do it even if I wasn't concentrating on making it happen.

Whew, at least I am not going to pass out from lack of oxygen. Now, how am I going to get home before my compromised mental state is discovered?

After carefully rehearsing the words in my head, I turn again to my colleague.

"Holly," I say, attempting to keep my voice calm but not stoned-sounding, "I'm feeling really tired and think I may be catching the crud going around the preschool. Can you let anyone that comes looking for me know that I have gone home for the rest of the day?"

Holly, an experienced mother of two, glances up only briefly from her screen as she replies, "Of course." She turns back to her computer. "It's almost impossible to not catch what they bring home from school. Between my two, one of us is always sick."

"Thanks, Holly," I reply.

She barely nods in response.

Whew, I passed for normal. Now to get out.

I stand up slowly, carefully, making sure I'm not wobbling, before starting the long walk out of the office. My head feels like it's floating several feet above my body as I navigate the narrow aisles between office cubicles. Keeping my eyes down to avoid

RISK

eye contact, I pray I won't encounter anyone and get caught in a conversation that I surely cannot manage coherently.

After a brief pause at the top step of the back stairwell, I again force my brain to focus on controlling my robotic body limbs: walk down the stairs, open the back door, navigate around the building, and cross the parking lot. Every physical movement requires intense concentration to execute.

I sink into the driver's seat of my car, flooded with relief. After several moments of deep breathing, I slap my cheeks and steel myself for the five-mile drive home.

I concentrate as hard as I can to operate my right foot on the brake and accelerator while continuously shifting my eyes between the windshield, the odometer, and the rearview mirror. Whenever I look at the odometer, I must either speed up from a twenty-mile-per-hour crawl or slow from a breakneck sixty; it's a struggle to adhere to the forty-mile-per-hour speed limit, all the while trying to stay between those pesky yellow and white lines. Crap, driving is hard.

Pulling into my driveway, I am again overcome with relief at having made it home safely—and having salvaged my career from total ruin.

But David's goddamn car is still here. My sanctuary is still occupied by an unwanted invader.

I enter the house to find him at the kitchen table, staring at his laptop and steadily chomping through yet another bowl of Froot Loops.

Walking past the kitchen, I say, "I think I'm catching something and am going to stay home sick today. Can you please pick up Seth from preschool this afternoon?"

With his mouth full of cereal, he mumbles back, "Yeah, sure," barely lifting his eyes from his computer screen.

For once, I'm grateful for his stunted communication skills.

Pot Candy (2014)

After closing the bedroom door, I crawl deep under the covers of my bed.

It takes all day to get through the effects of my accidental ganja trip. I spend hours crying quietly into my pillow. Once David finally leaves the house around noon, I succumb to periods of full-on wailing. Unable to sleep or eat, I only get out of bed to pee.

My friend, the medical marijuana supplier, has told me many times how much she likes the mind-opening clarity she experiences with pot. But I do not need clarity; I need denial. I need to keep my fear and self-doubt, however real or well-founded, deeply buried.

But the THC has stripped away all my defenses, allowing my brain to circle the same thoughts repeatedly like a hamster on a wheel, desperately running to nowhere.

I have ruined my life! I can't raise a kid. That is why I didn't have kids of my own. Why doesn't Seth talk? Why does he get so angry? Why does he hit? How am I going to get my loser brother out of my house, and is Seth going to self-destruct when he does move away? God, I need to get some exercise. I am just so exhausted. There is never any time. Lisa is going to leave me. Who would put up with this? I am no longer fun. I used to be fun. If the situation were reversed, I would not put up with this. None of my friends want to be around me anymore. I am going to be seventy years old by the time Seth is eighteen. My last good years are fucked! This is not what I had planned!

Fuck, fuck, fuck! What am I going to do!?

Finally, the high, and the desperation, run their course.

I force myself to get up around four o'clock to fix something to eat and take the dog for a walk before David brings Seth home from preschool. As the food and oxygen make their way through

RISK

my bloodstream, I complete re-entry into my body. A body that can once again perform automatic breathing and movement functions.

The fears are still there, but thankfully, they no longer feel insurmountable. I do not know exactly how I am going to face the challenges ahead. But faith in my ability to find a way has been restored—for now, at least.

There is little clarity, but I do know one thing: Seth needs me. He needs me to love him, protect him, and to fucking figure things out.

Chapter 4
Whitewater Pioneers (1970)

David and I watched from the shore as Dad, in his new-used whitewater C-1, floated sideways toward a large, frothing hydraulic. The closed-deck fiberglass boat was small and sleek, compared to our family camping canoe, and specially designed for whitewater. Dad maneuvered the craft with a single-bladed canoe paddle from a kneeling position, with a spray skirt secured snugly around his waist and the cockpit of the boat.

Dad slid down into the seething boil of violently recirculating water; the C-1 bounced like a bucking bronco a couple of times, and WHAM—the upstream side of his boat caught the current and he was flipped upstream so fast it looked as though he'd been yanked and rolled up into a window shade like a Looney Tunes cartoon character. Hence the name for this unplanned maneuver: being window-shaded.

As the upside-down boat continued to buck and bounce in the hydraulic, Dad stuck his paddle blade up to the surface and flipped the C-1 upright, a maneuver known as an Eskimo roll.

WHAM, window-shaded again.

This time, as the upside-down boat continued its wild ride in the hydraulic, we saw Dad's paddle float downstream, and soon after he popped to the surface, gasping for air.

RISK

After Dad's paddling companions pulled all the flotsam and jetsam back together, he clambered over the boulders along the riverbank, his five-foot-nine-inch frame and skinny white legs dwarfed by the thirteen-foot boat on his shoulder. He slowly worked his way upstream to get back in the river and participate some more in this "whitewater play."

From our perspective on shore, we were not quite sure why Dad was enjoying this. It looked like he was getting soundly thumped as he tried to figure out how to surf the river hydraulic in his new toy. But the goofy grin on his face made it clear he was having a blast.

It was inevitable that my dad's addiction to river adventure would lead our family from open-deck, family-style canoeing into the growing sport of closed-deck whitewater paddling.

Closed-deck whitewater boats include both one- and two-person canoes, with the paddlers using a single-bladed paddle in the kneeling position. One-person whitewater kayaks are paddled with a two-bladed paddle in the sitting position. The boats are relatively small in volume, just designed to carry the paddler and the plastic flotation bags filled with air that keep the boat from sinking if the paddler takes a swim. Constructed out of fiberglass and resin, they generally weigh between thirty-five and forty-five pounds.

Whitewater kayaking was a fringe sport when I was a kid, and the segment of the population drawn to it was inherently limited. There were no companies building whitewater kayaks and canoes until the early seventies, so boats were constructed by the paddlers themselves, using molds rented or purchased by their clubs.

The common denominators of whitewater enthusiasts were an attraction to a dynamic, challenging sport; the desire to be in the company of a small, like-minded tribe; a love of remote river canyons largely unspoiled by man; and an interest in escaping the

Whitewater Pioneers (1970)

realities of a mundane weekday life in an activity that involved intense focus and offered strong camaraderie.

Also, it was not really all that expensive.

It was the perfect sport for our family. It met my dad's need to immerse himself in raw natural settings on the weekends to offset the soul-numbing urban lives we led in the large cities we needed to live in for his work. Because of our sketchy financial status, we could only afford to live in lower-middle-class neighborhoods and had few amenities to amuse us.

Our weekend adventures were essential for Dad to keep his creative juices flowing. They were also a way to immediately establish a tightly knit group of friends in whichever new place our nomadic family landed. As a whitewater paddler, you were immediately part of a small, fanatic subculture that embraced newcomers with enthusiasm.

Dad sought out a local canoe club when we first arrived in California and found the Ventura Canoe and Kayak Club. We participated in a couple of family canoe trips with the club but soon found out there weren't many rivers in Southern California suitable for calm water open-deck canoeing. There were, however, several options for the emerging sport of whitewater paddling.

Closed-deck whitewater kayaking and canoeing required a completely different set of skills—but mastering those skills made it possible to navigate a much higher difficulty level of whitewater.

Soon after he purchased the C-1 for himself, a cheap deal came along for a used fiberglass whitewater-racing kayak for David and me to share. The boat only cost seventy-five dollars and was accompanied by a glamorous mystique: it had been manufactured in France and was brought to California by a club member on the US World Championship Whitewater Kayaking Team. Sleeker and smaller in volume than a regular river-running kayak, the whitewater-racing kayak was much more suitable for David and me, since we were still quite puny.

RISK

As Dad became addicted to this new sport, we started taking regular weekend trips, driving three and a half hours to the Kern River near Kernville, California.

Learning how to whitewater kayak was a pleasure/pain experience for me, a constant mix of fear and exhilaration. Kayaking upright and in the right place in the river was thrilling and fun. But upside down and in the wrong place in the river was terrifying.

There you are, legs trapped inside this little boat with a neoprene spray skirt holding you in, bouncing over rocks and through turbulent hydraulics with your head under the water, icy cold water blasting up your nose. At this point, you are expected to keep your cool, hold your breath, and attempt to execute an Eskimo roll, a coordinated maneuver performed with your paddle and hips that brings you and your upside-down kayak back into an upright position, ready to again take control of navigating yourself through whatever mess you are in.

It takes most people sustained time and effort to develop the whitewater reading skills, paddling technique, and head for keeping it together when the shit hits the fan to find whitewater kayaking fun.

I was deemed ready for my first river run at age thirteen.

I made it down the three miles of easy rapids without any mishaps. But I knew the real test was the infamous Ewing's Falls at the end of the run. The rapid was steep and long, and about halfway down, the powerful currents pushed my kayak sideways into a rock.

Panicked, I leaned upstream, the current caught the edge of my boat, and I flipped over, screaming. Because I had my head thrown back and mouth open when I went under the water, I smacked my front teeth on a rock. There was no question I was going to try out my sketchy Eskimo roll, so I bailed.

Swimming through the waves and hydraulics to the bottom of the rapid, I had no awareness of pain. But at the end, clinging

Whitewater Pioneers (1970)

onto the grab loop of Dad's boat as he pulled me to shore, I became aware of an intense throbbing in my mouth. While I sat on the beach waiting for the other boaters to retrieve my boat and paddle, I tentatively felt around with my tongue, fearing I had lost teeth. They were all still there, but I could feel a sizable corner missing from one of my top front teeth.

I learned two valuable kayaking lessons that day that I have never forgotten. One, always lean into your danger. Two, if you go upside down, tuck your face and body tight against the boat's deck until you are past all the turbulence.

I wasn't ready to quit. But I couldn't say I loved whitewater kayaking, either.

One of the most valuable life skills I gained from following Dad in this sport was overcoming fear. Although my stomach was frequently twisted in knots, I learned how to control and use that feeling. I learned to channel the emotional intensity of the situation into the energy needed to face the danger. I soon found that encountering a situation that scares you, and doing it anyway, can prepare you for other life challenges.

Of course, it helped that I had a safety net of adults providing instruction and making sure measures were taken to facilitate a quick rescue if I got in trouble. But still, it was primarily up to me to keep myself out of a terrifying swim.

I was a quiet and shy kid. But building inside of me, without me realizing it, was a new strength and confidence. I learned that by planning, developing skills, and sometimes just jumping into the current and taking things as they came, I could overcome my fear.

Learning to kayak also helped to put things in perspective. Some of the situations I had felt fearful of before in my everyday life, such as being the new kid in school, regularly thrust into drastically new environments and social conditions that I did not feel comfortable in, were not as daunting as before. I still felt awkward and nervous, but I would just tell myself that it was not as scary as when I had to run Killer Fang Falls, and suddenly those challenges seemed more manageable.

That first year of whitewater kayaking was also the year that Dad decided to divorce Mom.

One evening, Dad sat David and I down at our Formica kitchen table, placed in the middle of our tiny living room in the small, shabby bungalow we were renting in Van Nuys.

Looking down at the table he said, "I need to tell you that your mother and I are getting a divorce." Without looking up he rushed on, "We are never going to live together as a family again because of how sick you mom is getting, and I cannot make enough money to pay for her medical care. If we get a divorce, she becomes a ward of the state and will be eligible for aid programs to help get the equipment and care she needs."

I do not recall either of us asking any questions during this monologue. I do remember feeling a heavy weight settle over my entire body. There was a finality in these words, cementing what I must have already known on some level. I was never going to live with my mother again.

There is so much of our parents' personal experience that is hidden from us, or that we as children are just oblivious to, as we struggle with our own self-centered survival. But as we grow into adults and face our own struggles, we can gain a clearer perspective on our parents' experiences.

Even though Dad divorced my mother, he did not start dating again until one year after Mom died. When I asked Dad in my teens if he ever thought he would marry again, he said he was just too old to start over. But when he started dating again a decade later, I realized that even after the divorce, he had still considered himself married to Mom "till death do you part." The

Whitewater Pioneers (1970)

divorce indeed had been a financial decision necessary for our survival, not a separation of the heart.

This conversation about the divorce brought the reality of Mom's disease and the finality of our separation from her into laser focus. There was not much that could help me cope with the fear, pain, and loneliness that came with that. It was a much bigger emotional package than the fear associated with learning how to whitewater kayak. Our weekend escapes to the river, therefore, became a welcome and even essential distraction. At least the stomach-wrenching fear I experienced above each rapid helped dim the sadness and anxiety of living every day without Mom.

When Dad quit his job and packed David and me into the truck to head west for the summer in June of 1968, Mom left Cleveland to live with her parents in Bloomfield, Iowa. That summer, while David and I explored the Missouri River with Dad during the first phase of his effort to get his head back on straight, Mom faced the hard reality of being abandoned by her husband and knowing she'd never again live full time with her children.

I don't know what transpired between my parents during the two months we were on our western river safari, but at the end of the summer, Dad announced we were moving to Bloomfield, where Mom was now living with her parents, for the sixth-grade school year. I believe he made this crucial decision when Mom was teetering at a suicidal tipping point. It was not a good move for him, personally or financially, so he must have done it for her.

In 1968, Bloomfield was a small town of about 3,500 surrounded by a thriving agricultural community of family-owned farms. My grandparents' house was about five blocks from the town square, which featured a handsome stone courthouse surrounded by the typical variety of commerce needed to meet the needs of a small midwestern town. It was a peaceful place where

RISK

everyone greeted you when you passed them on the street. However, it was not a peaceful existence for the fractured Norman family.

David and I eagerly ran through the door of my grandparents' house and turned directly into Mom's bedroom, now in the large sunroom next to the living room. Mom's face lit up as I opened my arms to give her a hug and kiss, and although she could not hug me back, the joy in her big smile and warmth in her deep brown eyes expressed her love just as powerfully as a physical embrace.

I lowered the bar on Mom's hospital-style bed so I could sit down next to her and asked excitedly, "Did Grandpa cook pot roast for dinner?"

My watering mouth already knew the answer to this question, of course; my nose had detected the savory aroma of Grandpa's signature dish the second I'd entered the house.

Mom took a deep breath before answering, a necessary step because of the paralyzing effects of multiple sclerosis. "Pot roast," she said, "and we also have strawberry rhubarb pie for dessert!" Another big breath and then, "Hey, can you and David help me turn over?"

Because my mother was virtually paralyzed, she could not change her position in bed without assistance. David and I were familiar with the procedure by this point, and we quickly began working together: one of us pushed her hips up while the other pulled her shoulder and arm to get her body on its side, and then we repositioned the various pillows needed to hold all her body parts in a stable and comfortable position.

Once all the adjustments were made, she took another breath and said, "Thank you—now, how did that math test go at school?"

As we sat chatting, I reveled in the comfort of knowing David and I would get to spend the rest of the weekend with Mom at my grandparents' house.

Whitewater Pioneers (1970)

This was the same house in which my mother had seriously considered committing suicide only a few months earlier, though I was unaware of that fact, just as I was unaware of how crucial our presence was now in getting her past those dark thoughts.

Instead, my eleven-year-old self was self-absorbedly content that I was about to spend a glorious few days in a warm, clean house. A house full of comfy chairs and couches, antique armoires, and familiar ceramic knick-knacks and pastoral paintings decorating the shelves and walls. A house, timeless and changeless, that David and I knew intimately from our earliest memories.

It would be a whole weekend of basking in Mom's love, watching *Perry Mason* and *Bonanza* with Grandpa and Grandma and *Merv Griffin* with Mom, and gorging on our grandparents' home cooking. All of which stood in stark relief to our grim weekday life with Dad in a sad and lonely farmhouse ten miles outside of town.

The past year had been devastating for both my parents. The steady progression of the symptoms of multiple sclerosis had slowly and inexorably trapped my mother's joyous spirit and bright mind in a coffin made of her own inert flesh and bones. Just five years after her initial diagnosis, which had come when David and I were five years old, she'd lost the ability to walk or feed herself. Her physical disabilities had also diminished her intellectual pursuits in that she could no longer write, and her eyes could not track well enough to read a book.

Dad had reached his breaking point from the strain of coping with Mom's illness during the previous school year. Years later, he revealed to me that, overwhelmed by the severity of Mom's disabilities, he decided to abandon all of us. On that late winter day in 1968, he got in his car and simply started driving. His plan was to keep going until the authorities caught up to him and put him in jail. My mom would be put in a nursing home, David and I would be placed in foster care, and his worries would be over.

Five hundred miles later, his fevered brain finally came upon a different alternative, and he turned the car around. When he came home, Dad told my mother that he could no longer take care of her and take care of us, and that he had to make a choice. He admitted that the amount of attention she needed was beyond his capacity to provide, even with the hired help that came in for a few hours three days a week. He felt she needed to go into a nursing home.

The next few weeks were awful for all of us. During the many angry and tearful arguments between our parents, David and I quietly sought each other out in our respective bedrooms, trying to figure out what was happening and to find comfort, however small, in each other's presence.

We were aware, without really understanding why, that our family was unraveling.

Although her move meant the arguments were over, the next four months Mom spent in the nursing home while we finished the school year were not any better. It did not feel right, her living in that place with all those old people. I hated the smell, the fluorescent lights, and the squeaky floors.

By the end of the school year, it became clear we had all been treading water. It was time to jump out of the pool before someone sank to the bottom.

When we first got to Iowa, a week before the start of school, David and I stayed with Mom while Dad set up our new home. The only place he could afford was a run-down house on an abandoned farm about ten miles outside town. We would live in several dreary homes with Dad in the years to come, but this creepy, forlorn house was the worst.

Whitewater Pioneers (1970)

At the end of the week, Dad picked us up for our first night in our new home. As we pulled into the gravel driveway, my first sight of the two-story house with peeling white paint and blank, staring windows was not encouraging. Reluctantly, I pulled my duffel bag of clothes onto my shoulder and carried it across the sagging porch to the front door.

Fawn's frolicking tail-wagging and romping did little to assuage my dread.

The living room was furnished with a massive blue velour couch and a work desk made from a door placed on cinder blocks next to an old kerosene-fueled stove. The only other furniture in the downstairs central living space was a cheap Formica kitchen table surrounded by three mismatched chairs. No rugs, no pictures on the walls, nothing to make the house homey. Dad's bedroom was located behind a curtain he had placed over the entrance to a small room off the living room, furnished simply with an old iron bed frame and mattress.

Since there were no other rooms on the first floor, Dad led us upstairs to pick which of the four bare, cold rooms we wanted. David and I walked through the dusty rooms, each with mottled, peeling paint on the walls and cobwebs on the ceiling. I picked my room first, and Dad helped drag a mattress to my spot. After David had picked his room and we'd maneuvered a mattress into it, too, all three of us stood in awkward silence for a moment. There was no more furniture to move or stuff to unpack besides our clothes.

I looked at my duffel bag by the door. "Uh, where should I put my clothes?"

Dad walked over to the closet and gestured inside. "Well, we aren't going to be here long enough to buy dressers, so you can hang your nice clothes in this closet, and you can just keep your other clothes in your duffel bag."

RISK

Basically, we were camping—but without the benefit of sleeping next to a beautiful river or in a serene forest. I carried my duffel bag over to the closet floor and went back down to the car to get my nice clothes. Over the summer, my grandmother had sewn school outfits for me from JCPenney patterns my mom had selected, one for each day of the week. Hanging the brightly colored jumpers and skirts with matching jackets neatly in the closet made me feel a little better. At least I would not look poor when I went to school.

Because Dad had given away all our belongings before we left Cleveland, we had no toys or books to put away or posters to put on the walls. Since there was no electricity—or heat—in the upstairs rooms, we also had no lamps. David and I took turns at bedtime being the one to turn the light off at the end of the upstairs hallway and then navigate with our hand along the cold wall to find the door to our bedroom. The temperature in our bedrooms was almost the same as the outdoor temperature; as winter approached, we needed all the blankets and sleeping bags at our disposal to stay warm through the night. In the mornings, we scampered downstairs, school clothes in hand, so we could take turns standing by the gas stove to pre-warm our clothes before getting dressed. On the coldest nights, Dad hung a blanket over the doorway between the living room and the rest of the house, and David and I slept on air mattresses by the stove.

I dreaded the days and nights we spent with Dad in this barren, lonely place and eagerly looked forward to Wednesdays and Fridays, when David and I walked to our grandparents' house in town after school. On Wednesdays, Dad's grocery shopping day, we only stayed with Mom and our grandparents through dinnertime. But on Fridays we had the whole, delicious weekend in the comfort and warmth of our grandparents' soul-saving refuge to look forward to.

Whitewater Pioneers (1970)

When I was a young adult, a friend once remarked to me, "You always eat as if it's your last meal." The correlation between that characteristic and the periods of relative feast and famine in my childhood is hard to ignore.

In addition to discovering how different our homes were going to feel living only with Dad, our year in Iowa also demonstrated Dad's limitations in providing us with appetizing fare. Although we were both always lean, I now find some photos of David and me during our middle school years alarming, our thinness and pallor shocking.

A typical home-cooked dinner by Dad consisted of plain hamburger meat patties (with A-1 sauce and ketchup as condiments) and potato chips, or a casserole of tuna and rice mixed with a can of mushroom soup. Fresh vegetables, when offered, consisted of iceberg lettuce salad with a few chopped radishes and celery. We also ate a lot of fast food and TV dinners, the latter of which always looked way better in the picture on the box.

In contrast, Grandpa's Betty Crocker cookbook–inspired Sunday dinners of pot roast or fried chicken were always amply augmented with fresh or home-canned vegetables and fruits from his half-acre garden. The bounty from this garden included crisp green beans, snap peas, tomatoes, and sweet corn; homemade blackberry, raspberry, and strawberry preserves spread on soft white rolls; cinnamon sugar–infused tart applesauce from the sour green apple tree in the side yard; and pies. Pies filled with strawberry and rhubarb, cherry, or apple, with tender, flaky crust and dollops of vanilla ice cream melting over the top. The cookie jar, meanwhile, was a horn of plenty, the supply of homemade snickerdoodles rarely depleted.

In contrast to life with Dad, the memories of the abundance we feasted on during our visits with Mom have been heightened

RISK

to mythic levels in my brain in the years since—like the memories of the first meals experienced by survivors rescued from a lifeboat at sea or liberated prisoners of war. To this day, I can remember with clarity the flavors and textures that my grandparents produced from their garden.

While David and I were staying with Mom, Dad made himself scarce—writing comic book stories, preparing proposals for syndicated comic strips, and walking the dogs on desolate farm roads. As the wife-deserter, he was *persona non grata* with Mom's family. During his brief exchanges with my grandparents, seething anger and resentment was visible in the harsh lines of their faces; I'm sure he was eager to steer clear of them. And he had no friends in the area. Apart than me, my brother, and our pets, Dad lived in total social isolation in Bloomfield.

We got our second dog during our residency at the creepy farmhouse when a skinny little black and tan spaniel-like puppy showed up on our doorstep, barfing up grasshoppers. We all immediately fell in love with the intelligent and meek little puppy, who was the polar opposite of Fawn, our dopey and overly excitable lab. My dad, always a soft touch, said we could keep the puppy and that David and I could pick its name. We chose Biskit after our favorite food from our summer camping on the river.

Biskit gave my grandparents another reason to scorn my dad's common sense—*what was he thinking, adopting another animal when he could barely provide for us?*—but for Dad, our pets were essential to his quality of life and work. As the animals were critical creative tools for his trade, their expenses were included as itemized deductions on his tax returns. They provided endless inspirations for his cartoons, which relied heavily on the antics of dog and cat characters. Biskit, Fawn, and our cat, Spook, were the only playmates David and I had at the farmhouse, and Dad's only companions.

Whitewater Pioneers (1970)

Dad tried to make enough money for us to survive by freelance writing comic book stories for Dell Publishing that featured popular cartoon characters like Bugs Bunny, Daffy Duck, and Tom and Jerry. Since he made about thirty dollars a story and only sold two or three a week, our continued residency in Iowa was clearly not sustainable. Although he continued to send proposals for his own newspaper comic strip, he was never able to break into the larger syndicates where the big money was.

By Christmas, Dad had had enough; he announced his decision to relocate us to Southern California the following school year. He arranged for David and me to temporarily live on our aunt and uncle's farm so we could finish the sixth grade near Mom, and he went ahead to Los Angeles to get settled and begin a more lucrative freelancing job writing for television cartoon studios.

David and I finished out sixth grade at a one-room-per-class country school that was also attended by our three cousins (ages nine, twelve, and fourteen). At their home on the farm, we lived in fear of Aunt Dorothy losing her shit every other minute. Although living with our cousins was an improvement from our previous isolation, our thirty-year-old aunt was clearly stretched to her limit with five children underfoot during the long, cold months of winter.

Our previous visits to our cousins' farm had always been during the summer, when we were only allowed to be inside for meals and the hour before bedtime when we took our baths.

But now our rambunctious after-school inside play frequently resulted in my aunt stomping upstairs, ping-pong paddle at the ready for spanking whoever had not heeded her warning about not producing unacceptably loud banging, thumping, or shouting.

RISK

Although I did not understand why she got so angry with us at the time, I now have tremendous compassion for my young aunt. When I eventually became a parent, I struggled to deal with the brain-melting chaos that just one child can create when cooped up inside too long, much less in a pack. I cannot imagine the day-to-day stress my aunt felt caring for her own three children *and* David and me, while also coping with the impacts of Mom's illness on our grandparents.

Unfortunately, the subliminal effects of the stressors bombarding David and me resulted in us becoming bedwetters—another reason for our presence to drive our aunt completely berserk. In return, her stress steadily fed the chronic state of anxiety growing in my brother and me.

The cycle of pain and dysfunction that emerges from family tragedy spins like a wobbly top, banging into many nearby objects just before it falls.

Before moving in with our aunt, David and I moved back in with our grandparents and Mom for a couple of months. During this time, I began to gain a deeper understanding of my mother's life experience and who she was as a person, not just as my mother.

Because she could no longer physically read or hold a pen, Mom usually hired a neighbor kid to maintain her active correspondence with a large group of family and friends, but while we were living with her that summer, and after that, whenever we visited, David and I took over this job.

Letters had become my mom's lifeline to the outside world since becoming bedridden. Although they included their fair share of mundane and often embarrassing praise of David's and my accomplishments, they also included thoughtful conversations about worldviews and life philosophies.

Both of my parents were anomalies from their midwestern corn-fed upbringing, and their leftist tendencies were part of

Whitewater Pioneers (1970)

what brought them together when they met while pursuing liberal arts degrees at the University of Iowa. Many of Mom's letters were to members of her former river clan, the Ozark Wilderness Waterways Canoe Club (OWWCC). These were some of her most enduring friendships and the people with whom she most openly shared her liberal views on politics, feminism, and environmental conservation.

Growing up in Bloomfield, my mom's idea of experiencing the outdoors had been limited to driving to a lake in a state park located nearby. But this had changed dramatically while David and I were still toddlers, soon after our dad began taking off on weekend canoe trips in the Ozarks, leaving her home alone with us.

Although she had no concept of what he was up to, Mom presented Dad with an ultimatum after one of these trips. After returning home from his fun weekend, Dad found a two-page letter on the dining room table. In it, Mom stated, in no uncertain terms, that she was not going to tolerate being left behind while he played at being "the great white explorer." Her final words on the matter were "Either we all go, or nobody goes."

Consequently, at the age of two and a half, my brother and I, with our somewhat reluctant but determined mother, joined our father in his ever-growing pursuit of outdoor adventure on the river—the origin of my earliest and most vivid childhood memories.

Sitting on my wooden seat next to my brother in the middle of the canoe at age three, I trailed my hand in the clear water of the river. I enjoyed the feeling of cool water flowing around my skin and was fascinated by the ripple pattern my hand created on the water's surface. The river bent and turned, passing brilliant green forests and tall beige and gray sandstone and shale bluffs. Around the next bend, the river widened, and I saw the canoes in front of us disappear into a tall gray bluff on the side of the river.

RISK

Dad steered the canoe toward the bluff and a large black opening appeared.

From her seat in the front of the canoe, Mom said, "Look kids, a cave! Do you want to go in?"

"I guess so," I responded, uneasy but also curious.

Mom and Dad slowly paddled the canoe into the dark mouth of the cave. We heard the echoing voices and laughter of our companions as our vision temporarily went black. When our eyes adjusted, the light filtering into the cave revealed a large cavern looming over an emerald-green pool. We pulled up next to the other canoes in our flotilla, and the deep metallic clanks of the aluminum canoes as they touched reverberated, along with the sounds of water drips and paddle splashes, in the air. My uneasiness slowly abated as Mom chatted excitedly with one of the women in the canoe next to us, marveling at the beauty of the cavern.

"Maybe this is where 'the Echo' lives," Dad said, turning to me and David.

"The Echo?" my brother asked. "Who's that?"

"You know," Dad said, "the little man who repeats everything we say in the cave, and sometimes on the steep cliffs across from our river camp."

Our canoe was a magical ship, carrying us through a fantastical wonderland.

A little further downstream, I saw one of the canoes on our trip pulled over to the side of the river, its occupants standing on shore with a rope. The man on shore yelled out to Dad, "Be sure to angle hard left when you enter the turn so you don't get jammed up on that tree!"

"Okay," Dad yelled back. "Bette, draw left!"

Mom tried to pull the front of the canoe to the left with her paddle as we entered the swift current. There were no big waves or rocks, but the river bent at a sharp left angle, forcing the

Whitewater Pioneers (1970)

current to pile up on the right bank against a tree trunk that had collapsed along the river.

Dad yelled louder at Mom, "Draw harder, harder!" as our canoe gained speed, heading straight for the tree trunk.

With a sharp jolt and loud thunk, the canoe bashed into the tree, and suddenly, I was under water.

I popped up, sputtering, filled with panic.

"SAVE THE TWINS! SAVE THE TWINS!" I heard from multiple voices as I was swiftly swept down the river. But not for long.

Within moments a canoe pulled up beside me and I was lifted out of the water by my lifejacket and dropped on a gear bag next to my dripping wet brother. As our rescuers paddled us to shore, David and I shrieked, "Mommy! Get Mommy!" as we watched our mother disappear around the next bend of the river.

David and I were fussed over by several women in our group as a few men helped Dad pull our upside-down canoe over to shore. Eventually, Mom and two other members of our club emerged from the forest downstream. David and I ran over to embrace each leg of her wet denim overalls.

Mom tried to make sure to portage us around any significant rapids on our weekend explorations on the rivers we traveled in the Ozarks—the Current, Buffalo, and Niangua—but unexpected capsizes were an unavoidable risk. Fortunately, due to the capable hands of our friends in the OWWCC, quick and efficient rescues could be also counted on. David and I also learned an additional benefit to these mishaps: any time a capsize of the Norman canoe transpired, David and I were each handed a whole, bright rainbow-colored roll of Life Savers candy at the next monthly club meeting.

Participating in weekend canoe trips with the OWWCC changed my mom's world. Although she had been brought up going to church every Sunday, she did not establish a personal

RISK

relationship with her higher power until she began canoeing in the Ozarks. In an essay that I read as an adult years later after she passed away, she wrote that through the beauty and rhythm of nature and the river, she experienced a visceral spiritual awareness and connection to something greater. In the outdoors, God became real.

Both of my parents were grateful that they did not wait until David and I were a more "reasonable" age before embarking on whitewater canoeing adventures. If they had waited until we'd passed out of toddlerhood—a time when diapers were necessary and symptoms from mumps, measles, or chickenpox frequently and inconveniently manifested themselves on weekend canoe trips—my mother's illness would have prevented us from ever having these adventures together. As it was, for about five years, mostly before Mom's diagnosis, we all got the chance to explore rivers in the Missouri and Arkansas Ozarks together.

The memories of those five years of adventures sustained Mom through some very bleak times as an invalid, and her friendships from the Ozark Wilderness Waterways Canoe Club lasted a lifetime.

Living with Mom's illness meant my childhood was defined by a constant and evolving relationship with grief. First, I was a powerless child suffering the loss of my mother; then I became a helpless bystander, increasingly aware of the undeserved suffering she was experiencing. Whenever I visited my mother as I grew up, I experienced new and profound grief surrounding her illness. And not only because her physical condition continually deteriorated. As my empathy matured, my awareness of how her illness affected *her* life, and not just my own, became that much more acute. Over time, my self-pity was replaced by sadness for the suffering she endured, mostly without complaint. My mother was often physically uncomfortable, surrounded by acres of boredom,

Whitewater Pioneers (1970)

and frustrated by her physical dependency on others. As her daughter, this was painful to witness.

This continual relationship with grief provided a constant source of grappling with emerging questions in my growing adolescent mind. *What did Mom ever do to deserve this? How can there really be a God, or such a thing as karma?*

Multiple sclerosis's relentless attack on my mother's body taught me that life is not fair. Sad things happen to good people, I learned, and there is little we can do about it. This produced a keen desire in me to seize control of whatever part of living I could, since so much was clearly out of our hands. Her disability also spurred me to pursue athletics, because I had a heightened awareness that being blessed with a healthy body was a gift that could be taken away at any time.

I spent many nights throughout my childhood weeping my frustration and anguish into my pillow, as my awareness of Mom's suffering inexorably grew alongside my own physical growth. I also had a recurring dream during my visits in which she miraculously recovered and could walk again. It was always devastating to wake up from that dream.

I would not wish my mom's life experience on anyone; however, even trapped as she was in her increasingly ravaged body, Mom was a unique force. She had an enduring sense of humor and passionately shared her views as an early and vocal advocate for women's liberation and environmental conservation. From her I learned the importance of connections with friends and community and finding spiritual growth and solace through connection with the natural world. She taught me never to set my bar low because I was female. And to never let myself be taken advantage of.

I was nineteen when Mom shared with me that she had considered taking her own life nine years earlier. She told me the only reason she didn't was her overriding desire to see David and I grow up and provide parental guidance during whatever fractured

RISK

time she had to spend with us. She also told me how grateful she was that she had not made that choice. She was so proud of my achievements and saw me as the embodiment of her hopes. Through her love, I grew up perceiving myself as a capable, independent being with worth—the greatest gift a mother can give her child.

Chapter 5
A Quality Partner (2014)

One late Sunday afternoon, I walk in the door after a weekend at Lisa's house and stop dead in my tracks. The blinds are down, and David is asleep on the couch. Seth is sitting on the floor, still in his pajama onesie, surrounded by LEGOs, absorbed in making one of his fantastical flying battleship creations.

Almost every surface in the house, counters and tables, is covered in dirty dishes, open boxes of crackers, bags of chips, candy wrappers, soda cans, and pizza boxes. It seems every toy Seth owns is also scattered around the living room, as is a box of spilled cereal and a variety of food wrappers. I don't think they've left the house the entire weekend.

It is worse than usual. I feel smothered, hardly able to breathe in the stuffy air of dysfunction.

"Hello, sweetie," I say to Seth, forcing the strained greeting out of my throat, trying to keep my tone light. Still trying to keep it genial for Seth's sake, I say a little more loudly, "Hey David, let's start cleaning things up, okay?"

I cannot keep a slight tremor, forced by the suppressed fury I want to unleash, out of my voice.

"Uh, yeah . . . okay . . ." David mumbles, opening his eyes groggily.

RISK

Why is he so tired? And how long has he been sleeping on the couch, leaving Seth to his own devices?

He gets up slowly and shuffles into the kitchen. As he begins moving dirty dishes to the sink, I grab a garbage bag and start picking up trash, wanting to reclaim order out of the chaos as quickly as possible.

Removing a greasy pizza box off the pine coffee table, I see the wood is covered in a maze of red, green, and blue Crayola Super Tips markers. No coherent drawings, just chaotic scribbling. A project that clearly took some time to accomplish.

"Jesus," I exclaim, "what happened here?"

David looks over at me, rolls his eyes, and sighs. "Ahh, I dunno, he must have done that while I was sleeping."

I turn around abruptly, walk into my room, and close the door, hoping to take a moment to control my emotions. But behind the door, I am immediately confronted by my African djembe, a drum I loved, stabbed to death. The steak knife used to slash a big X across the head is still embedded in the cowhide.

Apparently, David has done a lot of sleeping this weekend, and Seth has run amok. I collapse on my bed and put my head in my hands, overwhelmed.

I need to call Lisa.

Because when Seth first came to live with me we still maintained our separate homes, I think Lisa did not initially perceive Seth and David's move to Tahoe as a significant threat to her lifestyle. This was mainly going to be my thing. She would be free to pop in and out of the situation and keep her life intact.

However, after the weekend the drum was brutally murdered, we agreed Seth should no longer be left alone with David.

Lisa begrudgingly started coming to my house on the weekends when I did not bring Seth to her house. They were horribly uncomfortable weekends, the four of us trapped in my

A Quality Partner (2014)

760-square-foot house. My small mountain home had been a cozy base for our daily outdoor explorations when it had just been Lisa, me, and our dogs. But now, every minute in it felt claustrophobic. I hated no longer being able to love my home.

Something needed to shift, and soon.

In December, four and a half months after David's arrival in California, Lisa and I escape for a dog walk at the lake on a cold, windy day. I desperately gulp the icy air, embracing the expanse of Lake Tahoe and surrounding beach and mountains. The cobalt blue surface of the lake is covered in frothy whitecaps. The myriad forms and shades of this beautiful lake have always been a delight to me, even during my most troubled moods.

As we trudge against the biting wind, our footsteps crunching on frozen sand and ice, Lisa puts it plainly: "Sue, you are going to have to do something about your brother. This is just not working."

"But what am I supposed to do?"

"You need to tell him to move out, to get his own place."

"I know, I know . . . I can't even stand to be in my own house anymore." I turn pleading eyes on her. "But where is he supposed to go?"

"I don't know, and I don't care," she fumes. Fierce blond Viking eyebrows arch over flashing green eyes, widened by her anger. "You are constantly stressed out," she continues. "You fly into rages over everything. We never do anything fun anymore. He has to go!"

My puffy eyes, already streaming from the bitter wind, become gushers as my anger overwhelms me. "God, I hate this situation. And I hate how I am now. I just feel trapped."

My chest hurts, a sharp ache consisting of equal parts disappointment and anger toward my brother. As well as fear and sadness, not seeing a clear path to protect Seth from more emotional turmoil. I cannot see solutions. I can only feel the pain.

At the sound of my broken voice, Lisa's becomes softer. "Well, the first thing you need to do is get your brother out of your house. He is not helping you or Seth in any way."

"But where—"

"Sue!" Lisa cuts me off. "He is a grown man. You have been helping take care of him for years. It is time for him to figure his shit out without dragging us all down with him."

Lisa has a perspective I do not. Like my brother, she is an alcoholic.

I did not know Lisa during her drinking years. We met after she had done the heavy lifting. The woman I knew did not drink and no longer went to AA meetings. But through "the work," she'd found other activities, many of which we shared, to take up the space her former addiction occupied. She also knew what happened to people who did not do the work. She had friends from AA who died from their disease.

Sometimes Lisa still craved a drink. She did not like parties and needed substantial time alone with her animals. She was susceptible to short-circuiting over what seemed to me trivial stressors and triggers, often surrounding borderline OCD tendencies. And when she felt anxious and uncomfortable in her skin, she often wished there was some quick fix.

But Lisa is also the person you wanted around in a crisis. When faced with the mountain instead of molehills, she became a different person. The minutia disappeared and she snapped into laser-like focus.

I learned this about her on several occasions, the first of which took place a year and a half after we started dating—on September 11, 2001. We were at the Newport Beach Airport, on our way home to Tahoe, when all the flights in the United States were shut down

A Quality Partner (2014)

that day. After watching the terrifying early footage on the television screens and then hearing the announcement that all flights had been canceled, she snapped into action—literally dragged me by the collar to the rental car booth, then convinced them to rent us a car even though they were all "booked" for incoming flights. Lisa was the first person in the whole damn airport that understood the magnitude of what was happening. Three hours later, there wasn't a rental car to be had in all of Southern California.

Around this same time, I also saw Lisa's ability to focus under pressure while doing her photography work.

Sitting high on a rock outcrop overlooking a water hole, I watched Lisa slowly walk around the wild horses already gathered at the far side of the small, muddy pond. Soon, multiple bands would be coming in for their evening happy hour.

She meticulously picked her way through the sagebrush, her camera, lenses, and tripod slung over her shoulder, and set up her tripod on the far side of the waterhole just as the evening light reached the golden hour. The colorful hides of the paints, grays, roans, and bays glowed as the setting sun began to light the clouds above. From my perch, I couldn't hear it, but I knew Lisa was furiously clicking away, face pressed against the camera, zooming in on the mares, colts, and stallions that caught her eye.

Suddenly I saw a trail of dust appear over a slight rise behind and to the right of Lisa. A new band was coming in hot. In addition, a group of four bachelor stallions, not yet powerful enough to have acquired mares for their own band, had positioned themselves between Lisa and the band she was photographing. These young two- to three-year-old teenagers, located on the lowest rung within the wild horse hierarchy, were standing right next to the trail the new band was coming in on.

I tried to wave to Lisa to let her know the shit was about to hit the fan but she, still focused intently on the horses in her view screen, didn't see me.

RISK

The stallion from the incoming band saw the bachelors blocking his path into the water hole and charged. In seconds, Lisa was surrounded by about twenty wild horses, all of them galloping in different directions, everyone but the charging stallion trying to get out of the way.

One of the bachelors began to run toward Lisa at full speed, either not seeing her or deliberately trying to use her to distract the stallion hot on his heels.

Now surrounded by dust and thundering hooves and fully aware of what was happening, Lisa stood up to her full five feet eight and a half inches, took off her gray Stetson, and stepped forward aggressively toward the bachelor, waving her hat furiously over her head.

Fifteen feet in front of her, he finally veered off.

And Lisa immediately dropped back down behind her lens and began shooting toward the two stallions that were now facing off, rearing and kicking, manes and tails swirling through the air. Immersed in a world she loves and understands, Lisa creates stunning equine photography. Simultaneously magical, spiritual, and grounding.

That's my girl, I thought. Fearless and focused. The person you want by your side in a crisis.

As I try to figure out how to manage the swirling chaos that Seth and David have brought into our lives, Lisa is once again showing me the path to navigate the danger that looms ahead.

David is no longer my responsibility. Seth is.

"You're right, you're right," I say simply. My voice calms, the pain in my chest eases slightly.

She puts a hand on my shoulder. "Do you want me to tell him? Because I will."

"No, no, I will do it," I say. "But I would like you there."

David is a little afraid of Lisa. She is formidable when she's

A Quality Partner (2014)

mad. He is less likely to blow up if she is around when I deliver this news.

Seth is about to be engulfed in a rancorous battle between his dad and me, but Lisa will help soften the blows. I am grateful that she is the person she is, able to step up with ferocity when it really matters.

She and I entered our relationship with the mutual understanding that neither of us wanted children. Before Seth, we were part of a community of happily childfree adults that spent their time with other childfree adults. We took for granted the fulfillment of uninterrupted adult conversations and activities, as well as the precious peace of silent companionship.

The moment Seth moved in with me, however, that life ended. And it is not coming back.

Chapter 6
Living Alone (1973)

David and I held hands in the backseat of Grandpa's Buick Skylark. Our sniffles were clearly audible as the powerful car sped silently past the bucolic landscape of cows and cornfields. Usually, we enjoyed driving in Grandpa and Grandma Norman's fancy car—a pleasant contrast to our noisy rattletrap, which reeked of wet dog and Dad's cigar butts—during our visits. But today the smooth, quiet ride of the car magnified our sadness during the three-hour drive from Cedar Rapids to Bloomfield, Iowa, where we were going to drop my brother off with Mom and Grandma and Grandpa Sager.

Grandma Norman fidgeted and groused the whole way, and our perpetually cheerful Grandpa was uncharacteristically quiet and somber.

I think most twins must have difficulty being alone. I believe nine months developing in the womb with another human being creates a core need for intimate relationships and a primal discomfort with just being with oneself.

Alone with Grandpa and Grandma Norman on the return drive to Cedar Rapids the next day—separated for the first time from my annoying, irritating, and dorky twin brother—I felt like part of me had been ripped away. David was my most constant

Living Alone (1973)

companion, the mirror, recipient, and audience of my actions. He and I were emotionally connected in a way I have never again experienced.

After sixth grade in Iowa, we'd moved with Dad to LA, where he'd hoped to get a good-paying job writing for television comedy shows. But in our two years there, he'd only managed to find seasonal contract work in the television cartoon industry, which came with no benefits. I don't think we had even basic health insurance.

With David and I now about to enter ninth grade, the reality of living on welfare for six months out of the year, carrying unpaid debts related to Mom's illness, and having no guarantee of future security was not something Dad was willing to keep taking a chance on in the hopes of making it "big." He felt returning to work for American Greetings in Cleveland was his only option to provide our family financial stability until David and I graduated from high school. And during our transition from LA to Cleveland, he again asked the family to take David and me for the first half of ninth grade while he got settled into work and established a home for us in Cleveland.

Aunt Dorothy had made it clear that she would not take us in again like she had during sixth grade, so—through a decision process I was not privy to—the family had decided David would stay with my mother and her parents in Bloomfield, Iowa, and I with my dad's parents in Cedar Rapids. Looking back on this, I'm sure my mom heavily influenced this decision because she understood David needed her more. But at the time, I felt rejected.

I loved Grandma and Grandpa Norman, but I cried myself to sleep every night for the first month I lived with them. I had never felt so adrift and alone, cut off from everyone in my immediate family—Mom, Dad, David, even the dogs. There was not much to fill the gaping hole left in the place my twin brother had long occupied in my life. And the knowledge that this was a

RISK

temporary situation precluded any efforts to overcome my painful shyness to establish new friendships at the school I attended for only three and a half months. What would be the point? And there were no kids my age in the retiree neighborhood where my grandparents lived.

The days passed with excruciating slowness. I crossed them off one by one on a calendar until the start of Christmas vacation.

When the first ninth grade semester finally ended, David and I spent another week at our mom's over Christmas vacation, making the most of the time we had before leaving her again.

I think this looming separation must have been particularly painful for David, having had our mother to himself for the past three months. Although I have no doubts about the depth of love and pride my mom had for me, I know that she had a different and equally deep love for David. She knew he was more vulnerable, and I think she felt an intense desire to protect him—and a deep worry over the limitations of what she could do.

After leaving the diesel-and-bathroom smell of the Greyhound bus we had spent the last twenty-four hours on—from Des Moines, Iowa, to Cleveland, Ohio—I was enveloped in a feeling of comfortable belonging when Dad opened the door to our stinky, dog hair–covered station wagon. It felt great to be back together in our adventure mobile again, as gross as it was. I was positively overjoyed to wallow in hairy and sloppy wet dog greetings.

"Oh, I missed you too," I said as I hugged Fawn, immediately plastering my clothes with a layer of blond dog hair. With Biskit's black hair, no article of clothing, regardless of shade, was safe in the station wagon.

Fawn's body wriggled into me as she buried her nose in my neck and licked my face, while Biskit quietly crawled between David and me and gently put her head in his lap. He murmured sweet nothings in her ear and petted her on the head.

Living Alone (1973)

But any sense of being back to the familiar, or home, dissipated as we walked into our lower-middle-class rental house in west Cleveland. This place was just as dreary and unwelcoming as our previous homes in Iowa and California had been, sparsely furnished with ratty Salvation Army furniture, containing merely the bare necessities to exist.

David and I trudged up the stairs to put our bags in our dingy, bare rooms and quickly returned to the living room.

"Come pick out which dinner you want tonight," Dad called from the kitchen.

David and I walked over to the counter to examine the variety of TV dinners he had pulled out. I picked the sirloin steak with mashed potatoes and peas and a brownie dessert, while David picked the fried chicken with French fries, corn, and apple cobbler.

"Do you want to trade desserts?" I asked David, knowing he would prefer the brownie.

"Sure," he said despondently.

I knew how he felt.

I imagine we were both missing some aspects of living with our grandparents in their clean and homey houses with home-cooked meals, wishing we could merge those two worlds somehow. But I could not have put it in words at the time. I only recently have come to consciously understand that after we stopped living with my mother, I never again felt a sense of safety and stability—characteristics I have since learned through counseling are essential for a child's sense of well-being—while growing up. Moving frequently, not only in location but also across a broad spectrum of American society, was illuminating once I gained perspective in adulthood, but at the time it was disorienting.

Life in our economically depressed blue-collar Irish Catholic neighborhood in west Cleveland again felt like an alien world, compounded by the added pressures and confusion of full-blown puberty. Our peers at school seethed with a mixture of hormones and bottled-up repression, having spent the first eight years of their education in Catholic school before entering the public schools in the ninth grade.

Our school district was a melting pot: predominantly Irish and Italian families, but also more recently arrived immigrants from Puerto Rico and Eastern Europe. Many kids at West Technical High School were learning to speak English for the first time. Our school dumbed down the classes accordingly and focused on grooming most of the students for trades rather than college. The boys at least got to take cool classes like auto or wood shop; as a girl, I was forced to take home economics and typing. The school was so academically unchallenging that David and I got all our homework done either during the boring classes or scheduled study halls.

A neighbor girl my age tried to befriend me, but I could not find much common ground with her; her interests were primarily makeup, cheerleading, and boys, while my main interest was sports. The problem was, I was too old for neighborhood street games, and because Title IX had not yet happened, there were no high school teams for girls other than the cheerleading squad. Even if I had been interested in cheer, I never would have gotten selected for that. Short and skinny, with buck teeth, freckles, and lank dishwater blond hair, I looked much younger than my age. My looks, social awkwardness, and tomboy interests ensured I was an oddball who did not fit in.

With no homework, extracurricular activities, or friends, David and I whiled away the time watching hours and hours of mindless seventies TV. *Green Acres*, *The Partridge Family*, *Bonanza*, *Mister Ed*, *I Dream of Jeannie*—you name it, we watched it. But that gradually became pretty much the only activity the two of us shared. A distance began to develop between us as we entered puberty and developed more distinct personalities, likes,

Living Alone (1973)

and dislikes. David was marginally more successful than I was socially: he found a couple of fellow nerds who also liked chess club and fantasy games at school, and they stuck together.

Of course, I was clearly a nerd, too; I just had not learned to embrace it yet. When not watching TV, I immersed myself in books.

Dad had hoped that moving us to Cleveland and giving us a chance to stay in one place for four years would allow David and me to develop the kinds of friendships and experiences he had enjoyed while growing up in Cedar Rapids. He had very fond memories of his high school years—specifically, his close group of friends, which he'd maintained from elementary through high school. But I could not find my people. Even more so than in LA, I felt isolated. Still a stranger in a strange land.

I never found home in Cleveland. But through my dad's ever-growing pursuit of escape through whitewater paddling, we found our way back to another home: the river.

Chapter 7
Class V Therapy (2015)

"Here, why don't you take a seat," Seth's psychologist says as we enter her office.

In another room on the other side of the hall, Seth is still happily playing with toy dinosaurs and action figures. We're in here without him so Mary, a heavyset woman with a motherly smile and warm brown eyes, can give me her initial assessment.

Mary leans toward me as she settles into the chair next to mine. "First, let me assure you Seth's behavior is completely understandable, and he will get better."

The relief I feel at her certain words, those of a professional, is so intense my eyes begin to tear.

Over the past two months, I've made myself sick with internet research. What I've read online has filled me with apprehension. Seth did not receive the stimulation and nurturing essential for healthy early childhood development, and I've been terrified that the parenting he received during his first four years of life caused irreparable damage to his developing brain.

"So, you don't think it's too late?" I ask, voicing my worst fears.

"No, not at all," she says firmly. "I'm not supposed to ever say this. But I've worked with kids who have been through so much

Class V Therapy (2015)

trauma that their spark has been all but snuffed out. They will suffer from any number of mental illnesses as adults and likely need therapy their whole lives. But Seth displays a lot of positive behaviors. He is curious, playful, and happy. Why, when that child smiles, he lights up the whole room!"

At this, I can only nod, tears streaming from my eyes. Mary gently gestures to a box of tissues sitting on a side table between our two chairs. I noticed earlier that the flowery pastel boxes seemed to be plentiful throughout the South Lake Tahoe Family Resource Center. Now, grateful, I snatch a handful.

"Seth's emotional development has been delayed because his little brain does not know how to process the grief and confusion he has experienced from the abrupt family separations he has had to endure," Mary continues. "Because he's experienced so little stability in his life, he snaps whenever he feels something going out of control in his world. He simply does not yet have the tools to cope with another child trying to play with his toy, or not getting to do something he wants."

The tears have stopped, but I take a moment to blow my nose one final time.

"But how do I get him to stop hitting?" I ask, anxiously wadding the used tissues into a ball.

"Well, as part of our treatment plan, I'll work with you and his kindergarten teacher to develop strategies for managing his impulse control issues. It will take time, but with a lot of love and a safe environment going forward, his emotional development will catch up."

"What do you mean by a safe environment, exactly?" I ask, latching on to that phrase. "I mean, he has never been abused, he's just been"—pausing briefly to consider the right word, I stuff the tissues into my pocket—"neglected."

"That may be," she says with a small shrug, "but neglect can be considered a form of abuse. I'm talking about how kids *feel*. For

RISK

instance, from what you've told me about his dad and his drinking, that's a problem. Kids can't feel safe around an alcoholic, no matter how much they love them. He will need someone else to provide him a safe, stable home."

"Oh," I said.

Someone else. Like me?

"This is why kids end up in foster care," Mary says. "They don't want to leave their parents. They are placed in foster care to take them out of an unhealthy situation. Of course, as you know, this is not always an ideal solution, either. It's always better if there is someone they have a strong relationship with within the family that can provide the stability they need. Seth is lucky to have you."

I nod weakly, not yet fully accepting my new reality.

Later, on the drive home, I struggle to wrap my head around what Mary told me. The role I thought I was going to play in Seth's life continues to shift. Not only is David showing no signs of wanting to move out of my house, but this is now the second therapist who's told me that Seth will not thrive living with his father.

A month ago, I started seeing a family counselor with David. I've gone from never seeing a therapist before in my life to seeing two different counselors every week.

In his youth, David was a bright boy full of innocence and promise. I see a lot of the boy I grew up with in Seth. But the young man who scored in the ninety-fifth percentile on his high school SATs has become an adult who can't hold down a job.

In his late fifties, David looks like someone ten to twenty years older. He is gaunt, and his movements are slow and stiff. His hair is completely white. Sometimes, his eyes are buggy and a little crazy-looking. He rarely smiles because he is missing teeth, and those remaining are stained and crooked. His clothes are often soiled, frayed, and ill-fitting, and he rarely wears socks. He

Class V Therapy (2015)

also presents a gruff and self-righteous persona to the world and flies into rants and rages at the slightest provocation.

In my own dime-store analysis of David, I thought he was a lazy, arrogant man who never learned how to manage what I had concluded was a classic case of Asperger's syndrome. I thought maybe seeing a family counselor with David would improve our ability to communicate. My goal was to have a safe place to talk with David about the steps he needs to take to become independent and how we could work together to provide the care and support Seth needs.

Instead, I've learned that my brother is sick.

A month ago, David and I had our first meeting with Kim, a family counselor provided through my employer's wellness program. Kim's office was furnished with a medium-size overstuffed couch for her clients.

David and I occupied the ends of the couch like two fighters at opposite corners of the ring.

Kim, a no-nonsense-looking woman with straight brown hair and a serious demeanor, pulled her chair out from her desk to face us both, pad and pen at the ready in her lap.

The tension that had been building between my brother and me since he arrived in California burst open within minutes.

After brief introductions to establish who we were and the nature of our relationship and living situation, Kim jumped in with the question, "So Sue, what is it you would like to talk about with David?"

"Well, the main thing is, I want him to get more serious about finding a job," I said immediately. "I don't feel like he is looking hard enough for work to afford to move into his own place sometime . . . soon."

"Can you be more specific?" she prodded. "What do you mean by soon?"

RISK

I paused for a moment, not fully prepared for this question. I wanted David out yesterday. It had been three months since his July arrival. But I also wanted to hit a high bar on the reasonability meter. "Uh . . . I think he should try to get into his own place by January."

David made a huffing noise on the other end of the couch, his face tight and angry.

After calmly writing her notes, Kim turned to David and asked, "David, what do you think about what Sue has said?"

"I have been looking for a job," David shouted. "I just haven't found anything that's good enough yet."

As Kim scribbled some more in her pad, I clenched my teeth. Many of our most heated arguments in recent months have been about his unwillingness to consider the numerous seasonal service jobs in the area. That day's was no different. Trying to create even more distance, I surreptitiously pulled the small couch pillow between my leg and the side of the couch and moved it under my left arm, scooching a few inches farther to my end.

"Well, how long do you think it's reasonable for you to live in your sister's house?" Kim asked.

"As long as it takes! As . . . long . . . as . . . it . . . takes!" David stated indignantly.

There was a pregnant pause as we both waited for him to elaborate.

"My son is living there, and I should be able to stay with him as long as I want," he snapped.

So much for improving our ability to communicate. The guy was just nuts.

But it was a week later, during our second session, when I developed a deeper understanding of the magnitude of my problem.

"Sue, you said you wanted to talk about your concerns regarding David's drinking," Kim began. "What are your concerns exactly?"

Class V Therapy (2015)

"Well, when David came out here, I made it clear that one of my house rules is that he does not drink any alcohol," I said.

"And why did you make that rule? A lot of people drink a glass of wine or a beer in the evening—why not any?"

"Well . . . because he has had problems drinking too much in the past," I replied, a little defensively. "It was just one of the conditions I thought was necessary to make sure he could be successful in making a fresh start out here."

"Okay. And do you think David has been following that rule?"

"No." I shot a look at my brother. "Last weekend I went to Lisa's home in Truckee and left Seth with David at my house. When we got back on Sunday night, Lisa discovered a half-empty bottle of vodka in a paper bag David had left on the kitchen table."

The counselor turned to my brother. "David, can you tell me more about your drinking?"

"Like what?" he asked gruffly.

"Well, for instance . . . how often do you drink?"

"Enough," he barked, glaring at the counselor. "When I need to."

"Can you be more specific?" she asked mildly. "I would like to know how much and how often."

I do not remember exactly what my brother said over the next few minutes of back and forth. But by the time the counselor finished her questions, David had admitted that he frequently drank hard alcohol, either Jack Daniel's or vodka, until he basically passed out. He drank alone, at home, always at night. He did this about twice a week.

I am still amazed by how forthcoming my brother was during this counseling session, only our second. It was as if he couldn't stop answering the questions, and answering them truthfully. Was that a cry for help?

Kim then asked, "David, have you ever tried to stop drinking?"

"Yes. Many times." David's voice had become noticeably softer. He sounded tired.

RISK

"For how long?"

"Sometimes several weeks . . . sometimes a couple of months."

"And David, how long have you been drinking like this?" She asked this last question gently. Up until this point, she had been calm but firm with David. This time, I could hear the compassion in her voice.

David's voice got even softer, more defeated. "Thirty years."

Kim slowly nodded her head, giving David a little time, silently acknowledging his pain. She obviously already had a good idea of what his answer was going to be.

David stared at the floor, all the anger gone from his face. He looked like he might cry. As I sat on my end of the couch in shock, I moved the small couch pillow into my lap and hugged it to my stomach.

I couldn't believe I hadn't known until this moment that my brother had been a pass-out drunk for thirty years. Including the year he'd taken care of Seth on his own in Cleveland, and at my house over the past few months. On my sporadic visits to Cleveland over the years, I had never seen him drink or seen any evidence of his drinking in his home. In my ignorance, maybe mixed with a healthy dose of denial, I thought his drinking problems had been limited to sporadic periods of severe depression. I thought he had been able to control it through the support and encouragement he received from his church community.

When we left the session that day, I made a point of saying goodbye to David in the parking lot instead of just storming off to my car. I had been so angry with my brother over the last couple of months, I had ignored the bigger picture. David was arrogant and delusional, but he was also unhappy and alone—and had been for a long time.

David did not show up to our third session, and our counselor took this time to be straight with me regarding the demons my brother was dealing with. I learned there is statistically about a 10

Class V Therapy (2015)

to 15 percent chance that he will ever stop drinking. The counselor also made it clear that his behavior will not change, and he is not likely to take personal responsibility for his circumstances, unless he does stop.

Furthermore, she told me that sibling relationships are the most difficult to work on because we learn our communication cues from each other when we are toddlers and never really grow out of that. David and I are still communicating with the proficiency of five-year-olds.

In other words, I am not the best person to provide the support he needs to get sober.

Driving home from my meeting with Mary today, all the pieces are coming together. Between my work with her and Kim, I now understand "The Issue." David needs to quit drinking and work at the AA program with integrity. I, meanwhile, need to stop my codependent bullshit with him and figure out how to protect Seth from his own father—especially his alcoholic behaviors, which are incredibly destructive to a developing young mind.

David is a brother I am beginning to despise, and a father that Seth loves with all his heart.

My subconscious mind figured all this out way before my conscious mind did, which is why the mind-opening benefits of THC opened a floodgate of pure panic two months ago. At that time, I simply was not yet able to face the responsibility of caring for a damaged and helpless young human being while simultaneously protecting him from another even more damaged human being. Driving home from counseling now, however, I'm realizing that if I'm going to give Seth what he requires, I need to be more than Aunt Sue. I need to become a mother.

Before this, I thought my most terrifying life challenges were behind me. I survived my own broken childhood and poverty. I overcame daunting financial challenges by obtaining two

RISK

degrees and working hard to establish a rewarding and stable career.

I also thought my past years of kayaking and rafting, especially those on Class V whitewater, had prepared me to face almost anything. Paddling taught me early that working hard for incremental gains is a successful path to achieving a larger goal. The definition of Class V whitewater is that a mistake can lead to severe injury and possible death. Developing the skills to meet Class V whitewater challenges as a young woman gave me confidence and strength that has allowed me to put most other life challenges in perspective over the decades.

But now at age fifty-six, which is six years older than my mother was when she passed away, I'm facing a challenge like none I've ever encountered before.

Since Seth came to live with me, I've found myself thinking about my mom all the time. I hope there is some form of an afterlife that allows her to have an awareness of this remarkable little being in my care. I swear I see her warm eyes and bright smile in his face sometimes. And although Seth struggles from the impact of all he has been through in his short life and is frequently thrown off-kilter by a lack of impulse control, he also has an inherent love of life. The same love of life that my mom somehow maintained through all her suffering. Mom was an amazingly resilient woman, never losing her ability to laugh and love, characteristics that continually pulled her up from the depths of despair. Despite Seth's episodes of anger and frustration at not being able to accomplish a task or a failed social interaction with a peer, at his core, he is also a happiness seeker.

I feel this inherent joyous spirit will be one of Seth's greatest strengths in life. And although I sense that I will frequently struggle with overwhelming frustrations and despair in my role and actions as a parent in the coming years, my hope is that I will find a way to bestow on Seth the parental love and pride that was

Class V Therapy (2015)

my mom's legacy to me. As she did for me, I want to pass on the fertile soil that will allow his effervescent spirit to flourish.

But at this point in my parenting journey, I feel I'm rapidly approaching a horizon line signaling the descent into a long, steep canyon full of danger, and I'm bumbling along with Class II proficiency.

I need Class V parenting and relationship skills, and I need them before someone gets hurt.

Chapter 8
Paddling through Puberty
(1973–1975)

I could hear my dad clacking away in the other room as I unpacked my gear bag in the bathroom.

As soon as we finished unloading the car from our weekend of kayaking on the Youghiogheny River outside of Ohiopyle, Pennsylvania, he'd sat down at his typewriter to get his ideas down. His creative juices always peaked on our Sunday evening drives back home from whatever adventure we had been on over the weekend. Chewing on his cigar, he chuckled intermittently on our four-hour drive home from the Yough as his head processed "funny" ideas for gag lines for the humorous greeting cards he was expected to produce each week for the Hi Brow Department at American Greetings.

Fortunately, because Dad needed to restore his inspiration, he transported us away from our dreary lower-middle-class neighborhood in Cleveland every weekend to a world where we all felt more at home: on the river.

Accompanied by the clicks of Dad's typewriter, I unpacked a bulky long-sleeve diving wetsuit top (with a front zipper and beavertail extension that was pulled under the crotch and clipped to the front), a Farmer John wetsuit, wool socks, canvas high-tops, a very stinky wool sweater, and a thin, not-really-waterproof, nylon

Paddling through Puberty (1973–1975)

paddling jacket. The Farmer John still smelled a little bit like urine since, obviously, there was no easy way to get through all that while on the river. It had to go in the bathtub for a thorough wash before getting hung on the lines in the basement with the other wet gear. The rest of my gear consisted of a life jacket and a football helmet. My paddle and kayak were already put away in the garage.

Even more so than in California, whitewater kayaking in the Midwest during the early 1970s was not for sissies. There was no such thing as Patagonia fleece or a dry suit back then. Although my gear kept me from freezing, the discomfort when my body was not in motion and my mind was not distracted by paddling was almost intolerable—itchy, soggy, and cold all at the same time.

For my birthday and Christmas present that year, my dad had offered to help me make my own kayak so David and I would no longer have to share. I'd picked out the color (purple), Dad had bought the materials, and we'd spent several weekends that winter at the shop of one of our fellow Keel-Haulers Club members, cutting fiberglass, squeegeeing resin, and sanding . . . until voila! A brand-new boat.

Although it was considered innovative at the time, I marvel now that I could paddle that beast. It was thirteen feet long and weighed about forty pounds. (For comparison, current kids' kayak designs are about five feet in length and weigh around twenty pounds.) At barely 100 pounds and only five feet tall, it took every ounce of my puny strength to hoist the Bronco on my shoulder and carry it up and down the steep and rocky access trails to the river. Dad insisted that everyone carry their own boat, which seemed unfair to me since mine weighed more than his or David's.

My ability to maneuver on the water was also limited by my lack of muscle strength and arm span.

When we'd moved to Cleveland with our newly acquired

kayaking skills from California, Dad had immediately joined the Keel-Haulers Canoe Club. Most of the club engaged in sedate canoe camping trips, but about twenty or so members were at the forefront of the emerging generation of whitewater paddlers.

Early whitewater paddlers from Ohio were not hip and trendy like the young guns you see in the whitewater videos and magazines today. The Keel-Haulers from Northern Ohio were never going to be the glam crowd in this already very fringe sport; most were down-to-earth blue-collar workers, already married with families, and most lived everyday Midwestern lives when not pursuing their passion for rivers and whitewater.

The Keel-Haulers were the perfect fit for the quirky Norman family. The club was warm and welcoming to newcomers, and we quickly became part of the like-minded community. As in California with the Ventura Canoe Club, joining the Keel-Haulers was how my dad saved me from an existence devoid of passion and belonging. Populated by folks as eccentric as we were, the club provided a community in which I would gradually learn to become comfortable in my own skin.

Our favorite places to paddle, remote and pristine river canyons, required drives of at least four or five hours. Our most frequent repeat excursions were to Class III runs on Slippery Rock Creek and the Youghiogheny River in Pennsylvania. On long holiday weekends, we ventured out to the New River Gorge and the Cheat River in West Virginia, which included a few Class IV rapids.

Those weekends, when we were engaged in various forms of outdoor adventure from sunrise to sunset, were the only time when my existence turned from a dull gray back to full living color.

"Who's going to go next?" I asked, sitting in the eddy at the top of Pillow Rock.

Paddling through Puberty (1973–1975)

Pillow Rock was considered to be the toughest rapid on the Lower Youghiogheny, and Kathy, Terry, and I had nervously scouted the rapid from shore while our fathers ran through before us.

Although Terry's dad and mine had navigated the rapid cleanly, we'd watched Kathy's father flip right above Pillow Rock and bounce upside down along the churning currents next to the rock for what seemed like forever before finally rolling his kayak back up after two failed attempts. I certainly did not want to repeat that mess of a run.

To my relief, Kathy said confidently, "I'll go. My dad just didn't have a strong enough ferry angle on the tongue. Just follow me."

Like ducklings, Terry and I followed Kathy's perfect line into the smooth tongue of current at the entrance, a path that enabled all of us to navigate the rest of the rapid cleanly, to the cheers of our fathers.

At the bottom, we all pulled into an eddy together with big grins on our faces.

"Whew, I'm glad that's over with!" I said, my heart pumping with adrenaline.

"Me too!" Terry chimed in. "And thanks Kathy, I'm glad you showed us the way. I think we ran that better than all our dads!"

Kathy laughed. "Yeah, it's all about getting the right angle on the tongue. Once you get that, the rest is cake."

"Just one more mile to go and then we can get ice cream to go along with that sweet run," I said gleefully.

Although I had developed no close friends from my school or neighborhood, I'd finally found my crew in the Keel-Haulers with two girls about my age. Kathy, Terry, and I had immediately bonded as uneasy accomplices in our fathers' passion for this often uncomfortable and terrifying sport. Although they both had moms, their mothers had no interest in joining their husbands in this crazy enterprise, so we were on our own in the male-dominated sport. In those days, only a handful of women in the entire country whitewater kayaked, and the few we knew in the Keel-Haulers were not much better than us. With no female role models, we were among the original daughters of the whitewater kayaking revolution. Facing fear and physical discomfort together, we shared the success of navigating challenging rapids and consoled each other after embarrassing and sometimes scary swims. Paddling made us different from most girls our age, and we enjoyed the status of that uniqueness.

During those weekends on the river with my best friends, sleeping in tents surrounded by woods or sitting around the campfire with the music of the river in the background, I felt grounded and at peace.

During my high school years paddling with Kathy, Terry, and the Keel-Haulers, a pivotal event occurred that fundamentally changed the trajectory of the sport of whitewater paddling in the United States and my interest in it.

In 1972, whitewater slalom kayaking was introduced to the world stage when the sport was included in the Olympics that year as a demonstration event. (Whitewater kayaking would not appear again in the Olympics until 1992, twenty years later, but has been a regular event ever since.) That year, an American, Jamie McEwen, broke into the European-dominated powerhouse of whitewater slalom athletes, winning a bronze medal in the whitewater C-1 division (one-man closed-deck canoe). Handsome and engaging, Jamie was a powerful inspiration to the budding junior whitewater paddling community.

Our club, and surrounding clubs in Pennsylvania and Maryland, hosted local kayak slalom races every year, and after Jamie's medal, interest in these events noticeably increased. Slalom paddling immediately appealed to Kathy, Terri, and me. Kayak slalom

Paddling through Puberty (1973–1975)

required making difficult maneuvers to get through all the gates, but usually without any dire consequences if you didn't make the move. You may have lost the race, but at least you weren't as likely to get munched in a hydraulic or slammed against a rock as when you missed difficult river-running maneuvers.

My dad was not that interested in racing, but fortunately, Kathy and Terri's dads were, and I joined them in traveling to as many races as I could.

Although David was part of our family paddling trips, he was not interested in racing. A distance began to grow between us as I developed intimate friendships apart from him for the first time. But I also began to flourish and come into my own as I competed alongside a multistate group of talented young paddlers—a sharp contrast to school, where I never fit in.

During my last year of high school, in 1974, autumn brilliance long gone, Dad sat David and me down to give us our last big life talk as a residential parent.

"So, kids," Dad said, "we need to have a talk about what you are going to do after you graduate next spring."

"Uh, okay," David said, shooting a glance toward me. We walked over to the cheap thrift store dining table where Dad sat and pulled out chairs on either side of him.

Dad took another small sip of his post-dinner Budweiser. He drank one each night and would savor each sip before swallowing it.

"Now, you know I don't have any money to send you to college."

I looked at David, then replied for both of us: "Yeah, we know."

"And at the end of next summer, I plan to bum around for a while. I'm going to leave Cleveland and work part-time for American Greetings as a freelancer."

"Where do you think you'll go?" I asked, wondering if we were invited.

"I don't know yet, but somewhere in the woods. It may be

pretty rough. I will probably live out of the station wagon at first, and then maybe Oz Hawksley's cabin in Montana for the winter."

That did not sound appealing, which he certainly must have known.

"So, you have a few options," he continued. "You can try to get part-time jobs to support yourself and go to college, but I don't recommend that, because it will be tough to make enough money for living expenses and go to college at the same time."

David and I nodded in agreement. We had been looking at Ohio University manuals provided through our high school but were daunted by the costs, clearly out of our reach.

"What's another option?" David asked.

"Well, you could bum around with me until you make up your mind. But I think there is a better option."

"What's that?" I asked.

"Join the Army," he replied.

David and I knew Dad had been drafted into the Army at the tail end of the Korean War. But he'd been drafted after college, after he married our mom, and he'd served his time as a clerk in Delaware.

David and I remained silent, taking in this idea. I had to admit, the thought of going out on my own in less than a year and supporting myself through college seemed impossible. And clearly, Dad did not want us tagging along on his self-styled sabbatical. I got it; at forty-six years old, after financially struggling as a single parent for the past eight years, he was undoubtedly ready to live life again on his own terms.

Joining the Army seemed a daunting prospect—but, I had to admit, the most appealing of the three options.

Seeming to read my thoughts, Dad added, "You will have to wait a while to go to college, but you can save up some money, and when you get out, you can use the GI Bill to help pay for

Paddling through Puberty (1973–1975)

college. Then you can focus more on your studies when you do go to college. I think that is your best choice."

"Can you get the GI Bill if you join the Navy instead?" I asked. I didn't know anything about any of the military branches, but the Navy seemed a little more glamorous, and I liked the uniforms.

"Well, the Navy and Air Force recruiting offices are downtown, and there is an Army recruiting station just a few blocks away on Lorain. I don't have the time to drive you downtown, so you should just go to the Army recruiting station unless you want the hassle of taking the bus." He shrugged. "There is really no difference between any of the branches of the military."

I will never know the validity of Dad's statement. Who knows what direction my life would have taken if I had ridden the bus downtown, but I did not have the confidence to do so. So, a few weeks later, I walked through the cold November wind to the Army recruiting station after school.

By the time I left the office, dusk was rapidly approaching. Alternating the jobs booklet from my right to left hand so I could warm the freezing right one in my pocket, I strode down the drab gray streets between our house and the Army recruiting station, eager to get home to give it a thorough examination. I was ready to spend the three years after high school as a soldier in the US Army.

When I came back to the recruiting station with my top choices in the jobs booklet selected, the recruiter gave me one lame excuse after another as to why none of those choices were available to me.

Finally, I suggested maybe we could make this easier, and he could just tell me which jobs were available. A little too quickly, he said I had the choice of being a cook, office clerk, or military police.

That recruiter must have seen me coming a mile away, a look of desperation and "no other options" stamped all over my face.

RISK

Since I was clearly easy pickings, he had only offered me the jobs the army primarily wanted women for. Of my three choices, the military police seemed like the best of the worst, and I signed the dotted line.

I would start active duty in ten months, on September 15, 1975, two days after my eighteenth birthday. It was hard to imagine how my life would change on this date, but at least I had a plan.

Just like that, my fate was decided in a sterile little office on Lorain Avenue, with a poster in the window of Uncle Sam pointing a finger at me and saying, "Go, Army!"

Chapter 9

Motherhood after Menopause (2015)

The face I see is an unfortunate reflection in the mirror, a sadly accurate and visible account of the toll the past year has taken. I always thought I would be one of those women who would age gracefully. Welcoming the lines of wisdom and sunspot blemishes reflecting a life well lived. Bull pucky. I feel like burying the face I see looking back at me in a bag of ice. My face feels puffy all over, and the swelling around my eyes creates a weird effect that makes me look part Klingon. My eyes are also bloodshot and red-rimmed and my skin dry and pale, making all the age spots and wrinkles stand out in stark relief.

Maybe I should get that BBL skin treatment, I think, but then almost immediately realize how impractical that is with the hefty monthly preschool tuition and other expenses I have taken on as Seth's sole provider.

The natural process of aging is one thing. It has been a shock how quickly menopause has affected my skin and muscle tone, sleep patterns and energy levels. It seems like one day I was a fit and active fifty-plus-year-old, almost immune to the effects of time, physically and mentally. Then, in an instant, it all changed. As menses began to cease, the aging process accelerated at a record pace.

RISK

I lived with a friend for a short while when I was in graduate school at UC Davis, a single mother in her early forties raising a ten-year-old son while working as a doctor in Sacramento. After she helped her son with his homework, piano practice, and put him to bed, she would get back to work, often staying up until one or two in the morning. She lived on four to five hours of sleep a night; she said she was used to minimal sleep from medical school and residency. I marveled at how she could manage it then, and I was still in my early thirties.

At the age of fifty-six, I am barely making it to seventy-thirty or eight every night. I breathe a deep sigh of relief every evening when Seth is put to bed and I can retreat to my room, utterly exhausted. But I spend most of the night reading books on my iPad, as sleep has become increasingly elusive.

I know the biological changes would have happened anyway, but it is clear the effects of mommy stress and anxiety are exacerbating the process. Motherhood after menopause is a double whammy.

The best I can do for now is splash my face with cold water, slather my skin in heavy cream, and put some ice cubes in a napkin so I can press them into my eyes while running around the house getting the start on another day. Today is a big one: the day I start applying for legal guardianship, taking the first step in committing to raising Seth to manhood.

Since he entered my home, I have had little success in maintaining any semblance of life balance.

Even during the few months when David was living here and theoretically helping with Seth, I was unable to maintain a regimen of regular exercise, alone time, and intelligent conversation with adult friends doing adult things.

I know every mother out there is probably saying, "Duh, welcome to the real world." But this was not *my* reality up until now. Some real coming to grips is required here.

Motherhood after Menopause (2015)

Also, David wasn't just unhelpful; he and I were in a full-on war, with every skirmish bloodier than the last. The brother that, for much of my childhood, was the person I was closest to is now someone I do not want to have in my life at all, whose very presence makes my skin crawl. David seems incapable of interacting with Seth in a manner that does not involve yelling. I understand why. Seth is challenging for both of us. But David has shown little capacity for the hard work of positive parenting.

The five months my brother lived with me was hell. In addition to his inability to find a job, every therapy session made it more apparent how broken he is. He would go on long rants in our sessions about how unreasonable I was for not wanting to give him any more money or let him live in my house for as long as it took for him to find work and move out. When he started going off to our therapist about what a bad father our dad was, I realized that my brother had decided he was a victim at an early age—not consciously, but that is the role he ended up sliding into.

Even though we had the same parents and shared the same traumatic experience when our mother got sick, David and I went in two completely different directions: he chose victimhood, and I unconsciously chose to become a survivor. A frequent subject of rumination when I experience middle-of-the-night insomnia is why David and I evolved so differently, whether Seth has inherited any of the "nature" that will lead him down a similar path as his father, and what I can provide as "nurture" to ward that off.

At least David is now out of my house. Although I now have full-time responsibility for Seth, a huge weight has been lifted. I can walk into my house and take full breaths for a change.

In February, I gave David the option of moving down to some raw land I own in the California foothills just outside Sacramento—a friend of mine was loaning me a very decrepit but workable pop-up tent trailer for the property—or finding his own situation. David decided the trailer would be better than his only

RISK

other option, a homeless shelter. I assumed that the primitive camp-living situation would force David to better his situation sooner rather than later. The interim would give him some time to find more consistent day labor work in Sacramento and figure out how to get into affordable housing.

Seth and I have had our battles as he's tried to process his feelings about David moving out. But as I've continued to be the only consistent adult in his life, we've also started forming a tighter bond. This has translated to him becoming simultaneously more confrontational *and* needier.

For example, he refuses to get dressed by himself. He only puts on his school clothes or pajamas if I put them on for him, stating loudly that I *have* to do it. Any resistance I show in doing things for him is met with fury. I think he is testing me; he wants me to show him that he matters. It's maddening. Already getting ready in the morning is such a production; dressing him like a baby is not something I want to do. But I also realize that this is his way of getting assurance that I care about him. I've had to accept that although he is five now, emotionally, he is still stuck at three. I simply hope this gap will resolve itself sooner or later, as my therapist said it should. In the meantime, I will keep using the techniques she is teaching me for "positive reinforcement." I never realized how difficult it is to parent positively when every impulse is to get mad at toddler rebellion and yell them into submission. And Seth is obviously a rebel.

Mary, Seth's therapist, made it clear that it was in Seth's best interest not to be living with his dad because he needs consistency, safety, and security. However, she said it was also vital that he have regular contact with David to know that David still loves him and is a part of his life on a routine basis. There is a biological bond between sons and their fathers, coded from generations of the evolutionary process. Although Seth spent most of his young life living with Gesi, his emotional tie to his father is much

Motherhood after Menopause (2015)

stronger. To provide the best situation for Seth, my challenge is to maintain that connection with appropriate buffers that keep everyone healthy. So, we go down to the property to visit David regularly. I have a comfortable camper there for Lisa and me, and Seth gets to see his dad.

Although applying for legal guardianship is not what I had planned for when I brought Seth to California, it feels good to have a resolution. It has become clear that David will not be a healthy live-in parent for Seth for quite a while, and probably not ever. Seth's mom, Gesi, is out of prison now, but still jobless and unable to secure a home and recover custody of her two other children.

Although I feel genuine empathy for Gesi, it is clear this twenty-three-year-old mother of three is a lost soul. She is not addicted to either alcohol or drugs, and I know she loves her children and wants them to live with her. In every conversation I have with her, she talks about all the things she is going to do to get her life together, and many times her goals seem reasonable. But although she is not an addict, the emotional impacts of her upbringing are just as disabling.

Gesi was raised in foster homes and orphanages. She doesn't know who her father is, and her mother is a mentally ill drug addict. There is a steady supply of reasons and excuses for why Gesi has not been able to get out of the cycle of generational poverty and family dysfunction that she came from. I do not pretend to fully understand what the true reason is, but I can see that once you are in that rabbit hole, it is hard to get out. Especially when you start having babies.

I understand why conservatives get frustrated with having their taxes pay for "enabling" social welfare programs and why liberals get frustrated with their inadequacy. I think Gesi has become too dependent on social welfare as a crutch, but I shudder to think where she would be if those programs did not exist,

RISK

much less where her children would be. Seth benefited from Gesi receiving prenatal care, including vitamins and nutrition assistance, because of those programs. Without that, his life might have been irreversibly compromised before he was even born.

I honestly wish that Gesi had the support and personal strengths to overcome her hurdles. For her own sake, as well as that of her other children. But I am past the point of relying on others when it comes to Seth. It is time to take matters fully into my own hands.

Just having a plan is helping me feel like I'm paddling out of the vast eddy I've been swirling around in for months.

The swelling around my eyes has gone down, but I'm still applying ice, alternating eyes every minute or so, as I drop Seth off at daycare and drive to my four-hour appointment with a counselor from Lilliput. I was surprised when they told me we needed that much time for our meetings.

Lilliput is a non-profit organization I found online that helps guide people through the process of petitioning for legal guardianship for their minor-aged relatives when it is apparent parental custody is no longer in the child's best interest. The status of "relative" foster care is known as kinship care in the state of California. California passed legislation in 1992 providing detailed guidance to the courts to carefully consider what is in the child's best interest during child custody cases. This legislation, some of the most stringent in the nation, was based on research data that showed that children who remained in the custody of parents with chronic drug and alcohol addiction did not thrive and often ended up with the same kinds of problems exhibited by those parents. This seems obvious, but in other states the process for establishing parental fitness is often not as robust and the courts favor keeping the child with at least one biological parent, usually the mother. The child's options

Motherhood after Menopause (2015)

are often also limited because foster care, especially good-quality foster care, is in short supply.

Lilliput is partially funded through state grants because research has also shown that children in foster care with a relative (aunts, uncles, grandparents) do better. Statistically, kids who are placed with someone who already has a strong connection with the child and a vested interest in maintaining a relationship through visitation with the biological parents have better outcomes.

My kinship care advocate, Moira, a compact woman in a plain white button-up shirt and blue jeans, meets me with a stack of forms almost two inches thick. She does not smile or waste a lot of time on niceties; she simply adjusts her thick, black-framed glasses and jumps into the stack of forms in a direct business-like manner.

After we have gone through about half the stack, I lean back in my chair and take a deep breath.

"Man, this is . . . a lot," I say. "Can we take a break?"

"Sure," she says. "Would you also like something to eat?"

She pulls some chips, granola bars, and bottled water from a bag she has next to her on the floor.

I am glad she's prepared, as I brought nothing. Her anticipation of my needs reinforces my impression of the capability of this woman that is helping me. "Yes," I respond, "that would be great. Also, can you tell me where the bathroom is?"

Alone in the bathroom, I still feel overwhelmed but also grateful for Moira's ability to present the paperwork efficiently. It makes the nagging worry about what I am getting myself into just a little bit lighter.

"I know what you will be going through," Moira says quietly after I return and start munching hungrily on a bag of Fritos. "I adopted my granddaughter when I was about your age. And I can tell you, what you're doing is going to save Seth's life."

RISK

The directness of this statement makes me pause my snarfing. There is a subtle change of timbre in Moira's voice that reveals the passion behind her words.

"Very few people nowadays are willing to take on the challenge of kinship care," she continues. "It is the main reason our foster care system is so overloaded. Because it is not going to be easy. The lifestyle you have become used to is going to completely change. You will have to make a lot of sacrifices, and working through the emotional challenges Seth is likely to experience will be tough. But I also believe you will never regret this decision."

"Thank you, Moira," I respond quietly.

Her delivery of the cold, hard truth, without mincing words, is exactly what I need. And the intimate knowledge we have just shared, of what her life experience has been and what mine will be, overwhelms me. This woman, a total stranger, is the first person I have met who really seems to understand what I am going through.

Moira also warns me the legal process of an adverse custody battle will be brutal. Desperately holding back every raw and bleeding emotional trigger in the courtroom's stern and formal atmosphere. Controlling each word and response to make sure I'm not the one sounding like the crazy person to the judge.

But along with tough talk about how hard this is going to be, Moira is just as emphatic in assuring me that I'm making the right decision. She tells me there will also be tremendous rewards that will make up for the challenges. Her granddaughter has turned out to be an accomplished young woman whom Moira is clearly proud of.

This is something I can understand. Although life has been relatively easy for me over the past fifteen to twenty years, I'm no stranger to sacrifice or enduring difficulties to achieve a goal. I know from my past that the best way to overcome fear and face a challenge with an unclear outcome or path to success is to pick

Motherhood after Menopause (2015)

a starting point and take baby step after baby step from there. And the current step is to establish full legal responsibility for Seth.

Unfortunately, the decline in kinship care in our country has been repeated to me on numerous occasions by social workers, counselors, and teachers. A generation ago, it was almost a given that kids would be cared for by their extended family in times of trouble. I wonder what that means as a statement of the evolution or de-evolution of our society. Possibly it is because many of those extended families are also compromised themselves, already overloaded with their own mental, financial, or addiction problems. Many friends have told me how much they admire me for choosing to take on this responsibility. But at my core, I do not feel that there was ever really a choice. Seth has no other family. This is something I had to do, or I would not be able to live with myself.

At the end of our session, I hug Moira with tears in my eyes. I think it would have taken me months to accomplish on my own what we have done in these four hours. But she has done much more than provide administrative guidance; she's given me affirmation. Although I'm facing the biggest and most significant challenge of my life, at least the path toward this step has been laid out for me, and I am not walking it alone.

After I get home, I take Roscoe out on a dog walk in the meadow next to my house in South Lake and call Lisa. Hopefully she is done riding her horse and is either at her house in Truckee or taking our other dog, Maddie, on her walk.

"Hey, what's up," she says, a little out of breath.

"Are you walking Maddie?" I ask.

"Yeah, but it's not too crowded, so we can talk. How did it go today?"

"Well, I got all the guardianship paperwork filled out. The

RISK

stack of forms was two inches thick. Thank goodness the lady from Lilliput really had her shit together, but it still took hours."

"Now what?" she asks.

"Well, I have to deliver it to the courthouse tomorrow, and then wait to hear back."

"How long will that take?"

"I have no idea; the kinship care advocate thought I would get temporary guardianship within a week or so, but it could take a few months for the hearing for permanent guardianship."

At this, there is just quiet on Lisa's end.

Although the support I got from Lilliput was godsend, I'm still navigating the support I can expect from my wife.

She and I engaged in numerous lengthy conversations about my nephew's dire circumstances throughout my four years of biannual visits to Cleveland. She supported me in my desire to be a more engaged auntie by helping David and Seth relocate to California. When I brought Seth out to California, she was on board. But this is not what she signed up for.

Lisa and I met through a dating service in our early forties. It wasn't love at first sight for me; I was admittedly a little intimidated at first by her broad shoulders, long, strong legs, and striking blue-green eyes framed by prominent Viking bone structure. I felt, well, a little puny and ordinary in comparison.

But considering the inherent uncomfortableness of navigating our blind date, the lunch went well as we stumbled through awkward gaps of silence. I appreciated that there was little pretension on her side of the conversation. It was even reassuring that she did not try to fill every space in the conversation.

Our second date, a dog walk at Fallen Leaf Lake, felt much more relaxed. We were both clearly more comfortable in our natural environment; our conversation flowed easily as we talked about our interests and origins, and the periods of silence were easier and more comfortable to absorb when walking.

Motherhood after Menopause (2015)

We eventually created a binding connection formed through sharing a sometimes adventurous, but more often simple, daily outdoor life.

Together we have shared many peak wilderness experiences on land, river, and sea. Our wilderness explorations soon included Lisa's evolution from wedding photography into landscape photography into her eventual niche as an equine photographer.

In 2008, thirty days after the defeat of DOMA in the Supreme Court, I got an email from the US Department of Agriculture letting us know that we could now include same-sex spouses on our health insurance policy—a change in federal policy I had never expected to see in my lifetime.

I called Lisa from the office and asked her if she wanted to get married. Neither of us felt the need to do it to validate our relationship; marriage was a heterosexual construct, after all. But it was a no-brainer to drop her horrendously expensive private insurance plan and add her to my sweet federal health insurance policy. And so we became a part of history in a wave of same-sex marriages around the country.

As we entered our fifties, our future together seemed straightforward: slight shifts here and there as our interests evolved over time, but mostly our same comfortable routines.

Our relationship wasn't perfect. We sometimes bickered and hurt each other's feelings. She is very neat; I am messy. Some of our strongest passions diverged—hers into owning horses, mine into more paddling. But we always seemed to have a strong foundation for resiliency.

A foundation that now feels primed to crumble under the weight of a five-year-old little boy in crisis.

Chapter 10
Passion (1975)

I don't know exactly when I started to love kayaking, but my passion was cemented during the final year before I left home.

Before my enlistment in the Army began in September, I was determined to push the bar an exponential leap forward with my paddling. While other girls spent their senior year planning for the prom, I focused on becoming a member of the small fringe community of whitewater kayaking elite—a sport that was destined to be the grounding force for my life for decades to come.

During this period, I physically transformed from a small and spindly waif into a still small but increasingly powerful young woman.

My transformation began in earnest when some slalom competitors in the men's division developed an exercise program for me and Kathy before the beginning of the school year. Over the fall and winter, she and I increased our upper-body strength with push-ups, pull-ups, sit-ups, and basic free-weight exercises.

By that spring, I could knock out ten to twelve pull-ups at a go (full extension without cheating) and bench press my 110-pound weight. Carrying my forty-pound kayak in and out from the river canyons got a lot easier, as my ability to drive it also improved.

Passion (1975)

Developing physical strength is an extremely potent way for a young woman, especially one who has as many insecurities as I did, to begin to own her power. I can't explain the phenomenon, but the more my shoulders and biceps grew, the greater my confidence and resilience in other facets of my life also grew. Feeling stronger in my body helped me feel stronger in my mind.

In May of 1975, the US National Kayak Slalom Team trials were held a mere four hours from Cleveland on our favorite river, the Youghiogheny. Kathy and I felt ready to enter our first national-level kayak slalom competition. We had no delusions of making the team, but we were eager to make our entry into the national paddling world—to see and be seen by the nation's best.

Scouting from shore before the practice run at the team trials, I realized that although the rapid was Class III, the maneuvers required to navigate the course had increased the difficulty to Class IV. Gates were strategically placed to force difficult moves around and through sticky hydraulics that generally would be avoided. The course was much more challenging and intimidating than any of the local races I had done before.

Sitting in my kayak behind the start wand, my heart began to race as the starter began the countdown. As soon as I broke through the wand, I felt off balance.

Barely a third of the way into the course, desperately attempting to navigate through a hydraulic, I flipped. Already short of breath from my efforts paddling through the first eight gates in the powerful currents, I panicked and pulled my spray skirt, not even attempting an Eskimo roll. Desperate for air when I came to the surface, I tried to breathe in, but the cold water seemed to have paralyzed my lungs, and I could only manage short, desperate gasps. Bobbing helplessly down the rapid through a series of breaking waves and hydraulics, I began choking as I inhaled water in my futile attempts to breathe. I thought I was going to drown.

RISK

Finally, at the bottom of the rapid, I saw a safety boater paddling toward me. Lauren was a fellow Keel-Hauler and a good friend of our family.

"Grab on," Lauren shouted as he turned his kayak to give me the loop of rope attached to the stern. I clutched the grab loop and let him paddle me to shore, too weak to help with even a feeble leg kick.

"Are you okay?" he asked as I crawled onto the shore.

"Yes," I managed to croak, still panting to replace the oxygen deficit.

"Okay, I'm going to help get your kayak and paddle. Just rest there till we get it back to you."

As I sat shivering and shaken on the shore, I saw one of the race organizers approaching me and assumed he was coming over to also make sure I was okay.

To my surprise, he barked, "You could have caused a huge delay in the race, grabbing on to the slalom poles like that! You're just lucky they didn't break."

"What?" I asked, befuddled. "I didn't grab onto any poles."

"Yes, you did!" he scowled. "You pulled on gates ten and fourteen."

"Oh," I said. "I don't remember doing that."

The official shook his head. "I think you better seriously consider not taking your second run. This is the national championships, for heaven's sakes, and the team trials for the world championships. If you're swimming and grabbing onto gates, you don't have any business being out there."

I still did not really believe I had grabbed poles until other witnesses corroborated the awful truth. From their description, I could have easily broken the cords and wires from which the gates were suspended, which would have held up the race for hours.

Dejected, I lugged my boat and paddle to the car and changed

Passion (1975)

into dry clothes. I remained in the car to have a good cry, hiding out in a puddle of mortification. I had publicly humiliated myself in front of spectators, race officials, and my fellow competitors. I had been seen in the worst possible way.

Then I got mad. Although I understood why the race official was upset, I also felt he could have shown a little more compassion. I'd thought I was going to die during that swim.

As I sat with that anger, I turned it toward myself.

Mortification turned into a hardened resolve. I absolutely needed to fix this. To come back and show that I did belong in the race, to my peers and that official. I got out of the car and began the ritual of suiting up.

After donning my paddle jacket, lifejacket, spray skirt, and helmet like a suit of armor, I was ready.

The energy coursing through my body during that second run was very different. Waiting behind the start gate, instead of letting my stomach churn with butterflies, I filled myself with anger. Gritting my teeth, I cursed silently to myself, *Attack, goddamn it. DO NOT HOLD BACK. Attack, attack, attack! Show that asshole you do belong here.*

When the starter yelled go, I burst out into the current with adrenaline-fueled strength, my teeth bared in a grimace. I approached every hard ferry and hydraulic with fury, repeating the silent mantra in my head, *ATTACK, DO NOT HOLD BACK, ATTACK!*

I did not have the skill to make a remarkable showing, but my second run was respectable. I finished in the middle of the women's class. My dignity was salvaged.

On the drive home after the race, Kathy and I giddily chatted about our plans for the summer, and it all involved slalom kayaking. We wanted more—and I was determined to work even harder so nothing like what happened during my first run at the

RISK

1975 Whitewater Slalom National Championships would ever happen again.

At the beginning of summer, Kathy and I participated in a girls-only slalom clinic, maybe the first ever to occur in the US, hosted by a rising kayak racing star named Linda Harrison.

Linda had won the women's kayak division at the 1975 team trials and placed fifth in the pre–world championships the year before. After seeing the depth of the European teams she raced against, Linda wanted to build up a similar force in the United States. She felt having more competition to train with would help her to become a stronger racer, like she saw was happening with the US men.

To this end, Linda decided to invite a small group of young female kayakers she had seen at the '75 team trials for five days of intense slalom training and coaching. Fortunately, I had redeemed myself sufficiently during my second run to earn one of the invitations.

The clinic was held on a muddy little Class I creek in Linda's backyard in New Jersey. Although the site was not glamorous, what I learned in that week surpassed anything I had learned in kayaking until then.

With Linda's focused coaching and paddling drills, using a lightweight racing kayak she loaned me for the clinic (weighing twenty pounds instead of forty pounds), the things I learned to do in a kayak that week were simply thrilling.

I learned how to do a three-stroke upstream gate, a two-stroke reverse gate, and downstream offset gates on one stroke.

I learned how to charge.

I became addicted to the intoxicating mix of strength and finesse that is the essence of whitewater slalom. The same addiction I've heard described in interviews with accomplished athletes in other adventure sports like slalom skiing, rock climbing, and

Passion (1975)

surfing. All sports that require a great deal of technique and power, resulting in the melding of mind and body in pure, exquisite focus.

Every day I got better and better, and at the end of the week I won the little mock race Linda put on as our final exam. Even though there were only five of us, I felt deliciously victorious.

The summer wasn't over yet. After Kathy and I spent a few weeks competing in local races and training at home, her father drove us to Ontario, Canada, for more whitewater slalom coaching at the Madawaska Kanu Camp, the premier location for slalom kayak instruction in North America.

At Madawaska, my paddling progression skyrocketed up the still steep incline of my learning curve. Not only did I get to use all the finesse skills Linda had taught us during her training camp, I also learned to integrate them into navigating a Class III whitewater slalom course. I learned that the essential strokes are the same whether in Class I or Class V whitewater. I also learned the beauty of integrating those strokes with reading whitewater so that each stroke is placed where it is needed to make it count. This added a whole new dimension to my slalom skills. When I got it right, it felt effortless, like I was at one with the wild and dynamic whitewater.

A couple of decades later, our instructor, who was a long-time national champion, wrote an article in which he described paddling a whitewater slalom course as a series of "sweet moments." A well-placed stroke entering an upstream gate slingshots you in and around the gate, and then another stroke jettisons you into the powerful currents to once again catapult downstream. Efficiently stroking from gate to gate turns into a whitewater ballet of movement, combining power and grace in a seamless dance. We were all in the grip of the same heady addiction, striving for those sweet moments, linking them together throughout an entire course.

RISK

I was at somewhat of a disadvantage compared to the other kids at Madawaska because I was stuck using my trusty but heavy and bulky Bronco. In contrast, most of the others had newer, sleeker, and more lightweight racing designs. But in some ways this made me better, because it forced me to be even smarter about reading the water and using the current, not wasting my strength trying to fight it.

At the end of each run on the full-length whitewater course, we carried our boats back to the start on a muddy trail almost a quarter-mile upriver. My physical and mental strength continued to grow as I paddled and lugged my Bronco in and out of the water.

Slalom racing helped my river skills rapidly progress. Instead of acting like a piece of flotsam being pushed down the river at random, I learned to read and feel the water. I learned to use my still girlish but rapidly developing strength to power myself when needed, and to use the current to my advantage—to work *with* the river rather than fighting it or drifting downstream at its mercy.

As the summer drew to an end, I relished every moment with my peers both on and off the water, realizing this would be the last time I would be in a kayak for a while. Within days of returning home, I was scheduled to board a Greyhound bus destined for Basic Training in Fort McClellan, Alabama. I tried not to think about it too much. I focused instead on enjoying the camaraderie and excitement generated from developing my skills alongside this fantastic group of kids.

The slalom paddling code we young paddlers lived by—put in the work, do not complain, do not make excuses, and never quit or throw a snit—had a powerful influence on me, and I have never forgotten it. Many of the young athletes I trained with came with natural athletic talents. But the main reason so many of them went on to have such great competitive accomplishments

Passion (1975)

is because they worked their asses off. They didn't rely on a coach for this motivation. They motivated themselves and each other to work harder and go faster, and it paid off.

Some of the kids I spent that summer with became national champions and also dominated world championships in the decade to come. A few of them were also innovative thinkers, and within the collective soup of their collaborative efforts they developed sleeker boat designs and advanced paddling techniques that revolutionized the sport.

I knew none of this at the time, of course, but I did know I was surrounded by greatness in our small fringe sport. It was going to be hard to leave.

We were only ten minutes into our drive back to Cleveland from Madawaska when David dropped the bomb.

"I've decided I'm not going to enlist after all," he announced.

"What?" I asked, dumbfounded. "Why?"

"Because," he said, "I cannot serve my country and serve Jesus too."

A few days before I was supposed to leave Madawaska, I'd gotten a call from David. He'd said he wanted to drive up and give me a ride home. I was supposed to come back with Kathy and her dad and didn't really want to change that, but David had been adamant, though when I'd asked *why* he would make this eight-hour round trip, he'd been evasive.

I'd thought maybe he wanted to spend some time alone together before starting our enlistments. After all, this was it. We were both leaving home for good. So, hearing the urgency in his voice, I'd finally agreed.

Now I knew why, along with his long Jesus-like wavy brown hair, he was also sporting a three-inch wooden cross on a leather cord. While I had devoted my summer to whitewater slalom kayaking, my brother had been recruited by a religious cult. A cult that required its members to live in a communal house, turn over most of their money to the "Family," and spend their free time proselytizing on the streets.

I was flabbergasted. We had not been raised with religion, and our only exposure had consisted of occasionally accompanying our grandmother to Sunday school.

We talked about it the entire four-hour drive back, and as David campaigned to save my soul before I was lost to the devil forever, it became clear to me that he was dead serious about his new vocation.

This drive was the first time I felt profoundly worried about what was to become of my brother. Although I had tormented him for much of our childhood, on some level I was also aware of how fragile he was. What was he going to do without me bossing him around when he needed it?

As fledgling adults, we were both desperately seeking our individual identities. But was this really the right path for him?

As we drove up to our house, I could see all my brother's belongings had been stacked in piles on the front porch.

"Uh . . . David, how did Dad react when you told him about your decision?" I asked.

"Well, he isn't happy," he replied.

We both sat and stared at the porch for a minute.

"Well, I guess I better go in and see what's up," I said.

I hugged my brother on the front porch and promised to call him later; he grabbed a couple of boxes and walked forlornly back to his car. What had the past month been like around here while I was at kayak camp?

Not pretty, I imagined.

My dad's expression was grim as I entered the house.

I stopped just inside the doorway. "Hey, Dad, are you okay?"

Passion (1975)

Keeping his eyes averted from mine, he said, "I'm sorry. I'm just so upset about what David is doing. The only way I could deal with it is to get all his stuff out of the house." Still looking anywhere but at me, he paced around the room. "You guys are responsible for your own decisions now, and there is nothing I can do about the dumb ones. But I can't be a part of it."

I realized he wasn't looking at me because he was trying not to cry.

It had been such a struggle for Dad to raise us on his own for all these years. The realization that it might have all been for naught, right on the eve of him finally realizing his own freedom again, was a disappointment I could barely comprehend. But the depth of his sadness was apparent, and my heart ached for both him and my brother.

Although David and I began life by sharing the womb, we clearly had a different genetic code from day one.

I've always made decisions based on establishing long-term goals, which I term "The Plan." This trait has turned out to be one of the most defining of my character. I have figured out how to be somewhat flexible with The Plan, to adapt and merge with the flow if fate, the goddess, spirit, or whatever has given the sign. But I need long-term plans or goals in place in order to set my course, and all alterations and course corrections are carefully considered and calculated before they are enacted.

Although I was entering my enlistment with some trepidation, it was a sound Plan—and, for me, less daunting than trying to face the world on my own at eighteen.

David, on the other hand, was always chasing the next "Big Idea." He was obsessively engaged with that Big Idea for the time he was in it. And he was a bright young man—he scored in the ninety-fifth percentile on the SAT. But all his Big Ideas promised significant gains for little work. When that turned out not to be

RISK

the case, he became disillusioned and would leap off in a radically new direction, eager to replace the failed idea with something better.

Right now, David was obsessed with his savior, which meant our mutual decision to enlist in the Army six months ago was no longer relevant. My Plan and his Big Idea had diverged.

The night before I left for basic training, my brother and a friend from the "Family" came over to make one last concerted effort to convert me to their faith. Dad allowed them in the house, but immediately retired to his room.

After about an hour or so of extremely awkward back and forth, aware that he was losing the debate, David's eyes filled with tears. "But Sue, I'm so worried about what might happen to you if you are not saved," he lamented. "Not only are we no longer going to live together as a family anymore . . . you won't be able to join me in heaven, either!"

Suddenly I realized what was really at stake for both of us. Our life together as a family was ending. Although we had gradually become less and less connected over the years, seeking out our own friends and interests, we were still twins. We had bonded before birth in our mother's womb. We had been each other's best friend—and, often, only friend—for much of our lives. We had shared the pain of my mother's illness and our family's financial struggles and relied on each other to buffer the loneliness we often felt. And now it was over.

"Oh, Dave . . . I just don't know what to say . . ." I said, my eyes also filling with tears.

We just looked at each other for a few moments, wiping our eyes.

"I really wish I could do what you want," I finally said softly, "but it would just be fake."

"It's just that I'm going to miss you so much," David said

Passion (1975)

dejectedly, "and I want you to find the peace and happiness I have found with the Family and my Lord."

At this, I laughed and reached over to grasp his hand. "Well, I'm going to miss not having my baby—by eleven minutes—brother to boss around anymore too. And don't worry, I'm okay. Even though I'm scared, I'm also excited."

"Well, you at least need to take this with you." David reached into his backpack, pulled out a book, and handed it to me. "And you have to promise to read it!"

I held the Bible awkwardly. "Uh, okay . . . And I will write to let you know I have not gone astray if you promise to write to me, so I know you are all right too."

"Okay." He nodded. "But promise you will resist, Sue. And I will pray for you."

"Yeah, yeah, I promise . . ."

My brother and I hugged, both of us in tears, and said goodbye. As we each embarked on our separate life journeys, he carried his worries about Satan and me, and I wondered how on earth my brother was ever going to figure out the world on his own.

I tossed and turned in my bed that night, anxious about all the unknowns that lay ahead. I was worried about how my family was going to survive without me and how I was going to survive without them. But the confidence I had developed over the summer was also with me, filling me with excitement about the adventure that was about to begin. I would no longer be a passenger on the twists and turns of the life Dad chose for our family. From here on out, it would be my responsibility to adapt to the currents and eddies of fate; my decisions were now entirely up to me.

Chapter 11
The Abduction (2016)

"The first competitors are a few minutes away from the finish line!" the announcer for the Donner Lake Triathlon booms into the mic, simultaneously ramping up the volume on crazed, head-banging music.

My phone vibrates in my pocket as Will and I move with the crowd toward the finish line.

Not being a swimmer, biker, or runner, I am here as a cheerleader and to keep an eye on a friend's eight-year-old son, Will, while she competes. I am bummed I don't have Seth, as initially planned, so the boys could hang out together.

I don't recognize the number and don't want to answer the call and risk missing my friend, who is likely to be in the top finishers. But something tells me I should. I secure a place for Will against the ropes next to the finish and ask him to keep an eye out for his mom, then reluctantly trot away from the cacophony.

David picked Seth up yesterday to go to the Carson Swim Center for the day. But then he called in the afternoon and abruptly told me he would not bring him back to me at Lisa's house in Truckee—that he was instead going to stay with friends in South Lake Tahoe and keep Seth for another day. He refused to tell me who his friends were, and he didn't share their address.

The Abduction (2016)

Not cool. I have become more and more anxious as the weekend progresses, wondering if this erratic behavior means David is drinking again.

Our relationship has become increasingly strained since I filed my petition for legal guardianship a month ago, less than a year after bringing Seth to California. I was appointed temporary custody based on my petition, and our court date for the judge to hear the case to decide Seth's permanent status is scheduled for early September, two months from now.

Still trotting away from the crowd, I push the button and force out a breathless, "Hello?"

"Sue, this is Heather. I want you to know I have Seth, and he is okay."

I stop in my tracks, clamping my hand over my other ear, adrenaline spiking through my body, as it repeatedly has over the past year dealing with my brother. It is not a pleasant feeling. The thoughts in my brain spin, and an electrical buzz tingles throughout my body. As my stress level has ratcheted up over recent months, my ability to manage it has steadily diminished. I am immediately overwhelmed with dread.

Heather is a friend from the South Lake Tahoe junior stand-up paddleboard team and the coach for Seth's age group of littlest "groms." She is also the wife of one of the pastors in the local church that David frequented when he lived with me. Her husband, Noah, has provided David with counseling related to his alcohol addiction.

"Wh-what happened?" I stammer. "Has there been an accident?"

"No, no, nothing like that," she says. "But I happened to see David and Seth as they were leaving after the service this morning and went over to say hi. For some reason, he blurted out that he was planning to take Seth to live with him in a homeless shelter in Sacramento, and to be sure and not let you know."

My adrenaline spikes higher. *What the fuck kind of crazy*

RISK

bullshit has he told Seth!? I think, but all I say is, "This is unbelievable! Where are they now?"

"Well, of course I immediately told Noah, and David has been in his office now for about an hour. He is still trying to convince him to not take Seth."

The adrenaline spikes again. *Damn it!* Panicked, I blurt out, "Should I call the police? Does David seem dangerous? Could he still take Seth?"

"No, no, I have Seth," she assures me. "He's at our house. He is hanging with the kids."

I breathe out a sigh of relief and my anxiety goes down a smidge.

In some respects, Heather and I could not be more different. She is the mother of five kids, and the whole family is actively involved in a traditional, fundamentalist Christian church. But she, Noah, and their kids are also very active in the mountain lifestyle, including my current passion, stand-up paddleboarding, also known as SUP, and the ease with which she and her husband parent their flock astounds me. I envy the harmonious relationship they have with their kids. Her homeschooled children are notably thoughtful and engaging, and Seth loves being around them.

Being around their family and some other SUP enthusiasts in their congregation almost makes me wish I could be a part of their church. But besides the fact that my nature-worshiping bent requires spending most Sunday mornings somewhere outside, the LGBT community and lifestyle are certainly not supported in their congregation. I could belong—but I would need to be forgiven, and likely pressured to be cured of my "sin."

I hastily tell Heather that as soon as my friend finishes her race and can rejoin her son, I will drive the hour and a half to South Shore to pick up Seth. We both express our hope that Noah can talk David off the ledge so the police will not have to be called before I get there.

The Abduction (2016)

I try multiple breathing exercises on the drive to lessen the buzzing in my brain and body. Deep breath in, count to seven, hold for two, slow breath out for another seven. I keep having to repeat the exercise over and over as I catch myself lapsing into quick, shallow breaths, practically panting. I can't stop worrying about what David has told Seth and how it will affect him, and what David might try to do if Noah is not successful in changing his mind.

I have been trying so hard to create a feeling of stability, security, and consistency for Seth, as various counselors have advised. Yet his impulse control issues have not improved at the preschool this summer. He rarely has a day when he does not hit another child out of anger and frustration. What kind of setback is this going to create, I wonder?

Walking up to Heather's house, I hear children playing in the backyard. Turning the corner around the house, I see Seth happily jumping on the trampoline with the whole clan. So far, so good.

Heather tells me that Noah convinced David to go back to Sacramento alone, and my old army duffel bag with all the stuff David had gotten from my house for Seth is sitting in the yard. The asshole didn't stay with a friend after all; he stayed at *my* house. I am relieved that Seth has been somewhere familiar and relatively safe but irritated at David's arrogance—and I suspect David was not sober last night.

After loading the duffel bag, I approach the trampoline. Seth barely acknowledges my presence, just shooting a quick glance in my direction. Not that unusual for him when he is playing with other kids.

"Hey Seth," I call, "we're going to leave in ten minutes, okay?" Although I want to leave immediately, I know that he needs warning before this transition.

RISK

Seth continues to bounce like a Mexican jumping bean and does not respond.

After ten minutes of awkward conversation, peppered with long periods of silence, with Heather, I say, "Okay Seth, it's time to go. C'mon out now, all right?"

Again, he ignores me.

I walk over to the trampoline, and one of the older kids gently takes hold of Seth's arm and bounces him to the entrance, where I quickly grab him.

As I hold him in my arms, Seth begins to kick his legs, yelling, "No, no, no! I don't want to go! Put me down!"

"Thanks for everything," I say quickly to Heather, and I start walking briskly to the car.

Seth continues to kick and now begins hitting me on my back while full-on screaming at the top of his lungs.

My adrenaline spikes again—and my heart breaks. Is this just a typical six-year-old tantrum at having to leave the party, or is he suffering some deep emotional trauma from being yanked around by his crazy father?

I have no idea what is going on in his brain, but he clearly knows that yesterday David packed up his things and told him he was going with him to Sacramento, and now, as he continues to sob quietly in the back of the car, I'm telling him we are going back to Lisa's house in Truckee.

He wants to stay with Heather and Noah and their clearly happy, fun, and functional family. I can't blame him. I wish *I* could live with Heather and Noah right now, too, and let someone who knows how to do this be in charge for a while.

I make a quick stop by my house to see what condition David left it in, leaving Seth in the car. At least he is quiet now, silently playing with one of his LEGO men in the back of the car.

All the drawers to Seth's toy boxes and dressers have been left

The Abduction (2016)

open, with stuff not chosen to go in the duffel bag in disarray in drawers or on the floor. I fear the packing process was not done discreetly, deepening my concern over the confusion this must have created for Seth.

On the drive to Truckee, I try to create a sense of normalcy. I say nothing to Seth about his dad or ask him any questions. Instead, I tell him we are meeting some friends at one of his favorite places, Zano's Pizza, and there is another little boy there for him to hang out with.

Seth seems a little off at Zano's and his mood is hard to read, but he eats a monstrous amount of pizza, and when I take him home for an early bedtime, he conks out in five minutes.

I, on the other hand, can barely eat anything, and there is no sleep for me tonight. The day's adrenaline deluge keeps my brain flitting all night.

Over the past year, as a post-menopausal lesbian caretaker of a young child, I have developed a growing sense of living in the cracks between several different worlds, no longer neatly fitting into any one tribe. To cope, I'm learning to appreciate finding grace wherever I see it, regardless of where it comes from.

When I talked to Heather at her house this afternoon, we both marveled at the near miss. If she had not spotted David and Seth across the room and followed her impulse to greet them, I would have eventually had to call the police late that night, sick with worry, not knowing if I was dealing with a kidnapping, car wreck, murder-suicide, or some other doomsday scenario spun from my fevered brain. Who knows how many nights Seth would have spent in the homeless shelter until the authorities could track him down, and what sort of ugly scenario would then have unfolded when they did.

Heather, of course, is convinced this was direct intervention from God. Whether it was a miracle directed by a higher power or merely a lucky intersection between Heather's gracious heart

RISK

and David's odd communication style, I have decided to not form an opinion on the matter.

I spend my sleepless night consumed by overwhelming gratitude for Noah, Heather, and possibly divine intervention. I also worry about the yet-to-be-seen effects of this incident on Seth, afraid it could be hell week (or longer) at Jubilee Preschool. But mostly, I obsess about preparing for what is sure to be an ugly showdown with David at our hearing in two months in the El Dorado County Family Court. What will I need to do to convince the judge in this notably conservative county to forcibly take away parental rights from Seth's biological parents, both of whom are vehemently opposed to my petition? Will the fact I'm married to a woman, and that Lisa and I do not live together and have never been parents before, weaken my position?

No amount of breath work helps to stop the incessant flit and spin, flit and spin, of my thoughts.

Jesus, it's going to be a long two months.

Chapter 12
You're in the Army Now
(1975–1979)

At the end of my senior year, my friend Kathy's mom wrote a letter to our congressman, asking that he make sure I was supported by the Army to keep up my promising slalom kayaking career. He must have thought she was a nut, but she did get a letter saying he was sure the Army would do what was best for me.

It did work out, but not at all in the way I anticipated.

Two days after my eighteenth birthday, at 10:30 p.m., the Greyhound bus discharged its load of new recruits in Fort McClellan, Alabama. Stepping into the floodlights' harsh glare, we were greeted by a cursing, screaming drill sergeant barking out a continuous litany of orders. With his pathetic pencil-thin mustache and puppy-dog eyes, the young drill sergeant looked like he was only a few years older than us. But he was doing his best to sound as intimidating as possible.

"Get off the bus! Hurry up, goddamn it! Come on, come on, come on! Line up on the yellow lines, you maggots! Stand up straight! What are you looking at? Don't look at me! Eyes forward, goddamn it! Do you understand me?"

A few unfortunate women yelled, "Yes, sir!" at this carefully staged question.

He walked up to within inches of the face of one of these

RISK

hapless souls and barked, "Don't call me sir! Do I look like a goddamn officer to you? Sheeeiit! I'm a goddamn sergeant! Staff Sergeant Jones! You will answer me with either 'yes, Staff Sergeant,' or 'no, Staff Sergeant!' And whoever calls me sir again is going to be very sorry! Your momma is not around to wipe your ass anymore, so over the next eight weeks you maggots will do everything I goddamn say, and maybe, just maybe, you will become a goddamn soldier in the United States Army!"

This treatment for new recruits was a deliberate, time-honored tactic to quickly drive all the attitude and inclination you might have about making your own decisions right out of your brain. You were now the property of the United States Army, and you would be told when to eat, sleep, go to the bathroom, march, and salute. No longer an individual, you were merely an insignificant cog in a giant machine and needed to be told what to do every minute. Because you didn't know jack shit.

I imagine every recruit finds the abrupt introduction to Army life a disorienting transition from whatever their life was before. I was certainly no exception. But compared to the uncertainty and chaos I imagined trying to make my way in the world on my own would have entailed, I found the constraints and structure of Army life a relief. I was okay with someone else telling me what to do, keeping me busy every minute, and providing for my basic needs.

And I was not alone. Sharing the basic training experience with dozens of other women also far away from their families and everyone they have ever known in their life leads to fast friendships. There are no established cliques in basic training to break into or the accompanying insecurity about being accepted that I had experienced throughout my nomadic childhood. Here, everyone was on equal footing. Decisions about who to make friends with started with the women who slept in the bunks next to yours.

I'd grown up among many different American subcultures and social classes, including Iowa farm kids, sophisticated Southern

You're in the Army Now (1975–1979)

California urban kids, lower-middle-class Cleveland kids of other races and ethnicities, and middle-class suburban kayaking kids from all over. The Army included a hodgepodge of all these classes and cultures, plus more. But one of the beautiful things about being fellow privates was that these external differences were pretty much erased. We were all the lowest of the low, and whatever status we'd had in our crowd back home didn't mean diddly squat.

For some of the girls, the reality of what they had signed up for came as a rude shock. Many found the discipline, the physical challenges, and the social interactions of boot camp extremely difficult. In contrast, I felt well within my element.

With my slalom kayak training, boot camp's physical tests were no real challenge. I quickly became known as the company jock. I excelled at every contest compared to my fellow soldiers, whether it was knocking out pushups, completing the half-mile running test, or navigating the ropes, walls, and barbed wire of the obstacle course. I knew from playing high school sports that I was just a little above average compared to the talented girls I'd played basketball and run track with. Therefore, my jock status at boot camp was more a reflection of how horribly out of shape and unathletic the typical WAC (Women's Army Corp) recruit was in 1975. But still, I couldn't help but feel a little bad-ass—or enjoy the universal respect it gave me.

And although learning to use a gas mask after walking into a room with real tear gas and counting to ten before putting it on, throwing a grenade, and learning to shoot an M-16 were somewhat intimidating, those challenges were no more difficult than many of the outdoor adventures I had grown up with—and they were not nearly as scary.

But you didn't necessarily have to be a good athlete or particularly brave to succeed in the women's Army. The most critical requirement was to get along with your fellow soldiers, and not ever, ever, challenge authority.

RISK

Away from everything we'd ever known, most of us were just looking for a little kindness and camaraderie. It didn't take much to learn that friendships were easily acquired if you offered this. Being by nature a quiet personality, an empathetic listener, and unconstrained by racial or class prejudices, in the Army—for the first time in my life—I made friends effortlessly.

After completing our ten weeks of basic training, about a quarter of the girls from boot camp moved on with me to military police school. This education primarily consisted of several weeks of military law classes, two intense weeks of unarmed combat training, and many hours at the shooting range.

It was over before I knew it.

The five months of basic and military police school training had passed quickly, and until the last two weeks, none of us knew where we were going to be sent for our permanent duty station. The class before us was sent to Angola, and there were rumors that we might be sent there too. But by the time we graduated, the Angola situation had calmed down, and I was part of about 20 percent of my class that received orders for Germany.

While many of my classmates with these orders were horrified, having no desire to be that far from home, I was elated because Hermann, the owner of Madawaska Kanu Camp, had told me that Germany was absolutely the best place I could get assigned to continue slalom kayaking.

Germany was the birthplace of whitewater kayaking and slalom racing. Whitewater kayaking first began there in the early 1900s with the development of "Faltboots," folding kayaks made from a waterproof fabric stretched over a light wooden frame. By the 1920s, intrepid German and Austrian boaters were flocking to lakes and rivers all over Europe, transporting these lightweight, collapsible boats by train and bus to explore wild river canyons not previously seen by the human eye.

You're in the Army Now (1975–1979)

Unfortunately, there was a fifteen-year halt in participation in the sport when, in 1933, Adolf Hitler and the Nazi party began the dismantling and co-option of German society's core institutions, including religion, sports, and social clubs, as a strategy to ensure their grip as a totalitarian dictatorship. By weakening society in this way and offering the Nazi party as a replacement, they eliminated those who would eventually oppose its even darker schemes for the future. Who knows how the trajectory and progression of many adventure sports would have been altered if not for this one man's aspirations?

It was not until 1946 or 1948, depending on the region, that the Allies gradually lifted the ban on river travel in Germany and paddle clubs were again allowed to form. Not coincidentally, this is when returning American soldiers began to bring both "Faltboots" and whitewater kayak exploration to the United States.

At any rate, I was overjoyed at the prospect of being assigned to the veritable "Mecca" of kayaking, where champions of whitewater slalom were practically household names.

"Hey! Norman!" a voice snapped behind me. "The captain wants you to report to his office as soon as you're off duty."

Blearily waiting in line to turn in my weapons belt at the armory window, I turned to look at the captain's weasel-faced administrative assistant, Sergeant Walsh.

"Okay," I replied, wondering why he had such a sour expression on his face and why he was here. "What's it about?"

"You'll find out soon enough," he replied curtly, his eyebrows scrunched together in an angry scowl. "Just go as soon as you're done. He's waiting for you." He turned and stomped away.

Shit, it sounded like I was in trouble. My groggy brain spun in circles, wondering what possibly for. I had just finished my seventh night in a row of working MP duty on the midnight-to-eight shift. Only able to grab a few hours of sleep during the

RISK

day in my shared four-person barracks, I was almost delirious.

It was highly unusual for the captain of our ninety-soldier company in the 793rd Military Police Battalion in Nuremberg, Germany, to request to speak to one of us lowly enlisted ranks in person. After turning over my belt with the .38-caliber revolver, wooden baton, and handcuffs, I scampered up to the captain's office.

Sergeant Walsh gave me one last stink-eye glare as he signaled me to go in.

"Specialist Norman reporting, sir," I said crisply with a brisk salute. I stood ramrod straight at attention in front of his desk and kept my eyes up, staring above the captain's head at the picture of President Jimmy Carter on the wall.

"At ease, soldier," he replied, which was the signal I could relax. Somewhat.

I moved my arms behind my back and slid my left foot to a wider stance. But I had to keep my thumbs interlaced, and my right foot had to stay planted where it was.

He stared at a letter on his desk for another moment or two. Making me wait. Finally, he peered up at me and said grimly, "Specialist Norman, I don't know who you know, but you must have friends in pretty high places."

I stared back at him in stupefaction. "Excuse me, sir? I . . . I don't know what you mean," I stammered. My mushy brain flailed, attempting to process this ridiculous statement.

He scowled at me for a few moments, eyes squinted and lips pressed tightly together in a thin line, before tossing the letter toward me across his desk. "You mean to tell me you don't know anything about this?" he asked accusingly.

I picked up the letter and read the following:

Commander
Co A, 793d MP Bn

1. The application received from you for the attachment of Norman Sue E, E-4 to this organization has

You're in the Army Now (1975–1979)

been carefully considered, and I am exercising my option as the approval authority to override your recommendation of disapproval. This is necessary as a consequence of shortfall of applicants to staff the Armed Forces Recreation Center for the summer program and is done under the provisions of USAREUR REG 28.110.

My mind reeled as I realized that the application I had submitted a few months ago for a temporary assignment to teach kayaking at the Armed Forces Recreation Center (AFRC) had been approved, even after my commanding officer had recommended against it.

After finishing the letter, I looked up at the captain, my lips quivering a little as I tried to suppress a grin. "Sir, I swear I don't know anything about this. I . . . I don't know anyone." I even giggled a little, to my embarrassment, as I blurted, "I . . . I'm a nobody."

He stared at me for a few moments, and then his face relaxed—apparently satisfied that this freckled and buck-toothed nineteen-year-old girl-soldier, who could still pass for sixteen, was not lying.

"Well," he said resignedly, "it's out of my hands now. Get a copy of the letter with the details you need to prepare from Sergeant Walsh. You're dismissed."

"Yes, sir, thank you, sir," I said as I snapped back to attention.

No longer able to keep a grin entirely off my face, I saluted, executed a brisk about-face, and stepped quickly out of the office. After getting my letter from the even more darkly scowling Sergeant Walsh, I skipped up to my room.

My earlier brain fog was gone, replaced with both excitement and wonder. Could there be such a thing as a kayaking fairy godmother?

I zipped across the clear, swift water of the Loisach River, sprinting toward another swimmer. Squinting against the glare from

RISK

the towering snow-capped peaks surrounding the quaint Bavarian enclave of Garmisch-Partenkirchen, I could see the now-familiar expression of terror etched on his face. The whites of his eyes bulged in sharp contrast against his dark skin. His teeth were equally brilliant as he gasped for air between his desperate cries for help.

Uh, oh, he's panicking, I thought. *Got to keep my distance.*

"No, no, do not swim for my boat," I yelled as I carved a turn just out of reach of his flailing, muscled arms.

Before launch, I had carefully explained to the class that for me to assist a swimmer, they needed to hold on to the grab loop on the back of my boat and float or kick while I paddled them to shore.

But the swimmer before me was in pure survival mode. I knew from experience that if I let him get a hold of my grab loop, he would likely climb onto my boat, and me, in a panic-driven impulse to escape the boulder-strewn, frigid alpine whitewater—and then we'd both be in trouble.

"Swim to the shore behind that tree," I shouted, pointing to an eddy at the side of the river that presented the safest exit route from the Class II rapid. I used my command voice, the one I'd learned in military police school: a booming voice, pulled from deep in my diaphragm, that was meant to penetrate even the most reptilian brain, whether it be calling off a police dog in the middle of an adrenaline-fueled attack or a man terrified of drowning.

I floated next to the swimmer, continuing to point and bark commands, until I was sure he understood where to go. And—thank God—I could tell he knew how to swim. Sometimes they didn't.

Today was Tuesday, the most challenging day of the week for our kayak school. On Tuesdays, our class consisted entirely of infantry or special forces soldiers involuntarily participating in a week of required outdoor-based skills training. Of their week of

You're in the Army Now (1975–1979)

rock climbing, orienteering, and backpacking, whitewater kayaking day represented the most difficult challenge for many soldiers.

Learning to navigate a continuous Class II section of an icy cold alpine river, in a whitewater kayak, in one day, is challenging for even proficient athletes with strong swimming skills. For these soldiers, many of whom had grown up in the inner city or a remote rural community and never learned to swim, the experience was downright terrifying.

The Loisach was not an ideal river for teaching whitewater kayaking. Although the difficulty of the section of the river we used in our classes did not exceed Class II, there were virtually no pools—areas of deep, slow-moving water between the rapids. Because of its continuous gradient, a capsized swimmer and his gear kept flowing swiftly downriver until someone actively rescued them.

Once I was sure my current swimmer had his self-rescue under control, I scanned the river to see if my fellow instructors had retrieved his paddle or kayak.

I quickly determined that the situation was . . . a total shit show.

One of my instructors, a strapping young man from Montana, had also capsized. Although Matt was doggedly swimming himself and his equipment to shore in his own self-rescue, it was going to be a while before he would be of any help. Two of my other instructors—Judge, a scrawny small-town boy from Indiana, and Mike, an athletic Asian American from LA—were clumsily working together to rescue another student swimmer and his kayak. My last instructor, Ambrose, a fast-talking city boy from Chicago, was busy herding the rest of our eight students into nearby eddies. Ambrose had been an instructor in the program the year before and therefore had the most reliable paddling skills. He was also a few years older than the rest of us, with a good head on his shoulders, so I decided it was safe to leave the group with him and try to rescue gear.

RISK

Looking downstream, I spotted two paddles and an upside-down kayak bouncing merrily over the waves, already several hundred feet away.

"I'll get the gear!" I yelled as I spun my kayak in a 180-degree pivot turn.

I loved my Prijon slalom racing kayak for river rescues. With its lightweight, sleek construction, it flew across the currents like a water bug, which was good, since time was of the essence. Splicing my boat's stern underwater, my bow flying into the air, I charged downstream.

I plucked the first paddle out of the water and nestled it against mine in one movement as I continued to stroke toward the shore. Once I got close, I launched the paddle in a javelin throw onto the bank, then spun back into the current.

After rescuing the next paddle, I raced downstream toward the kayak, grimacing as I watched it bump over a picket fence of jagged, low-lying rocks. *Damn it, more fiberglass work tomorrow.*

The kayak had flotation bags in both ends, but the waterlogged boat hung low and heavy in the water. I pulled up next to the upside-down kayak and tipped it on its side so half the cockpit was above water. I then slipped the front end of my kayak into the cockpit and angled the now semi-connected boats toward a clear path to the shore. Because the rapids were relatively calm by this point, I could push the heavy boat into an eddy quickly. Since no one was there to help me, I grabbed onto a nearby bush to hold myself in the eddy while I popped my spray skirt and scrambled out of my kayak. After emptying enough water out of the capsized kayak to get it safely on land, I jumped back into my boat and began to work my way back up the river, hopping and skipping up the eddies and across the currents like a spawning salmon.

At least this is keeping me in competition shape, I thought. Eddy

You're in the Army Now (1975–1979)

attainment was one of the workouts we did to improve our strength and boat-handling techniques for slalom racing.

I had descended about a quarter-mile downstream while retrieving the floating gear. As I worked my way up around the bend in the river, I spotted the two swimmers slowly clambering down the shore to retrieve their equipment. My four instructors—all in their boats, thankfully—were escorting the rest of the class carefully down the river, barking out instructions on when to lean and where to point their kayaks, and encouraging them to paddle hard into the eddies.

My arms ached with exhaustion.

Dear God, I pleaded, *no more swimmers.*

We somehow managed to get everybody down to the spot where I had pulled out the capsized kayak without further mishap. Once there, I decided to get everybody out of the river so we could take a breather and assess the damage.

The kayak I had rescued had incurred multiple fractures from hitting rocks and was no longer seaworthy. Both swimmers had bruised legs and egos, and one was bleeding from his temple from hitting a rock while upside down in his kayak. He did not show any signs of concussion, but understandably, neither he nor the other swimmer wanted to resume the class. They were exhausted and still shivering despite the bright early-summer sun.

I looked over nervously at the squad leader, who had been following us in an Army truck on the road next to the river. Seeing our group congregating on the riverbank, he had parked his vehicle and strolled down to join us. I wondered how much of the carnage he had witnessed.

"Hey Sergeant, can we go up to your truck for a minute?" I asked tentatively, wanting to get out of earshot from his squad.

My stomach squirmed as I pondered what to say. Although

RISK

I was a mere enlisted grunt, it was my call who should stay on the river. I had found the squad leaders, who were sergeants and exceeded my rank in the military chain of command, often reluctant to let their soldiers bail.

This situation we had just experienced was not unique. In fact, it had happened pretty much every Tuesday during the required adventure skills kayak training. The first couple of times, I had not dared to stand up to the squad leader and insist on evacuations. It had never ended well. The terrified soldiers, now entrenched in reptilian brain, could no longer absorb instruction or escape their fear. They just kept swimming, and with instructors diverted to rescuing, other students were also more likely to capsize.

I had concluded that forcing anyone who was not a willing participant to learn how to whitewater kayak was not only stupid but also dangerous.

Steeling myself to sound more confident than I felt, I said firmly, "Sergeant, I will need you to evacuate two members of your squad."

"Well, if only one boat is damaged, why can't one of 'em keep going?" he asked with a scowl.

There is also the damaged self-esteem and ability to think straight, I thought to myself, but it was futile to explain that. The soldiers might need to learn to suck it up for combat, but teaching them that certainly was not my job.

"Well, you should have someone check out the guy who bonked his head," I replied, "and both of their legs are both pretty banged up from the rocks. They are also freezing, and I think another swim could make them hypothermic."

He continued to look at me skeptically but did not respond.

Now's my chance, I thought. *Be bold.*

"It puts both of them and the class at risk to make them continue," I said, consciously lowering the timbre of my voice to sound more authoritative. "I'm going to have my instructors bring

You're in the Army Now (1975–1979)

their equipment up to your truck and tie it in," I concluded. Then I abruptly turned away, ending the discussion.

As I walked away, I prayed, *Please don't say anything, please, please.* I could feel eyes boring into my back, but thankfully, he let me go without further comment.

Becoming the head instructor of the Armed Forces Recreation Center Kayak School was a crash course in leadership that required me to develop my self-confidence and decision-making skills. I found out soon after I arrived that the Army had conducted a worldwide search to find someone with enough kayaking skill to replace the previous head instructor who was rotating out. They had been considering canceling the program when the application I sent came floating in.

During the first four weeks teaching my fellow instructors how to kayak, the river flows were still high, the weather chilly, and water temperatures arctic. Fortunately, they were all excellent swimmers. Although they never used their advanced life-saving skills to rescue students, they could at least self-rescue most of the time. They swam a lot.

Because the alpine lakes were filled with recently melted snow, learning how to do an Eskimo roll was almost impossible. Flipping upside down meant an instant ice cream headache and the beginnings of hypothermia after about three attempts. Every flip resulted in a swim.

Two days a week were reserved for teaching my instructors how to put fiberglass patches on their boats as their bodies recovered from bruises and scrapes.

Even after this first month of training, none of my instructors had mastered a reliable Eskimo roll or edge control in the current. Their second month, our first month of teaching students, was a total yard sale: multiple students and instructors capsized within moments of each other in a single rapid as I churned back and forth across the river, yelling instructions and pulling equipment and people to shore.

It was not until I worked for a kayak school in the United States a few years later that followed a gradual progression in skill learning over several days that I fully realized how out of control the one-day AFRC kayak program was. Frankly, we were lucky no one died.

Finally, after two months, most of my instructors became decent kayakers. We still had many student swimmers, but with my instructors able to stay in their boats and proficiently perform river rescues, the action on the river was reduced from total chaos to controlled mayhem.

Despite the rocky start, the two six-month summer assignments I spent in Garmisch as a soldier kayak instructor for the Army were magical. Being the only woman hired for both summers within the Garmisch AFRC, I was a little starved for female friends; few women in the United States, much less the Armed Forces, had the requisite sports creds for the AFRC.

But I was used to playing with the boys. And I fell in love with one of them.

Although I had experienced many crushes in high school, I had never dated. Shy and awkward in oh so many ways, I was not on anybody's radar. But my first year in the Army had suddenly provided a lot of opportunities to grapple with dating men. After all, we women were a small pool of fish in a sea of sharks. These brief episodes had mostly been a struggle for me. And I was still years away from understanding or even acknowledging the attractions I also felt toward women or knowing what to do about them.

But Greg, a permanent staff member with the AFRC office in Garmisch, was special. A little bit older than me, and one of those guys who was friends with everybody, he was kind, athletic,

You're in the Army Now (1975-1979)

handsome, and at ease with exploring Europe beyond the base. Our romance was spent exploring the Alps in our backyard and other beautiful environs and villages in southern Germany, Switzerland, Austria, and Italy. It was a glorious feeling to be adored and respected by someone I was also attracted to. Greg was my first, and he was an ideal boyfriend for that time in my life.

Garmisch, the sister city of Aspen, Colorado, was an idyllic locale for a vacation, let alone a military post. The scenery around this quaint Bavarian village nestled at the base of the Alps was spectacular, unlike anything I had ever seen. My time there cemented a critical realization about my future: when I returned to the United States, I was going to live near or in the mountains.

I grew up during my three years in the Army. During this time, I explored communication nuances in both intimate relationships and friendships among people from many diverse backgrounds. I further developed the confidence in myself that had begun during my senior year while pushing the limits in kayaking. And as I was forced to face new and unexpected challenges, including being thrust into a leadership role at a young age, I became stronger and more resilient. It was but the first of many times I would use the grit I'd developed through paddling to face challenges outside of my kayak.

Without kayaking, my Army experience would have been very different—smaller and grimmer. Kayaking was the key to unlocking doors, magical doors to opportunities that would enrich my life in many surprising ways in the years to come.

I still have the letter sent to my commander announcing my assignment to the Armed Forces Recreation Center. I keep it in a small box of my most treasured keepsakes. A reminder that although you can't control what fate throws at you, continuing to step up to the plate and expanding your skill sets can't hurt. And that whenever your fairy godmother throws you a bone, you should chomp on it.

Chapter 13
Day in Court (2016)

About a dozen people are sitting around me in the courtroom, and I try to match up the opponents. Which of the grim-faced people seated on the left side of the aisle are fighting the equally grim-faced sitting on the right? No one is looking at each other, so no clues there. I try to determine relationships based on ages and physical resemblances—anything to distract myself, to try to calm my nerves.

Katie, a soulmate friend visiting from Colorado, is sitting to my right. Lisa and Julie, a long-time river sister, sit to my left. I have known Katie and Julie for over thirty years. I feel fortunate to be surrounded by this trio of powerful and unique women.

As people continue to file in, a woman with bleached blond hair in a tight-fitting matching black jacket and short pencil skirt totters past us down the aisle on shiny gold-colored high heels. Wielding a thick stack of papers in one arm, under prominent cleavage, and a briefcase under her other arm, she navigates to the table reserved for plaintiffs' attorneys.

Katie leans over and whispers, "That woman's a lawyer? She looks like a prostitute!"

No matter the situation, Katie can always make me laugh. It is one of her superpowers. At least I feel better about my decision to represent myself in today's proceedings.

Day in Court (2016)

David is wearing a suit and tie, and I wonder where he got them. Probably from some organization that helps the indigent in Sacramento, or maybe he found them at a thrift store. The suit is about one size too big on him, and his footwear—pink and white athletic socks with worn, scuffed black loafers—drags down the whole look he is going for. One of the telling marks of a homeless person, I've learned, is an inability to maintain appropriate socks and footwear.

He also looks like hell. His face is haggard, and his eyes have a buggy look, though I'm not sure whether that's from drinking or not sleeping well at the homeless shelter.

No children are present. Their fate will be decided behind these closed doors, by the judge wielding the gavel.

I feel any reasonable judge would rule in my favor, but I can't shake lingering anxiety. One of the witnesses I have called to testify on my behalf is my friend Gwen. She and her wife and kids have provided considerable support for Seth and me over the past year. I have turned to them to take Seth in for several extended overnight stays when I've had to work out of town, and he considers their children to be his new siblings. But Gwen also happens to work for Child Protective Services, and (without sharing any specifics) she's talked about a few cases she's been involved in where she felt judges exercised terrible judgment in returning kids to biological parents' care. Parents that Gwen thought were clearly not good for the child. She said some judges in our county are very reluctant to separate children from their biological parents absent evidence of blatant physical abuse.

As I listen to the cases preceding mine, I begin to feel better about my chances. This judge has clearly been doing this for a while. I can tell he has heard the same stories many times before. He is not gentle on the fools and quickly cuts off the testimony when either the petitioner or the defendant gets off track from providing facts and evidence relevant to determining what is best for the child in each case.

RISK

I believe my witnesses will be crucial to my case. They include Gwen; Seth's preschool teacher, Amber; and my ace in the hole, Pastor Noah—who, although he is David's pastor, not mine, agrees that Seth should remain in my care.

When Noah's turn to speak comes, he describes for the judge the role he played as a counselor for David in the last year, meeting regularly with him to provide guidance so that David could resume his parental role for Seth fully. Noah's core belief is that God's intention is that children be with their biological parents, and he feels that David's deep love for Seth and desire to be a good father are sincere and genuine. Given this, he admits, having to testify at this hearing is hard for him. He believes strongly in the natural world order and the concept of a traditional family. He also firmly believes in redemption, and God's grace and strength to facilitate that. I know at his core that Noah thinks it is God's desire for David to be healed and to once again become Seth's custodial parent.

After listening to Noah ramble a bit about his hopes for David, the judge point-blank asks him, "What do you think is best for Seth right now, based on your experience with both his father and his aunt?"

Noah takes a deep breath and exhales slowly. "It goes against every core belief I have to say this. I truly hope David will continue to work to become the kind of parent I know he wants to be. But he is not ready. He cannot provide a stable home and the parenting that Seth needs. Seth is much better off living in Sue's care until David can complete the work he needs to do."

Kaboom.

In my closing statement, I summarize for the court why I feel compelled to petition for guardianship and admit that this is an action I wish I did not have to take.

My voice trembles a little as I begin, "I never wanted to be a parent, and it has been extremely hard to give up my old life.

Day in Court (2016)

Taking in a young child, especially with some of the behavior issues Seth has, has been more difficult than I ever imagined. It has been extremely difficult for my marriage, disrupted my friendships, and affected my ability to work effectively and pursue my passions."

In the middle of the statement, I briefly describe some of the reasons I felt I needed to remove David from my home and why I now feel compelled to legalize my parenting role. Toward the end of my statement, I pause to take a deep breath. My voice gets stronger as I conclude, "I love Seth with all my heart. He is an amazing, joyful little being, and I'm willing to do whatever it takes to provide him the love, security, and stability he needs to heal from the emotional trauma he has endured so that he can thrive in this world."

When it's David's turn to give his closing statement, he chooses to rant about an incident that occurred a month ago.

Startled out of her slumber when Seth ninja-jumped her for a love hug one morning, our dog, Maddie, snapped at Seth, breaking the skin in two places on his face. The whole thing scared the shit out of all of us. Although the wounds were superficial and easily treated with antibiotic cream and bandages, and although a remorseful hug-out between Seth and Maddie took place soon afterward, David reported the incident to CPS. After a short conversation with me, CPS immediately closed the case.

But now, in classic form, David demands that the judge override CPS's decision.

At this demand, the judge, who has been relatively dispassionate through the proceedings up to that point in our case, becomes visibly irritated. "I do not consider this incident to be relevant to the proceedings, Mr. Norman," he says, more than once.

But David will not let it go and becomes increasingly belligerent toward the judge as the minutes tick by.

Finally, the judge says, "Mr. Norman, if you do not drop this issue, I will have the bailiff remove you from the court. Have I made myself clear?"

There is a moment where I wonder just how far David might go. I cannot believe my good fortune—that he has so willingly demonstrated for the judge the dysfunctional and irrational behavior that led us to be in this courtroom in the first place.

After this last reprimand, he wisely zips his lip and silently glares at the table in front of him.

At that point, the judge quickly moves on. "Well, I have heard enough to give the court my decision in this case."

There are several minutes of preamble, establishing for the record his authority to make the decision, but finally, he states the words that will change my life forever.

"Permanent guardianship of minor to Susan Elizabeth Norman is granted. The court finds that the permanent guardianship to Susan Elizabeth Norman is in the child's best interest."

It is hard to describe the emotions that go through me upon hearing those words and watching the court reporter transcribe them into the court records for all eternity.

Although my rational mind knew coming in here today that I had a solid case—a knowledge that was only reinforced by David's self-destruction at the end of this hearing—I still experience a powerful release of pent-up anxiety at this announcement. The tension that has built up over the past year, especially in the two months since the attempted abduction, whoosh out of my body. I feel joy. I feel exhausted. I feel like crying.

Beside me, Katie takes my left hand; Lisa, on my other side, puts her hand on top of my right.

It's done. I am now the sole legally responsible parent for Seth, for better or worse.

I do not yet know to be afraid.

Chapter 14
What It Takes to Be a Champion (1981)

I slowly paddled up to the start wand for my second race run, my breaths long and deep. Consciously relaxing my facial muscles, I focused on directing the tingling electrical buzz of energy coursing through my body for the task ahead. Regardless of what happened, it would all be over in four minutes. All the months of training, hours of course memorizing, and minutes of agonizing pre-race butterflies were behind me now. Just seconds remained before I'd take one last run through twenty-five gates of rambunctious Class III whitewater.

I peered nervously up at the sky as the tree branches began to wave from a light breeze. Dark storm clouds were quickly building overhead.

"Racer start in ten seconds," the starter announced.

I gently sculled my right blade in the water in a forward stroke position, ready to explode.

"Three . . . two . . . one . . ."

As the beeps began, I burst forward with a powerful stroke to break through the wand and into the current.

Paddling swiftly downstream through gate one, I reached out with a forward sweep to angle toward gate two, an upstream gate in the eddy. I drove across the eddy line, planted a draw stroke that whipped my boat around the inside pole, and followed up with a sweep stroke that launched me back into the current and ferried me across a wave to gate three. With a reverse stroke, I sliced the back end of my kayak under the inside pole and slid through gate three backward, then used a forward sweep to slip the front end of my boat under the same inside pole.

With my kayak now positioned at a downstream angle toward gate four, I stabbed two hard forward strokes and lifted my boat's edge to punch through a sharp reversing hydraulic.

Reading the water and always thinking two gates ahead, I concentrated on placing my strokes as efficiently as possible. I worked my way across currents, over hydraulics, and around rocks, navigating through the course as quickly as I could without hitting the poles, which would result in costly penalty points added to my running time.

My focus intensified as I came up to the lip of Nantahala Falls. The next four gates, numbers twelve through fifteen, were the crux moves on the course. Offset through the big drop, the gates required precise maneuvering. Gate twelve was a reverse gate on the left side of the river, just above the drop. The next two were hard-offset downstream gates on the right side through the falls, and gate fifteen was an upstream all the way back and to the left, just below the drop.

On my first run, I'd gone through gate fourteen too straight, afraid of getting stuck in the big hydraulic just below it. When the water cleared from my eyes after punching the hole, I had to scramble to ferry over to the eddy below gate fifteen. I'd made it, but I was low, and it had taken at least ten seconds to work my way back up the river to get through the gate.

I gritted my teeth and powered harder than I had my first run in and out of gate twelve. This resulted in a better line to thirteen, and even better into fourteen. After fourteen, I kept a

What It Takes to Be a Champion (1981)

hard angle toward gate fifteen. If I set my angle too hard, I ran the risk of getting caught sideways in the hole between fourteen and fifteen—a hydraulic, usually avoided when just paddling the river, that was sharp and steep and could easily cause a flip, or a time-wasting and nasty side surf—but if I ran it too straight, I would get blown downstream past gate fifteen again.

I lifted the upstream edge of my kayak and powered into the hole with a hard downstream stroke, and this time when the water cleared from my eyes, I was headed straight toward the inside pole of gate fifteen. My adrenaline surged as I propelled myself in and up through the gate on a single draw stroke. I was finished with over half the course now, and so far, the run had been fast and clean.

I made it through gate twenty-two before the storm cut loose. I bobbed and weaved to get my head and shoulders through the last three wildly swinging gates on the course as the storm unleashed a torrent of wind and rain. I heard the crack of thunder and was dimly aware of an almost simultaneous lightning flash in my peripheral vision. But nothing was going to break my focus now.

I sprinted across the finish line, gasping for breath, muscles spent. I'd left everything on the course.

Soaking wet and shivering, I decided not to hang around in the storm to see my official score. Even with the wind on the last few gates, I knew I'd been much faster, and accrued fewer penalties, in this second run than I had in my first. I'd done my best and now wanted only to get warm and dry, so I quickly paddled the half-mile downriver to the cabin where I was staying.

After changing into dry clothes, I crawled into bed and succumbed to a state of complete and utter exhaustion. Regardless of the outcome, after ten days of not properly sleeping or eating, the 1981 US Whitewater Canoe and Kayak Slalom Team trials were finally over.

RISK

≋

Slalom kayak racing came back into my world in 1980, the summer after I got out of the Army. I had gotten a job for a few weeks teaching at a whitewater kayak school owned by Roger Paris in Carbondale, Colorado. Roger (pronounced Ro-jey) had been on the French National Team back in the day and still used slalom gates to teach paddling technique. In between classes, he'd spent some time coaching me. By the end of my time at his school, he'd convinced me that I was good enough and still young enough to pursue whitewater slalom racing at the national level. I decided to give it a shot, and at the 1980 nationals on the Kern River in Bakersfield, California, I met back up with the kids I had paddled with in high school.

Only now, quite a few of them were world champions.

A documentary of these whitewater racers' experience, *Fast and Clean*, premiered at the 1980 national championships in Kernville. This documentary rocked my world. Even by current standards, the film was a classic. It presented the human drama of the thrill of victory and the agony of defeat at their best. And the characters in this drama were people I knew and admired. After viewing this Cinderella story of the United States's emergence as a world power in the European-dominated international whitewater-racing scene, I decided to jump on the wave.

I arranged my life around this goal. I left my boyfriend, Greg, behind in Utah and moved to Colorado to be closer to other slalom paddlers. Stretching out obtaining a bachelor's degree in watershed science at Colorado State University over the next five years, I took two full semesters off from school to train and compete. I worked part-time when I could—as a maid, a house painter, a kayak instructor, a raft guide, a waitress—and lived cheap. I made just enough money to pay the bills and feed my paddling habit. I drove crappy cars, lived in crappy houses with

What It Takes to Be a Champion (1981)

many roommates, and for long periods I mostly subsisted on bean burritos and peanut butter and jelly English muffins.

There was no financial sponsorship of whitewater paddlers, either through the national sports organizations or corporations. Those that competed in the obscure fringe sport of whitewater kayaking did it because they loved it.

Just before Christmas that year, my grandfather called to let me know my mom had passed away. This news was simultaneously devastating and a relief. She'd died from pneumonia because she had grown too weak to breathe effectively. By this point she could no longer talk, could barely swallow, and did not recognize most people. I did not mourn her passing; it felt merciful. I did, however, mourn the life my mom would have had if she had never been afflicted with multiple sclerosis, and the life I would have shared with her.

My grandfather did not expect me to come to the very small funeral he organized in Bloomfield. He knew I did not need closure, having processed the loss of my mother steadily over the past seventeen years. With every visit I'd witnessed the loss of more function, the progression of her slow death, and I had grieved.

My mom's illness has always given me profound gratitude for having a healthy body. And I was not going to waste it. When I was not in school or working, I paddled. I didn't think there was anything more satisfying than a whitewater athlete's lifestyle: eat, sleep, paddle, and repeat.

Whitewater slalom racing, usually set on Class III and IV whitewater, is an incredibly dynamic sport. If the athlete is not in the zone, meaning not using the water and precise paddling technique to efficiently zip from gate to gate, the experience becomes an exhausting battle against the river—always a little late, fighting for every move.

But when you're on, it's magic. Flying into eddies out of a

RISK

rushing jet of whitewater with a well-timed draw stroke and then using that momentum to slingshot through the gate and back into the current in one or two strokes. Shazam, a sweet moment. Achieving the exhilarating feeling of time slowed down, working powerfully and fluidly with the river to create a magical dance. Linking those sweet moments from gate to gate through all twenty-five gates of the course.

That was the addiction, and I was all in.

Resting in my cabin after my race run, I was thoroughly enjoying the sensation of my warming body lying under the covers on my bunk and the almost liquid feeling of relief pouring through my every cell.

For the 1981 Worlds, the US Whitewater Canoe and Kayak Team governing organization had created a new and particularly grueling team selection process. The intent was to help ensure that a deserving paddler did not miss out on making the team because of one bad day. But the resulting team trial format was one of the most emotionally and physically exhausting experiences of my life. Four separate races were held over two consecutive weekends in two different states. The winner of each day earned a berth on the team.

For my class, the K1-Ws, the first three races were predictably won by the established top women in the field.

That meant on this last day, about eight of us "best of the rest" were still left, hoping to snag that fourth-place spot. Although there were two favorites—women who had qualified for the team in '79—everyone knew that spot was up for grabs.

In about ten minutes, I thought, I'll rally and go back to the racecourse to see the results. It was apparent the quick-moving storm had passed. I figured they'd probably had to stop the race for a little while, but by now the rest of my class had likely finished their second runs.

What It Takes to Be a Champion (1981)

I was relieved that the storm hadn't greatly affected my second run, despite the gyrations required on the last three gates. I had been fast, including during the very tricky line through Nantahala Falls, and had only hit two gates on my entire run. That second run—and everyone else's—would decide the results of the race.

Just as I was getting out of bed, I heard an urgent knock at the door. Hoping it was someone coming to tell me the results (maybe I had won!), I opened the door to see my friend Chuck in the doorway, wearing a cheap poncho and soggy tennis shoes and dripping wet from head to toe.

Chuck was a fellow Westerner who had also trained in DC that year, competing for the downriver and slalom team. He was also a paddling legend, having qualified for several previous national and Olympic teams in various canoe and kayak disciplines. Throughout the spring, he had made a point of giving me advice and encouragement. I knew he was rooting for me as one of a few fellow Westerners he thought had a chance of breaking into the eastern racing monopoly.

But Chuck did not look congratulatory. Instead, he said urgently, "Sue, you have to come back up and take another run."

"What? Why? Did they lose my time?"

"No. But they didn't stop the race for the competitors that were behind you, and the gates were blowing sideways during their runs."

"But my run was fine!" I whined. "The wind only affected the last three gates. I'm happy with my second run."

Becoming more irritated, Chuck replied, "That doesn't matter. They have decided to throw out all the second run scores and have the entire class redo their runs."

I felt like crying. I could not face the thought of crawling back into my cold, wet paddling gear, carrying my boat back up to the starting line, and dealing with those nauseating butterflies in my stomach again.

RISK

"No, no, no—I just can't do it," I cried. "I'm exhausted!"

Chuck frowned at me. "You have no choice," he said in a commanding voice. "I'm going to drag you up there if I have to. But believe me, you do not want to quit now. You will always regret it."

I gaped at him, struck by the passion in his voice. Chuck was not my boyfriend, and he had nothing personal to gain from this. Hell, he had his own race to focus on. But he could recognize when a friend and a relatively inexperienced competitor needed help to make the right decision, and he was stepping up to deliver that help.

He gathered up my soggy paddling gear from where I had strewn it, stuffed it into my hands, and barked, "I'm giving you two minutes to suit up," and slammed the door.

I scrambled into my gear as fast as I could. When I came out the door, Chuck already had my boat on his shoulder and my paddle in his hand.

Seeing me ready to go, his face broke into a wide grin. "Let's go!"

Chuck jogged the entire half mile back up to the race start, carrying my gear. As I struggled to keep up, blood and oxygen began flowing through my body again.

As my mind also came back online, I realized how grateful I was that he had helped me get back in the fight.

Of *course* I did not want to give up and leave my fate to chance.

It wasn't until later that I fully understood how vital Chuck's simple act of support was to me—not just at that moment, but also in showing me how to present in life.

What I learned from my friend that day was the importance of achieving your goals through your best effort, and that the effort is often more important than the ultimate outcome. I also learned the value of recognizing when a friend needs help to face a challenge they find overwhelming, and what a difference it can make when support is offered and accepted.

What It Takes to Be a Champion (1981)

Well, I wish I could say that my third run was the winning run. But as it turned out, the entire women's class, including myself, were too exhausted to put together a race that could beat my first run of the day. Even with its mistakes, my first run score held up through all the re-runs, by a thin margin of a few seconds.

I would have made the team even if I had not taken the re-run. But I would not have fully earned it. Chuck had enabled me to qualify for the team with dignity by ensuring I had put in as much effort as the rest of my peers.

Because of him, I could go to the world championships in Bala, Wales, in just two months with my head held high.

I wish I could have told Mom. But of course, I knew she was already proud.

"I really thought I would have it after first runs," Linda said quietly.

I looked over at her in alarm. Her dark brown eyes were cast down, her voice weak, defeated. She slumped in the cramped passenger seat of our rental car, the heavy drizzle outside creating a light pitter-patter, the windows completely fogged.

"Linda," I said urgently, "there are still second runs. You can do it!"

From the backseat, Yuri chimed in, "Jeez, we all had crap first runs. You know this race will be won on second runs."

"Yeah," Linda replied, but her voice was not convincing.

The hours between first and second runs of a slalom race are a unique phenomenon on the space-time continuum. Those two to three hours or so drag infinitely slowly as you try to fill every second with positive thought. You pace up and down the riverbank, analyzing every move on the twenty-five-gate racecourse yet again. Later, you find a quiet space to practice calm, deep breathing, attempting to control the electrical energy buzzing through your body. Then you find a dry, warm place to do some stretching, keeping your muscles and ligaments limber. You force down food and drink that you know your body needs, even though your stomach heaves slightly with every swallow.

Especially if your first run was crap.

Well, that first run was still valuable as an additional practice run, you tell yourself. Every competitor only gets one practice run on the racecourse before the competition. So, the kinks often still need to be worked out on first race runs.

Yuri and I exchanged glances, knowing that the mental path Linda was on was not good. For any of us. We *needed* to maintain a positive headspace.

This was the first world championship for Yuri and me. However, Linda was a veteran. She had won a bronze in the 1977 world championships in Austria and another bronze at the 1979 world championships in Canada. She was a beautiful paddler. Tall and lanky, she had a smooth, graceful, and deceptively powerful paddling style. She was a gold medal favorite coming into this race, the 1981 World Kayak and Canoe Slalom Championships on the Tryweryn River in Bala, Wales.

The first bronze had been an exciting accomplishment for her and the sport. It made her the first woman from the United States to win a medal at an international race in whitewater slalom kayaking, a sport dominated by Europeans. And her performance had not been a fluke. Over the next two years, she'd continued to show she clearly had the talent and fitness to compete with the Europeans during other international races. Her second bronze had been a crushing disappointment because she had gone to the Worlds in Canada to win.

Her championship race at Bala was supposed to be the one. The redemption race, where Linda would finally bring home the gold medal she had been seeking for six years.

But now, her lack of confidence was palpable. I had watched her first run, and it had not been the same Linda I had trained and raced with all year. Instead of her arms effortlessly and seamlessly

What It Takes to Be a Champion (1981)

whipping her boat through the gates, her paddle strokes had seemed jerky and cramped. She'd also racked up careless gate touches, incurring ten-second penalties with each hit.

"Well," Yuri said, putting her rubber boots on in the back seat, "I think I'm going to go take another look at those upstream gates at fifteen and sixteen in those ridiculously narrow eddies. Do you guys want to come?"

"Yeah," I said eagerly. I knew what Yuri was thinking. We needed to get away from the suffocating negative energy Linda was filling the car with before getting contaminated by it. And maybe getting out of the vehicle and moving could help Linda get out of her head.

A head filled with doubts and fears. Visualizing defeat instead of victory. Racked with dread. It was a feeling I knew well.

We shook out our wet ponchos as best we could before putting on the slimy cold plastic. I climbed out of the car into the cold gray drizzle, hoping we could enter a new, more positive vibration in the dense energy of the space-time continuum between our first and second runs.

Linda and I were coming into the race from radically different perspectives.

This was my first world championship. I felt like a winner just being there. I was already successful because I had earned a spot on the US World Whitewater Kayak Slalom Team. I had a team uniform. I had marched in the parade of nations with the other athletes. It was all exciting and glorious.

My goal was to not come in last, and at best place in the top third of the class.

But Linda had come to win a gold medal. Anything less would be a disappointment. I did not envy the pressure that was on her. Of course, I was still nervous. But there would be very few eyes on my run. All eyes would be on hers.

RISK

Entering my second run, I felt stronger, more confident, ready to unlock the tricky, narrow moves gate by gate.

The Tryweryn was a narrow stream, bordered by sheer sod banks. The dark tea-colored water and the start of the racecourse originated from a reservoir—and the Bala slalom course started off with a bang. The first four gates were set in the reservoir spillway just before the spillway plunged over a ten-foot drop into the river channel below. The hydraulic at the bottom of the waterfall was steep and explosive, popping slalom kayaks out erratically, putting them in unpredictable positions. There was only a fraction of a second to adjust to whatever angle the pulsating hydraulic put your kayak in to attain the upstream gate set just below on the far left shore.

On this second run, I came out of the drop lined up perfectly and was able to navigate a fast, clean line through gate five. My confidence continued to surge as I put together fast moves from gate to gate.

Approaching the tricky upstream at gate fifteen, I turned my kayak to enter the eddy with a hard upstream ferry angle. During my first run, I'd entered the eddy pointed more downstream, creating a powerful upstream arc off my draw stroke as I crossed the eddy line. But the eddy was so narrow the sharp point of my kayak had plunged into the sod bank before I could finish the turn. I'd even gotten stuck for a moment. Pulling myself out with a backstroke, I had not only lost time but had also had to paddle up through the upstream gate with an embarrassing little clump of grass-tufted sod stuck on the front of my kayak.

But this time, I employed a new strategy—and it worked perfectly. I snuck the bow of my boat under the inside pole, pulling myself up and out of the gate in three strokes. I even heard a few people cheer as I powered downstream.

My almost flawless run continued until gate twenty-two. This reverse gate was set in an eddy in the middle of the river.

What It Takes to Be a Champion (1981)

My adrenaline was running high, and I powered over to the gate a little too fast. Turning upstream in the eddy, I had to flatten my boat to sneak the stern under the gate and navigate the reverse gate in the required backward position. But because of my speed, the sharp edge on the side of my boat grabbed the slow eddy water harder than I was expecting, and I flipped upside down. I rolled up quickly, my lungs almost bursting from oxygen debt. But I was below the gate.

I kept it together to finish the last three gates of the course in good form. But I knew I was going to receive a fifty-second penalty for running gate twenty-two upside down.

It was both a disappointing and exhilarating run. Except for the mistake at gate twenty-two, I knew it was the best run I was capable of—frankly, one of the best slalom runs of my life. My teammates and coaches who had watched me on the upper part of the course congratulated me. I had paddled well where they had seen me. But as they say, close only counts in horseshoes and hand grenades. Although I couldn't have hoped for a better run on twenty-four out of the twenty-five gates of the course, that fifty-second penalty would cost me.

But I had no time to dwell on my race. It was time for me to cheer for my teammates.

Because I was a first-timer with no cred, I had been seeded early in the competition. This gave me time to quickly get changed and run to the top of the course to watch the medal contenders.

Two of my teammates were in the top seed. Besides Linda, another teammate, Cathy Hearn, was also a gold medal favorite. In fact, Cathy had won the gold medal in the 1979 Worlds.

Cathy had a very different paddling style than Linda. She was incredibly powerful, with heavily muscled arms and back. Cathy was not as graceful as Linda, but every single stroke showcased her formidable strength. With her sleek racing helmet, form-fitting life jacket, long blond braid, blue eyes, and sharp cheekbones,

RISK

she looked like a kayaking Viking warrior. She attacked the river with her paddle wielded like a lance.

But during one of Cathy's slalom practices a couple days previously, she'd had a terrifying experience in the spillway drop: flipping over, losing her paddle, and then getting shoved by the current into very shallow water on the far right side of the river. She'd tried to exit her kayak, but the water was so shallow that the back of her life jacket was hitting the bottom of the river, so she was trapped in her boat, upside down, unable to get out, until a spectator on the shore finally ran out into the water, grabbed her arm, and pulled her upright.

I knew Cathy and Linda were coming into their second runs with psychological challenges. I also knew they were two of the best paddlers on the course, both capable of winning.

Linda started her run two positions ahead of Cathy. I could tell immediately this was not going to be her day. Her strokes were jerky, her face constricted in a desperate grimace. She hit a gate with her back and another with her paddle before she even entered the spillway. It was as if the synapses between her arms and her brain were misfiring.

Linda was my mentor, the person who had taught me the most in developing my own slalom technique. Although my arm span was almost a foot shorter than Linda's, I sought to emulate her graceful technique, reaching as far as I could to get the most from each stroke.

She was also a friend. I loved her goofy sense of humor as much as I admired her paddling prowess. She had an infectious, braying laugh and a large, toothy grin. And as intense as she was about her own training, she'd always supported Yuri and me, her protégés. It was from her that I had learned the fundamentals of slalom early in my career.

I felt the pain I knew she was going to experience at the end of this run—the loss of her dreams. Linda had made it clear this

What It Takes to Be a Champion (1981)

would be her last World Championships, and this was not how it was supposed to end.

I turned my eyes back up to the top of the course, ready to watch Cathy's run. As the reigning world champion, she was the last paddler in our class.

After Cathy cleanly navigated through the gates in the spillway, I saw immediately she was taking no chances as she powered over the top of the ten-foot waterfall. She had decided to not risk flipping by hitting the bottom of the drop with an aggressive forward stroke, keeping her boat pointed straight downstream. This strategy worked as intended, keeping her upright. But it also resulted in blasting her some distance downstream before she could turn her boat toward the upstream gate on the left side of the river. I counted one-one thousand, two-one thousand . . . counting off the seconds it took Cathy to grind her way to the side of the river and up against the current through the upstream gate. The gate wasn't even in a real eddy, just a slower current than the middle of the river.

She pulled into the gate when I got to twelve-one thousand, and my heart sank. Surely, she had lost the race with her conservation strategy. It would be tough to recover from that many seconds of lost time.

But unlike Linda, Cathy still looked solid and confident. The expression on her face was both relaxed and determined. Serious athletes and coaches have long known that when you grimace, you compromise the oxygen flow your body needs to perform in a sport. Cathy was a master at not losing her cool.

I was not as close to Cathy as I was to Linda. But she'd always been supportive, albeit more distantly, and I felt lucky when I could train with her. I was fortunate to have two world-class women to paddle with in my own country.

Now, seeing the race was not over for Cathy, I began to run down the side of the river to view as much of her run as was

RISK

humanly possible. She was nailing it. Cheers rose from the crowd as she tirelessly powered in and out of each gate, fast and clean. Everyone knew they were watching a potential medal run. She crossed the finish line strong, her last stroke as powerful as her first off the start line.

At the end of the day, Cathy did not win the gold. But she did win the silver with that run. She also won a bronze medal in the slalom team event with Linda and Yuri and a bronze medal in the downriver kayak team event.

Even with a fifty-second penalty, I finished barely within my goal, placing fifteen out of forty-five competitors—a testament to how challenging the course was. And I was in notable company. Linda finished twelfth, and Liz Sharman, the 1979 silver medalist from Britain, placed fourteenth. I did not feel I had disgraced myself, but I knew both those women were crushed by their result.

Cathy displayed the power of staying in the moment on her second run. Keeping the hounds of doubt and worry at bay until the finish line was crossed. Focusing her effort on the matter at hand, regardless of the outcome. I will never forget it. Cathy's ability to recover from such a costly mistake on gate five of a twenty-five-gate course displayed focus at the highest level.

Not giving up after a mistake doesn't always pay off. But it was part of our coaching and race ethic to never quit during a slalom run, to not dwell on a pole hit or coming in low in an upstream gate. Because someday, at one race, it would pay off.

Linda ended up disappearing from competition a couple years later, and I often wondered if her disappointment drove her to let that part of her life go.

We have all seen the phenomenon at the Olympics, especially in sports that require lightning-fast reflexes: the golden ones, hyped so intensely before the event, going down in flames. Every

What It Takes to Be a Champion (1981)

time I wonder, will they be forever scarred? Or will they be able to put their experiences in perspective, savoring the victories and beauty of their sport over memories of their defeats?

Cathy kept on competing. She won her last world championship medal, a bronze, in 1997.

She also ended up having a child very late in life. A daughter, only a year younger than Seth. We went on a five-day river trip on the San Juan River together in 2016. There was an openness and connection in our relationship that did not exist when the competitive fire of our youth still blazed. We are both women who began our journey into motherhood after fifty. We both know what it feels like to be mistaken for our child's grandmother. On our river trip, it was great to talk to someone my own age about our parenting challenges and learning. In some ways, her daughter was very much like Seth—strong, stubborn, and exuberant.

Competition is a tricky endeavor for gauging one's merit or experiencing joy. Even after winning a race, there is always the next one to be lost. Without a genuine love of the sport, the endeavor can never be as satisfying. But in my case, I found the joy came from savoring the entire web of the experience. A web full of friendships and memories that would last a lifetime.

I struggled with controlling race nerves throughout my racing career, which frequently resulted in race results that were not on par with the abilities I demonstrated during training. I rarely mastered the ability to tune out the distractions and achieve the kind of focus necessary to lay down the best run I was capable of.

Although I found it challenging to control negative thoughts during a heated, fast-paced, four-minute slalom race, I did learn I could use the mindset of not losing focus because of mistakes or setbacks to achieve success in more prolonged efforts. Efforts in which there were more chances to get back on course. That mindset helped get me through college with few financial resources and through tough assignments in my work.

RISK

It is absolutely a mindset required for parenting, a long, tortuous path filled with small defeats and wins. As in slalom, you must use setbacks and mistakes as opportunities for course adjustments, while never losing focus on what awaits downstream.

Chapter 15
The Aging Athlete (2015)

Clutching my paddle in one hand, I fill my arms with a beach blanket, a bag of sand toys, another of snacks and water bottles, jackets, and a large plastic dump truck that won't fit in a bag. Seth toddles along behind me as we walk the short distance from the car to the two six-man outrigger canoes. It has been a year since I brought Seth out from Ohio to live with me, and this is the first time I have come to practice since he arrived.

I am pent up, eager to get out on the water and experience the exhilaration of moving my muscles and filling my lungs, surrounded by the breathtaking beauty of Lake Tahoe.

Since moving to the lake twenty-five years ago, I have never taken for granted that I have peak experiences at my fingertips.

As a mid-level manager in a government bureaucracy, I spend my days in meetings, on the phone, or on the computer. Working on tasks I could accomplish in any office setting. It is important work, work I find meaningful. We are protecting and restoring the Lake Tahoe environment. But I am an office rat.

If I spend the entire day without movement, I know my body will feel toxic, my brain tired and cluttered.

Before Seth, it was easy to create the balance I needed. Within minutes from the office, there are places where I can hop on a bike, skis, or watercraft and get the movement I crave in a stunning alpine landscape. It is a life I have created by choice and with a bit of luck.

My team is already there, busily getting the canoes ready to take down to the water, when we walk up.

"Hey, I'll come help in a minute, after I get Seth set up," I announce.

Seth has scampered ahead of me and starts climbing on the canoe.

"Hi, Seth," Trudy says, "it's nice to meet you."

But Seth does not respond to casual adult overtures, so he stays silent and does not make eye contact.

"Careful, honey," I say. "Let's go play over here while they get it ready."

I wish I could have gotten here earlier and had some time to introduce Seth to everyone, but unfortunately, I am late. When coordinating almost a dozen people to complete a weekday workout in time to get home for dinner, timeliness is essential. I know I need to hurry.

The group is quiet, not as much chatter as usual. John and Mary have grim expressions on their faces, but that is not uncommon. I wonder what I might have missed before I got here, but, caught up in my own logistics, I don't dwell on it.

After I get Seth settled on the beach blanket, surrounded by toys and snacks, I trot over to help move the canoe down to the water. Pushing and pulling the 44-foot-long, 350-pound fiberglass canoe on rubber rollers over the sand and into the water is a task that requires all of us.

When both canoes are floating in the shallows, I quickly set the seat order for the paddlers in my canoe while John sets up the paddlers in his boat.

As my crew starts moving into their seats, I announce, "The babysitter isn't going to be here for about fifteen minutes, so I

The Aging Athlete (2015)

thought we could warm up in front of the beach. That way, I can just have Seth sit in the boat with us a little bit."

I feel a little bad for directing our warm-up to stay close to the start, as we usually warm up on our way, heading out toward Emerald Bay. But there are no bad views on Lake Tahoe, so I figure it's not a big deal.

I plop a milk crate in front of my steering seat at the canoe's rear for Seth to sit on and put on his lifejacket.

Seth appears to enjoy looking down into the depths, dangling his fingers in the water as we cruise along the shore. I wonder what is going through his head as he stares into the clear, green-tinted water, the ripples in the sand clearly visible more than fifteen feet below. Paddling on Lake Tahoe often feels like flying. I have experienced vertigo on my paddleboard, staring down into deep areas of the lake where the bottom is still visible dozens of feet below.

Seeing Seth similarly mesmerized, I smile and relax into my strokes.

Pulling back to the pier fifteen minutes later, I am relieved to see a young woman matching the babysitter's description on the beach. She is a friend of one of our younger members, in her early twenties, and we have never met. But there is no time for pleasantries; the crew is waiting. After a hasty introduction, I leave Seth with her, trusting Seth to behave and be safe. Seth quietly watches me paddle away. Already in his five years of life, he has grown used to being left with unknown adults.

Despite the nagging unease I feel at leaving Seth for the first time since I brought him to California, I am soon filled with the joy of paddling an outrigger canoe. The remaining snow on Mount Tallac beams in front of us as our canoe skims across the water. The crew is paddling well, blades entering the water together in a strong, steady rhythm. The sound of the water

RISK

slapping against the canoe is broken only by our rhythmic call and response for side changes. For changes, seat three calls "Hut" every fourteen strokes, matched by the entire crew chanting "Ho" in response on the next stroke. After the fifteenth stroke, everyone switches their paddle to the opposite side in one seamless motion, re-entering the water at the same time.

An outrigger paddling workout can be both exercise and moving meditation.

When we return to the beach, Seth is happily building sandcastles with the babysitter, and I feel better than I have in weeks, my body and brain restored.

I founded my outrigger club in South Lake Tahoe around 2001. Although I was ready to take a break from raft racing, I was far from ready to give up paddling. And outrigger canoeing is a perfect sport for an aging athlete, someone past their prime, maybe with an old injury or two. It provides a low-impact form of strength-building and aerobic exercise, as well some low-stakes competitive thrills.

Compared to other clubs in the Northern California Outrigger Canoe Association (NCOCA), our club is small. We only have about eighteen paying members, and it is often difficult to fill our two six-person boats for each workout. But most of our members are fit and athletic, and we do well competing in the amateur NCOCA racing circuit. Our crews frequently place in the top three.

In my early fifties, I was still competitive in the world of outrigger. I had honed my skills as a steersperson, handling the Bay Area's tricky currents and the open ocean. I had the skills and fitness to sit in any seat on a competitive team, whether setting the pace in seat one, cementing the blend in seat two, pushing the boat from seat three, four, or five, or steering from seat six.

I actively raced with my club and was also frequently asked to

The Aging Athlete (2015)

join crews with other clubs that had a seat that needed filling in the big races. I competed in the twenty-six-mile Catalina Crossing from Newport Beach to Catalina Island (the de facto national championships of outrigger) five times, including one time on the winning crew. I also competed in the forty-two-mile Na Wahine O Ke Kai (The Women of the Sea) three times, paddling from the island of Molokai to the island of Oahu. This event was the largest all-women's paddling race in the world, typically hosting 700 competitors and presenting one of the most challenging courses in the world because of the winds, waves, and currents crossing the channel between the islands.

Outrigger provided the exercise I needed to keep my body and mind in balance; it was also an essential component of my identity as a competitive athlete.

An identity that allowed me to receive some degree of respect and admiration for my physical prowess, even over fifty. An identity I had carried with me through various forms of paddle sport since I'd started training for slalom racing as a teenager.

Although I couldn't say why, I feel a slight sense of dread about attending the club meeting the next week.

It doesn't take long for my premonitions to be validated.

Mary jumps right in. "Sue, we need to talk about the problem you are creating for the club by bringing Seth to the workouts."

"I don't understand. What problem?" My face gets hot.

"It's not appropriate for him to be at the workout," she says. "Some of us don't think it's safe for him to be in the canoe."

At this point, I had put Seth in the canoe twice—only during our warm-ups, and only on the rare days when there was no wind and we were staying close to shore. I was eager to have him experience the feeling I still remembered from when I was young: the peace of gliding along the water in a canoe.

Seth had spent virtually no time outdoors before coming to

RISK

Tahoe. Immersing him in nature was a key strategy I planned to employ for healing whatever wounds he carried in his psyche.

"What do you mean 'not safe'?" I retort. "He's wearing a life jacket, and our chances of flipping during our warm-up on a flat day are pretty much nil."

I look around the room, trying to figure out how many people feel this way. Only seven of our eighteen members are present, and I suddenly wonder if this is why we have such low attendance today. Obviously, there have been conversations about this topic, and maybe some members have chosen not to be part of the confrontation.

Everyone here is silent, looking away. Letting Mary do the talking.

Hoping to cut off more unpleasant debate, I offer, "Well, if it makes you uncomfortable, I can stop bringing him into the boat, but it seems silly."

John, Mary's husband, retorts, "It's not for you to decide, Sue. You need to ask the club before you make decisions like this. You have never asked if we were okay with you bringing Roscoe, and dogs shouldn't be in the canoe either."

Roscoe is a twelve-pound Chihuahua-Maltese mix. I have occasionally brought him in the canoe during workouts when I've known there will only be light wind. Each time, he's curled up in the milk crate I've placed in front of my steering seat and slept the whole time.

As a steersperson, coach, and founder of the club, I've admittedly had a sense of entitlement in some regards. It's never even occurred to me to ask what people thought about my bringing Roscoe or Seth along in the boat.

I feel my face getting even hotter. I realize I've been arrogant in assuming I can just make these decisions without discussing them with my team and getting consensus—but all I can feel right now is resentment and frustration.

The Aging Athlete (2015)

"Well, I'm sorry I didn't ask," I say defensively, "but I honestly didn't feel it was a big deal. I don't understand how it affects our workouts. I will just leave Seth on the beach from now on."

"No, Sue, you don't get it," Mary fires back. "Kids don't belong, period. This is adult time. We don't want him there at all. My paddling time is very important to me, and having a kid there is disruptive and changes the energy. It's a distraction."

I stare at her in astonishment. "Well . . . I, I don't know how I'm going to be able to paddle then," I stammer.

"That's not our problem. Figure it out. You need to get a babysitter at home. And if you can't, you shouldn't come to practice."

I realize that John and Mary don't want to hear the logistical reasons why I can't get care for Seth at home. I am living with Seth by myself. The time it would take to pick him up from his daycare, drive him home, and then drive back to the paddle site would take almost an hour. There's no way I can leave work that early. Plus, I would have to add an hour to the babysitting time, which I cannot afford.

I wonder how many people really do feel bothered by Seth's presence on the beach but also realize it doesn't really matter. In a club this small, if even a few people agree and I ignore their wishes, it will create a toxic social environment that will kill the club. And John and Mary are key players; they are strong athletes, and John is the only other person in the club that can steer competently in rough water.

With a sinking pit in my stomach, I realize that as Seth's sole caregiver, I have no options here.

I have to give up paddling outrigger.

As a primary form of recreation and exercise, I continue to paddle, both in a one-man outrigger canoe and on a stand-up paddleboard. I set modest goals for competing in amateur competitions

RISK

in those sports as a masters athlete. But as I try to find the time and energy to train as well as coordinate logistics for Seth's care during workouts and races, I feel my biological clock ticking faster and faster.

My biological clock is not driven by a maternal drive—quite the opposite. Thrust unwillingly into a maternal role while my body goes through the chemical changes induced by menopause and stress, I have slammed into the biological clock of the aging athlete. I've become acutely aware that my time is running out.

By the time Seth turns eighteen, I will be seventy. Some of the fittest members of our outrigger club joined the club because they were enjoying their recently newfound freedom as empty nesters. With their adult or nearly adult children no longer dependent on them, they started paddling outrigger as part of their active lifestyle renaissance in their late forties and early fifties.

But I'm going to have to live out my dwindling years as a masters athlete also as a parent.

During my first two years as Seth's caregiver, exercise often felt like a slog. My muscles ached. I panted. I felt sore after workouts in ways I never had before.

I was battling the loss of estrogen due to menopause, compounded by increased cortisol due to psychological stress. I recently learned that as cortisol, the hormone produced by stress, goes up, estrogen goes down in equal measure. Research has shown that estrogen decreases are linked to brain fog, depression, anxiety, insomnia, and declines in muscle mass and connective tissue elasticity. I was living proof of all of the above.

My body's weakness forced me to reduce the intensity of whatever activity I engaged in. Consequently, I rarely achieved the endorphin or adrenaline high I was in search of.

Eventually, after moving in with Lisa and gaining her support in caring for Seth, I was able to increase the quality and

The Aging Athlete (2015)

frequency of my exercise. But I still had to adjust to a new normal.

I often modified my sports activities so I could exercise with Seth. Up until he was eight, I frequently carried him on my back so we could do longer hikes. Carrying him also served another purpose: as soon as I hoisted Seth up, he immediately melted onto my back, laying his head on my shoulder. Occasionally friends suggested I should make him walk more. But they didn't understand. It wasn't always about him needing a rest. It was about bonding. Bonding through physical contact, surrounded by the sounds, sights, and smells of nature, feeling supported and safe. He would have plenty of time to push his boundaries and toughen up.

When stand-up paddleboarding, I attached my leash to a foam surfboard and towed him behind me. I hauled him on a sled for cross-country skiing and later pulled him on his skis, like a sled dog. I did all I could to figure out ways for me to get exercise while also giving Seth the support he needed to participate.

I gradually changed the intensity of my workouts, going less often and less hard. I now exercised for wellness, not for performance—just to keep my brain and body healthy.

Although for now I was still waiting for Seth, soon I would be struggling to keep up.

Chapter 16
Dirtbag (1984–1986)

The term "dirtbag" was coined in the rock-climbing community. It can be defined as "one who forgoes material comforts and defies societal norms in pursuit of a nomadic life of outdoor adventure." For many, it is a badge of honor. To this day, many men and women in adventure sports proudly live the "dirtbag" lifestyle.

As a member of the US Whitewater Kayak Team in the early eighties, I was part of a rising wave of adventure sportswomen in America, a wave generated during an era of expansion in adventure sports culture. During this time, the growth of adventure sports was fueled by rapid improvements in equipment technology and a growing number of young people seeking their unique place in the world through pushing their boundaries in the outdoors. And for most adventure sports, corporate sponsorship or funding through a national sports organization was virtually nonexistent.

Over the last month, my teammates and I had traveled across Europe on a shoestring budget. Three of us pooled our money to rent a Renault Le Car, the cheapest option available. It took us over an hour to figure out how to cram ourselves, our kayaks, and all our gear in and on this tiny yellow tin can of a vehicle. We putt-putted through Europe at an average speed of forty miles per

Dirtbag (1984–1986)

hour, barely making it over some of the Alps' highest passes and leaning to the high side every time the car alarmingly tilted and swayed with a moderately stiff wind. In high winds, we just had to stop and wait it out.

We camped wherever we could, slept three or four to a room at the cheapest hostels, and gorged on crusty loaves of French bread, *brötchen,* and croissants, and a variety of *fromage,* meats, and fresh vegetables in communal picnics rather than eating out. Of course, we saved some money for bier and pomme frites, and for the inevitable party that occurred after each race. Luckily for us girls, our drinks were often heavily subsidized by the French, German, Swiss, Italian, or other amorous members of an international team. After all, everyone knew alcohol helped overcome language barriers.

Since the dollar was strong, my meager savings were enough to carry me through the month. But with what I had left, about $150, I knew getting to my kayak instructor/raft guide job in California before my money ran out would be a tight squeeze.

After a very long journey from Europe, I stayed at Dad's house in Cleveland for three days, soaking up free meals, sleeping, and finally wearing clean clothes again. Enjoying the sensation of just not doing. Anything. As a young athlete in my twenties, I had the energy to go through life at hyperspeed. The past few months had been a fantastic ride. The long hours of training, the excitement of international travel, racing, and parties, and some harrowing experiences both on and off the water had been a delicious adventure. I'd embraced all of it.

But now that it was over, I was thankful to have this short break from my pell-mell life. A life that was soon going to have to rev back up. Money had to be earned before college started again in the fall. I desperately needed to get back to work.

I did not overtly tell my dad about my money problems, but

RISK

fortunately the truth came out when one of his dogs ate my shorty paddle jacket, drying on his backyard fence.

When we discovered the tattered remnants, Dad apologized and offered to compensate me for it.

"That's actually great," I responded with a laugh, "because I need money more than I need that jacket right now."

He looked at me for a moment. "Well, how much will you need to replace it?"

"Uh . . . I think twenty-five dollars will cover it," I said.

Pulling his wallet out of his back pocket, he replied, "Well, I think I should give you fifty. It looks like you have had that jacket for a while, and sometimes things can cost more than you think to replace."

Along with the precious fifty dollars, Dad and his wife sent me off with clean laundry and a big bag of food. Enough to get me to my next stop ten hours away: my grandparents' house in Cedar Rapids, Iowa.

Driving across the country in a rattletrap car without air-conditioning was not new to me, and I had a system.

I stopped at the nearest convenience store and loaded up on the necessary supplies.

Minutes later, I headed out with a big icy cup of Pepsi nestled in my crotch—both to keep it well within reach for sipping and to help keep my body cool from the outside. I placed my Hershey's chocolate bars (with almonds, because *healthy*) on the bench seat just to my right, where I could easily pick up a gooey piece about every ten to fifteen minutes. Next to the chocolate bars was a fresh new pack of Marlboro cigarettes, the third cornerstone of "the system."

I limited myself to one ciggie per hour because, of course, I was an athlete. While I smoked, I held the cigarette high in my left hand to get as much smoke as possible—that was not getting

Dirtbag (1984-1986)

sucked down into my lungs—wafted out the window. After all, I didn't want my car to smell nasty.

I listened to the radio when I could get reception, sang when I couldn't, and did some mighty powerful thinking while riding the high provided by my steady intake of nicotine, caffeine, and sugar. Luxuriating in my indulgence in these shameful vices, known only to me and the open road, I repeatedly re-ran the courses I had competed on over the past couple months, the twenty-five gate sequences still emblazoned on my neurons after hours of racecourse memorization. I analyzed what went right and what went wrong, and how I would train differently for next year. I performed mental calculations regarding how much money I could expect to earn over the next two months, and how far that could carry me into the school year. I pondered what part-time job to get when I started school again, and what my upcoming classes would be like. I was the star of my very own picture show, playing endlessly in my head, as the miles of freeway, cornfields, and grain silos rolled on and on.

I awoke at 6:00 a.m. on my last day of driving as the first light streamed into my back window. My mouth tasted like an ashtray, and my stomach was shaky from the previous day of caffeine, nicotine, and chocolate. I calculated I had about five hours left to get to Coloma, where a job, a refrigerator full of food, and a place for my tent awaited me. Back to my temporary river home, where I would spend the rest of the summer working seven days a week teaching kayaking and raft guiding on the South Fork of the American River.

I couldn't wait.

Three hours from Coloma, just outside of Lovelock, I heard a knocking noise from my car's front passenger side. It started out sounding like playing cards flapping against a kid's bicycle spokes. But as the miles progressed, the noise got louder and

RISK

louder and started sounding more like what it was: metal grinding against metal. The grinding sound was more audible with speed, so I slowed down to what seemed the least destructive pace—around forty to fifty miles per hour. I later found out I had a broken wheel bearing that was slowly getting pulverized to metallic dust.

I had no credit card, no Triple A, and had spent my last dollar on my last tank of gas. The only money I had left was some spare change tossed onto the front floor of the car—less than two dollars. I had no choice but to keep driving for as long as the car could go.

Seventeen miles from Coloma, I applied the brake pedal while descending the steep, windy road to the confluence of the North and Middle Fork of the American River canyons—and nothing happened. I frantically pumped the pedal, and finally got some pressure after five pumps.

I put the car in first gear, slowing my speed down to a ten-mile-per-hour crawl. I kept testing the brakes, but each time required a greater number of pumps. Realizing the brakes might stop working altogether before I got to the bottom of the long three-mile descent, I unclasped my seat belt and cracked the front door, keeping my left hand on the handle—ready to jump, tuck, and roll before the car plummeted over the cliff into the steep river canyon below.

When I got to the bottom of the hill, it took a dozen pumps to get enough brake pressure to take the corner turn onto the bridge. Climbing out of the canyon and through the flats beyond, I kept the car in first gear, continuing my creeping ten-mile-per-hour pace.

I ignored the numerous drivers that blazed around me where they could, horns blaring and fists shaking. Bathed in sweat, I reached over to roll down the passenger-side window. The car was rank from the smell of the toxic combination of caffeine and

Dirtbag (1984–1986)

nicotine in my bloodstream, now seeping out my pores. I couldn't get any relief from the over 100-degree temperature.

Would this drive never end? I peered hopefully into my Pepsi cup, but the last shard of ice had been sucked down long ago.

That last seventeen miles was easily the longest two hours of my journey—all fourteen days' worth—from Brussels, Belgium, to Coloma, California.

Finally, I turned my clanking, rattling Dodge Dart into the entrance of Ultrasports Kayak School. I'd given up pumping the brakes about five miles back. They were gone. Coasting into the parking lot at three miles an hour, I threw the gear shift into park and the car jolted to a stop. I was home.

Wiping the sweat off my brow, I opened the door and walked over to the shaded picnic table where my friends and colleagues were eating lunch.

"What in the hell is wrong with that car?" my boss, Mark, asked, laughing and shaking his head.

"Hell if I know," I replied. "Know any good mechanics?"

Ed, another kayak instructor, jumped in. "Yeah, my brother can fix it. And from the sound of that car, you will be glad to know he also has a tow truck."

"Great." I walked over to the refrigerator in the open-air camp kitchen. "I'm starving. When can I start working?"

"An advanced kayak class starts tomorrow," Dave said. "You and I are teaching it."

Just then, Julie and Kelley, fellow raft guides and my two besties from the previous summer, walked up from the river trail.

"Hey sister, you're back! How was Europe!?" Kelley cried. "Man, you look hot—and not in a good way."

"Yeah, I'm a little thirsty, and I need a dip," I said, grabbing a bottle of water out of the fridge. "Just let me make a sandwich, and then let's go down for a swim and I'll tell you all about it."

RISK

The resiliency of youth is both a product of a strong mind and body and the intense, durable friendships and willingness of people to help someone on the upward trajectory of their life. When you're young and healthy and surrounded by friends, it does not take so much to keep on truckin'. Back then, knowing I had guaranteed income and would get to hang out with my people for at least a few months, maybe a year, was all it took.

Later that night, listening to the quiet shurr and shush of the river outside my tent, my body relaxed in a way it hadn't in months. I was back on the river, among family. I didn't need a car or a house for a while. Over the next two months, I'd make enough money to carry me into the next semester and simply enjoy having fun on the river. Life was good.

I spent the next two years alternating between competing and teaching kayak classes. But after a final summer of international kayak slalom racing in the 1986 Europa Cup, I knew it was time for a change. I was twenty-eight, time was running out on using my GI Bill benefits, and it was clear I had reached my competitive peak.

Although I'd qualified for the third position on the US Whitewater team that year, I generally placed between the top ten and fifteen in the European races that summer. Not good enough to warrant continuing in the sport.

It was time to figure out what I wanted to be when I grew up.

So, in the fall of 1986, I started a master's program in water science at UC Davis.

I arrived in Davis after having worked raft guiding and teaching kayaking on the South Fork of the American River in California for about six weeks. Between what I'd saved from those earnings and my GI Bill stipend of $400 a month, I entered graduate school with meager funds.

Fortunately, while on campus registering for classes, I saw a

Dirtbag (1984–1986)

powerful V-shaped torso walking toward me across the quad—and, to my surprise, realized I knew the guy it belonged to. Dan was a downriver kayak racer who had dated a good friend of mine when we were all back East training and racing together a few years earlier. He was also a fellow dirtbag.

Dan had just finished his graduate program and was wrapping things up to move to Tahoe. When I told him I was looking for a cheap place to live, he looked at me for a moment with his striking twinkly blue eyes and said, "Well . . . I'm not sure if you'd be interested . . . but you could take over my place."

I paused before answering. I was thinking about where Dan had lived back in DC: in the turret of a dilapidated boathouse on the Potomac River. That could only be reached with a ladder from the roof of the second floor.

"Maybe . . ." I cocked my head. "How much is the rent?"

"Well . . . the rent is only fifty dollars a month," he said. "It's ah . . . it's an abandoned house."

Of course it was. But damn, the price was right.

"I guess I could look at it," I replied, both curious and desperate.

The house was located only one block from campus. Convenient—I wouldn't have to drive to class. But it was a dump, with peeling paint, a few cracked windows, and large swaths of shingles missing from the roof.

We stopped in front of the walkway to the front door, and Dan looked around surreptitiously. "You have to make sure no one ever sees you go in and out. So we have to wait until that guy over there is out of sight."

Once no one was visible, he said, "Okay, let's go," and we walked briskly up the walkway. While Dan inserted the key in the door, I had a brief moment to glance at the bright pink notice tacked to the door, clearly announcing the house was condemned, before we slipped into darkness.

RISK

Blinds covered all the windows, so it took a minute for my eyes to adjust. But it didn't take long to take it all in. I could see several places where the drywall was cracked and peeling off the ceiling and a wall. An old, tattered couch and some broken chairs scattered about the living room were covered in dust. The air smelled musty and dank.

"So, there is only one room in the house that is livable." Dan started walking toward a door at the end of the living room. "C'mon."

I followed him through the dilapidated kitchen with a peeling linoleum floor to a bedroom that actually looked . . . okay. It was a small room, but it did not smell, and the floor, ceiling, and all the walls appeared to be intact.

Dan pointed to an orange power cord that ran over the sill of the room's one window. "That cord is plugged into the neighbor's house for your electricity. You just need to pay him ten dollars a month."

I nodded slowly. "What about water?"

"Well, water comes in, but it doesn't really go out very well. So, you can't shower here. You can pee in the toilet; it will drain out eventually." He looked awkwardly down at the floor. "But for anything else, you have to go to the coffee shop down the alley."

"Oh . . . okay." Was I really considering this?

"It's only half a block away, and they open early and stay open late, and you don't even have to go into the shop—a door opens into the alley," he said quickly.

"I think I'll just go check that out while I think about it," I said. "Is that okay?"

"Sure," he said. "I'll just pack up a few more boxes here. Just remember to look out the window first to make sure no one will see you going out."

"Okay, I'll be back in a minute."

Well, it is *a step up from living out of a car or a tent*, I rationalized

Dirtbag (1984–1986)

as I walked down the alley to the coffee shop. I had done that more than once. I could at least try it for one academic quarter. I could save a lot of money. After all, I only needed a place to live for a few nights a week, since I would be going home on the weekends to my girlfriend's house in Coloma, only an hour and a half away.

Besides, I figured I would be spending all my waking hours on campus. In between classes, I would study at the library, eat at the campus cafeteria, and shower at the gym. And Dan was right; the coffee shop bathroom was close enough, and clean. Basically, I just needed a place to sleep.

When I came back into the room, I said, "I'll take it."

Four months later, in December, the limitations of living in an abandoned house had become stark. I used an adapter for the power cord to plug in both my lamp and a toaster oven while I struggled through a take-home final exam.

A loud hum emerged from underneath the chair as the toaster oven kicked in again, sending warm air up around my legs. However, the heat did not make it up past my waist. I blew on my hands, staring in frustration at the convoluted page of numbers in front of me. It was one o'clock in the morning, and I was only halfway through my Differential Equations final.

I generally consider myself to be intelligent—above average, anyway. My undergraduate program in watershed management at Colorado State University had been rigorous but manageable, and I'd finished with a respectable 3.8 GPA. But the water science graduate program at UC Davis, with its heavy emphasis on civil engineering hydrology, was kicking my butt. The Diff-EQ class, easily the hardest, was almost incomprehensible to me.

I finally gave up at six in the morning. Lying down, I was too exhausted to sleep, the rows of numbers, letters, and mathematical symbols still dancing across my eyelids. At least I could warm up under the covers for a couple of hours before going to campus to turn in my exam.

I lost ten pounds during that first quarter at UC Davis. My biceps and shoulders shrank as I transitioned from an amateur athlete's life, training two times a day, six days a week, to a struggling graduate student's sedentary life.

I came home to Coloma on the weekends, strung out from lack of exercise and mentally exhausted. My girlfriend soon started meeting me at the door with a joint. She learned early on that if I was going to be bearable over the weekend, I needed to spend Friday evenings off task, and a big fat doobie was the fastest way to get me there.

On Saturday mornings, restored, I started on the mountain of papers I had lugged home to grade for my teaching assistant job, as well as the coursework I needed to complete before Monday. Since our house was next to the South Fork of the American River, I took breaks between my studies to get out on the water every Saturday and Sunday, rain or shine. Often, I simply put into the river right in front of the house, paddled upstream and eddy hopped for about forty-five minutes, then turned around to go back home.

Although I was no longer in training, paddling was now my meditation. The rhythmic motion of moving my paddle through the water further calmed my overworked brain. On Monday mornings, I drove back to Davis, ready to grind through another week.

That summer, instead of raft guiding and teaching kayaking, I got a student internship with the State Water Resources Control Board, my first foray into working on rivers as part of a massive government bureaucracy. I spent all day in front of a computer, compiling water quality data and recording the health of waterways throughout California in a state wide database.

Dirtbag (1984–1986)

The following summer, I worked as a temporary hydrologic technician with the US Forest Service in Lake Tahoe. This time, I collected data in the field to record the health of streams through stream morphology measurements.

All the years of paddling on rivers and my current studies were coming together in a fascinating way. I learned how to see a river through a different lens, using scientific metrics to measure, analyze, and assess a river's health.

Toward the end of that second summer working in hydrology, the goddess of rivers returned. The Forest Service was named in a class action suit claiming the predominantly white male–staffed agency was not doing enough to recruit women and minorities. The courts agreed. In the fall of 1989, I was one of about fifteen women who applied for ten new entry-level permanent hydrologist positions in Forest Service offices throughout California. I received offers from three different forests.

I chose the position in Lake Tahoe, and thus began a twenty-seven-year career working to protect and restore watersheds and rivers in one of the most beautiful backyards in the world. My job allowed me to turn my lifelong passion for rivers into a paid vocation. My role at the Forest Service combined passion and science in one complex and satisfying soup, providing the sustenance to support a life inextricably entwined with the river.

Chapter 17
Isolation (2016)

I didn't realize how mind-numbingly boring parenting a child was going to be. Here we are in the middle of another endless weekend, with me stuck trying to figure out how to entertain a six-year-old. I can't do any of the activities I used to do, like going on a long hike up to Dardanelles Lake or stand-up paddleboarding to Emerald Bay. I certainly can't drive down to Santa Cruz to surf and hang out with my posse of child-free lesbian friends.

Christ, I can't even go for a thirty-minute run in the meadow next to my house. This morning, I sat Seth on the bench in front of the house while running three-minute laps around the block. It was good to finally feel blood and oxygen coursing into my brain, which has felt all week like it's lying in a stagnant pool due to lack of exercise.

But afterward, I succumbed to his adamant requests to take him to the playground. Again. So, here we are.

God, I hate the playground.

After I push Seth on the swing for a while, he sees that two other children have arrived and scampers over to the playset. It's cold, so the playground is empty except for the newcomers and us.

As I walk over, the mother makes eye contact and says hi with

Isolation (2016)

a warm smile. I smile back, but I'm already dreading engagement in yet another awkward mommy conversation.

My attempts to converse with the other moms at the playground, or open house days at the school, or Easter egg hunts and other kiddy zones, are uncomfortable.

Admittedly, I am part of the problem. I can't help but come from a place of judgment: What compelled all these women to do it? Why did they choose to have kids? To give up their independence? Give up all the precious hours they could spend doing so many other satisfying, interesting things?

For this. Standing around as a bystander and referee while the *kids* get to live it up. I just don't get it.

I can see them wondering about me, too, obviously too old to be Seth's biological mom. Maybe the grandmother? It's hard to know at what point I should attempt to explain our situation.

But this time is different.

The woman, young and pretty, with long brown hair pulled back in a ponytail, walks closer to me and extends her hand.

"I'm so glad to meet you! My kids know Seth from the Boys and Girls Club. My name is Amy, and that is my son, Jasper, and my daughter, Ari."

"Oh hi . . . I'm Sue. That's good . . . ah . . . they are friends with him, then?"

"Oh, yes! They talk about him all the time."

This is the first time anyone has said anything like this in the two years Seth has been with me. Seth does not make friends. He gets in trouble. I get calls from the school or Boys and Girls Club about three times a week. Almost always about him losing his temper and hitting another child. He is dangerously close to being expelled from the Boys and Girls Club.

"That's great." I glance in his direction. "He sometimes has difficulty making friends."

She smiles warmly again. "Yes, I know . . . they've told me he gets in trouble sometimes. There are some tough kids at the Boys and Girls Club. They know how to push buttons."

"Yeah . . . he's easily triggered."

"So, you're his aunt, right? My kids told me he calls you Aunt Sue?"

"Yes," I nod. "But I'm also his legal guardian."

"Well, we should get the kids together for a playdate sometime," she says, pulling out her phone. "If you give me your number, I can send you my contact info."

"Sure, sure . . . that would be great," I say, feeling both flustered and excited. My first playdate. Well, Seth's first playdate. But still, my first mommy friend.

A milestone.

Amy turns out to be a good friend. It is a different friendship from what I am used to; instead of it being driven by mutual adult connection and interests, it is primarily driven by the relationship between our children. But it saves me.

For the next two years, we share playdates, including a few where Seth sleeps over at her house. For my part, I take the kids to the beach or the sledding hill to get her kids out of the house while she is working as a massage therapist. Sometimes, when our schedules match, we take them all out together.

The mother of four children, Amy is a lovely, caring person, unperturbed by Seth's occasional outbursts. She is untidy in her relationships and her home. All her children have different fathers, and her house is an explosion of piles of laundry, toys, and half-eaten food. But she is devoted to her children, and they are happy. She is also sincere and open-hearted. Although she struggles with money and is often overwhelmed by her work and responsibilities, she feels sorry for me. Recognizing that I find motherhood difficult, she is always generous in her offers to help. To take Seth into her fold.

She is also an anomaly.

Isolation (2016)

Who knows why—whether it's my personality or Seth's, or maybe age or class differences, or mismatched lifestyles—but I find it hard to connect with other moms. And as a mom, it is also difficult to connect with old and new friends who are not active mothers. Women my age, with similar lifestyles and interests. Women who prefer to engage in stimulating conversations and adventurous activities that do not involve children.

I often do not feel like a whole person. I sometimes feel I am becoming a shadow.

One of the only times I get some sense of being back in a world that feels familiar is when I'm on the river, especially on multiday raft trips. Then, for a precious few days, Seth and I can coexist in an environment where we find mutual satisfaction. Both of us are equally fulfilled by adventure, beauty, and camaraderie. Plus, on the river, I have help.

Our first multiday river trip is on the Rogue River in Oregon, with three members of my former competitive rafting team and their families. Beth and Juliet, who both became parents by choice thirteen years ago, easily include Seth in their general corralling and directing of children on the trip. I even see them taking Jules, who is not a mother, aside after she experiences a frustrating incident of misbehavior involving Seth to explain why Seth requires more patience than the other kids. In addition to being the youngest and the only boy on the trip, he is the least compliant. It is a relief to have these women and their partners step forward in providing adult guidance without drama.

Seth enjoys every aspect of being on the river. He crows with delight through the rapids. He sits in the raft with his arm over Jules's pit-Lab mix's shoulder, singing songs in the calm sections. He scampers around, accumulating a new stick and rock collection on every beach. He is fascinated by the river-worn shapes and smooth surfaces. He builds sandcastles, embellished with his

RISK

treasures. He frolics in the pools on the side hikes, watching the older kids with fascination as they jump off rocks and slide down natural water slides—nature's playground, more diverse and fascinating than even the best city park.

And he loves camping, seemingly as much as I did as a kid. In the summer, Western rivers with sandy beaches that are warm, windless, and bug-free are simply the best for camping.

It is our second night on the Rogue, and I've decided not to pitch the tent. As the light begins to fade, I lead a yawning Seth up to the nook I have set up for our camp. Our pads and sleeping bags lie on a tarp.

He stares at it. "Is that where we're going to sleep?"

"Yep."

"Where's the tent?"

"Oh, we don't need a tent, buddy. This way, we can see the stars."

He tightens his grip on my hand and pulls me a little closer, holding his stuffed puppy to his chest.

"Are you scared?" I ask.

"A little," he admits.

"Well, we are going to be right next to each other, and all our friends are around us," I reassure him. "Besides, all the animals here are friendly."

His face turns up to look at mine. "What about bears?"

He did not miss the fact that the black bears are infamously a little too friendly on the Rogue, as he watched us move all our food after dinner inside the electric fenced enclosure provided upstream from our camp.

"Well, they are only interested in our food, not us. In fact, I think we are safer outside of the tent. They can smell us better and will keep their distance."

The sky grows dark in the time it takes to brush our teeth and change into pajamas. We crawl into our bags and gaze up at

Isolation (2016)

a night sky glittering with stars. I try to point out the few constellations I know: the Big Dipper, Orion, and the bright star of Jupiter. It is the first time Seth has seen stars, and he stares solemnly up into the expanse.

I wonder what he is thinking, feeling.

After a while, he says, "I think I'm ready to go to sleep now; can you read a story?"

"Sure," I say, and grab my iPad.

Tonight I read *The Going to Bed Book* by Sandra Boynton. Ms. Boynton is a very successful cartoonist and writer. She also happened to marry Jamie McEwan, the bronze medal winner in whitewater C-I in the 1972 Olympics—one of my childhood heroes. In the book, the cute animal characters are all on a boat together; the last line reads, "And they rock, and rock, and rock, to sleep."

I wonder if Seth still feels the motion of the raft, like I often do at night on river trips. The body-brain connectors still feel the rhythmic movement even hours after being off the water.

When I finish, he snuggles down in his bag so his head is completely covered, and presses his body into mine.

For the first time since I brought Seth to California, I feel at peace. Maybe I can do this parenting thing. We just need to do more of this: spending quality time away from the busy, complicated world that can be so hard to fit into. Like my dad did with David and me, escaping our impoverished and dreary urban life to ground ourselves in nature.

I really need to buck up and stop feeling so sorry for myself. I am so much better off than Dad was. Although it was never my intention to be a parent, I will retire in a year, with adequate financial resources to raise a child. I can maintain a good lifestyle for both of us.

We also live in a beautiful home, surrounded by nature. Our escapes are not nearly as dramatic. It's just hard because he is so

RISK

young, and I have no idea what in the hell I am doing. But I think the more time we can spend outside, where we can be ourselves together, the better we'll both do.

My life experiences on the river have provided the grist of my resilience as I now grapple with understanding and managing the impact of Seth's emotional trauma. Along with my love, I want to provide a fabric of experiences that will help him find resilience and equilibrium in his own struggle.

My life on the river continues with this vulnerable and fragile little being who is now my sole responsibility. Like the river, navigating the treacherous path of unexpected motherhood will include times of feeling anxious, out of my comfort zone. But we will also find these precise, blissful moments of peace and euphoria. From both, I hope to forge the skills needed for our journey.

I spend a few more moments gazing at the stars before closing my eyes and listening to the river's soft burbling, letting the sound trigger my body's phantom memory of the day on the water, as I rock, and rock, and rock, to sleep.

Chapter 18
Risk (1989)

With the engines screaming at full throttle, the Aeroflot plane lumbered down the runway. The pine trees at the end of the runway loomed larger and larger as the front of the aircraft rose with excruciating slowness. *The plane isn't going to make it!* Gripping the armrests, I held my breath as the bottom of the plane appeared to practically brush the tops of the pine trees. With relief, I joined a collective cheer as our overloaded aircraft cleared the forest below.

After sitting for three hours on the tarmac in Moscow, watching the Russian crews laboriously load a veritable mountain of food boxes, dry bags, and paddles into the hold of our two planes, we were airborne.

A member of Team Costa Rica cranked up the volume on a boom box, and as salsa music flooded the space, several Ticos pulled members of our team into the aisle for an impromptu dance party. Everyone began to cheer and sway with the music, and more people squeezed into the aisle.

A voice squawked over the loudspeaker, but the thick Russian accent was drowned out by the noise of our celebration. Soon an anxious stewardess appeared at the front of the plane, frantically waving to get our attention.

RISK

"Za pilot, he says you are making too much shaking of the plane," she shouted. "Pleez, sit down!"

"Yikes, that's sketchy," I said nervously to Kelley in the seat next to me.

"Yeah," she replied, eyes wide. "I think we may be way over the load limit. I don't think they pay as much attention to that stuff here. They probably should have put more of our gear in the trucks."

In addition to the gear they'd crammed into the planes, we had also watched the Russian Army load a convoy of trucks to carry the big stuff. Every truck had been filled to the brim with rafts, frames, oars, kayaks, stacks of lumber, bundles of canvas, and hundreds of cardboard boxes.

I shook my head. "I don't think there was any more room. Besides, I would hate to be the one whose gear bag fell off a truck in the middle of the night between here and Siberia."

Kelley laughed. "Yeah, that would suck."

Our two planes were carrying two hundred paddlers representing ten different countries. We were one of the largest delegations of outsiders to visit Russia since the initial thawing of the Cold War. Our three-hour flight from Moscow to Barnaul, the capital of Siberia, would cross five time zones.

As participants in the 1989 Chuya River Rally, our contingent of 200 paddlers from mostly Western Bloc countries was on its way to meet 300 more paddlers representing Russia and other nations from the former Soviet Union. Far from the eyes of the world in all respects, we would come together on the banks of the remote Chuya River, in the heart of the Siberian wilderness—one of the most isolated regions on earth—ostensibly to facilitate world peace through a mutual love of the river and river sport.

On the plane with me were nine other members of the US Women's Whitewater Team, including two of my closest friends, Julie Munger and Kelley Kalafatich. We were the only women's

Risk (1989)

team participating in the rally. Therefore, we were not only representing our country but also our gender at this historic event in the fast-growing realm of whitewater rafting.

After landing in Barnaul—safely, thank God—we traveled for three days by bus to finally arrive at the banks of the Chuya River. Each visiting team was quickly paired with a Russian team representing one of many small paddling clubs. Although this was the event's first time hosting international guests, the Chuya Rally had been in existence for over a decade and marked the kickoff for the short and intense Siberian paddling season.

A sister or brother team was assigned to host every team visiting throughout the event. This was not only to facilitate cultural exchange but also to help us navigate the intricacies of camping in the Siberian outback. The race coordinator introduced our team to Sasha, a slight, wiry man with bright blue eyes and an equally brilliant gold tooth glinting through his shy smile. As we began to pick up our gear, intending to carry it to our camp, Sasha and his friends leapt forward, grabbing the biggest, heaviest bags for themselves. Staggering under their loads, they led us—carrying only our daypacks and light duffels—to the section of tundra designated for our combined team camp.

After dropping our bags at our tent site, Sasha signaled for a few of us to follow him to pick up our provisions for the week from the food tent. There, we were given four large cardboard boxes and a two-foot diameter wheel of grayish-white cheese.

When we got back to our camp, we opened the boxes to see what was inside.

After surveying the goods, Maryanne, a tall southern gal on our team with a dry sense of humor, turned to me with a wry smile. "Sheeit!" she drawled, "I don' think I brought enough food for all y'all. What in Sam Hill are we expected to do with this stuff? I already told y'all, I don't cook."

RISK

I had laughed at Maryanne earlier when she showed me the vast suitcase she had brought packed with jars of peanut butter, jerky, crackers, dried fruit, gorp, and other staples. I wasn't laughing now.

The cardboard boxes contain unwrapped loaves of hard-crusted bread, slightly rusted cans with no labels, huge bars of chocolate, and an array of tired-looking vegetables—potatoes, beets, onions, cabbage, carrots, and leeks.

As my teammates and I stared at the boxes in dismay, our Russian companions quickly took charge: After letting us know through sign language that they would take care of the meals, they carried the boxes over to where they already had their wares stored next to the campfire with a huge iron pot suspended over hot coals. Then, as if to make sure we understood that we were going to be okay in the food department, they scooped out bowls of everything-but-the-kitchen-sink soup.

We sat down for our first meal from this ever-evolving and bottomless vat of hot borscht with thick slices of cheese and bread. The bread and cheese were almost unpalatable on their own, but when submerged into the delicious, brothy borscht, they made a hearty addition to our dinner.

Everything about the camp was indicative of how resourceful, inventive, and downright tough the Russians were. They did not have Patagonia, Sierra Designs, or North Face gear. Their ratty old canvas tents were heavily augmented with sheets of plastic and tarps. Their outdoor and paddling clothing consisted of stinky wool, flimsy windbreaker jackets and pants, and heavy rubber boots. No Gore-Tex, neoprene, fleece, or Capilene on any of these guys. It reminded me of the kind of gear we'd used fifteen years before, during my early days of kayaking with the Keel-Haulers Canoe Club in Ohio. Except back in the US, we'd always been close to a warm car and restaurant after paddling.

I did, however, immediately began to covet a simple accessory

Risk (1989)

the Russians all wore: a small but thick foam pad worn on a belt around the waist that was used as a cushion when sitting on whatever cold rock, log, or piece of ground was available. We had no camp chairs, and none of my clothing could keep my butt warm or dry.

After watching me awkwardly stand as I ate, a member of our Russian buddy team presented me with a "butt cozy" so I could finally sit down.

I couldn't have been more delighted to accept it.

As the sky began to darken, the Russian teams stoked the fires and brought out guitars and bottles of clear liquid fire. It was time to party. I joined several of my teammates and our host team to wander through the camp and visit the various campfires where people were congregating.

What I learned that night: every Russian apparently knows how to sing, and how to do so from deep within their soul.

They launched into alternatingly boisterous and mournful songs between vodka shots, pouring their warm hearts out into the broad, bright canopy of stars over our heads.

The music and vodka, it turned out, transcended the need for language.

After a couple hours, I had exceeded my vodka limit—even though I had turned down nine out of every ten offers. I decided to stagger back to my tent before I got to a point where I might not find it.

Snuggling into my down bag, I wondered how long our comrades would stay singing by the fire, which was probably warmer than the wool blankets within their raggedy shelters. I never found out, as I immediately fell into a deep and contented slumber, surrounded by our community of 500-plus paddlers.

Once again at home, despite being nestled deep within the unfamiliar and remote Siberian canyon of the Chuya River.

RISK

My eyes opened to bright blue light flooding the cozy dome of my tent. The sun was out for the first time since our arrival in Siberia. Hopeful, I reached my hand out to feel the tip of my nose.

Nope, still cold.

After awkwardly dressing inside my sleeping bag, I crawled out of the tent. Squinting, I shaded my eyes to survey my surroundings: tundra grass sparkling with ice crystals and tents covered in sugary frost. I reached back into the tent to grab sunglasses before eagerly walking over to our communal camp's fire. It was already ablaze; possibly it had never gone out.

The first day of the competition was not scheduled until the next day, but the previous night I'd been invited to join an international group of about a dozen kayakers to explore a Class IV river gorge located upstream.

After a steaming bowl of hearty borscht, accompanied by a strong and achingly sweet cup of black tea, I was fortified, warmed inside and out, and ready to get on the river.

While loading our gear on the shuttle bus, my eagerness to paddle a new river was somewhat tempered as I looked around and realized I was the only woman.

I turned to my friend Eric. "Hey, just how difficult do you think this run is, anyway?"

"Well, from talking to the Russians," he said, "the rapids are steep and technical, but there are big pools in between." Observing the worried frown on my face, he added, "Don't worry, this is definitely within your ability. And besides, they said all the rapids can be portaged."

"Well, that's a relief," I said. "I sure didn't like the look of some of the gnar we passed on the bus yesterday."

In this male-dominated sport, it was essential to know men

Risk (1989)

who were competent in assessing risk and consequence, both for themselves and those they were paddling with. It also helped if they had the self-confidence to not be susceptible to testosterone-fueled group peer pressure.

Eric was one of those guys. And in addition to being one of the more skilled paddlers in our group, he was a leader in the emerging field of swift water rescue.

If he thought I could do it, I probably could.

Despite the border of ice along the riverbank, I was warm and cozy in my dry suit, and it felt great to finally be moving and on the water. Eric's beta was spot on. Most of the rapids were "read and run"—within our skill level to navigate on the fly—and the few rapids we scouted had clear lines that required just the right amount of challenge to keep things exciting.

Our bright red, blue, green, and yellow kayaks darted in and out of eddies, dropped over steep chutes, and bounced and surfed through the waves. Our colorful boats, helmets, and life jackets stood in stark contrast to Siberia's severe winter hues, providing a brief, vibrant bloom as we passed through the river. Our river play felt somewhat out of place in this barren land where most human endeavors clearly focused on survival.

We were almost at the end of the run when we caught up to a group of Russian rafters we'd seen at the put-in, including one group riding a large and ungainly *plote*—a homemade raft, made from trees harvested on site and homemade bladders made from truck tarps and plastic and steered by two large sweep oars, like the raft in *The Adventures of Huckleberry Finn*. But instead of drifting down the flat, sedate Mississippi River on this monstrosity, these men were running Class IV whitewater with it.

Pulling into the eddy where they were already beaching their rafts, we got out of our kayaks to join in scouting the last significant—and apparently most difficult—rapid.

RISK

The Russians looked wet and cold. Their worn windbreakers and rubber rain gear clearly were not keeping them dry. Even encapsulated as I was in my kayak, my toes were already numb in my neoprene booties, so I could not imagine how cold their feet must be in their wool socks and sneakers.

Scrambling over the rocks alongside one of the groups, I took a closer look at their bulky homemade life jackets. Like their rafts, the jackets were entirely fabricated out of raw materials. Nylon fabric was stitched around square-shaped foam blocks and attached to nylon straps and buckles. They looked both uncomfortable and flimsy. As I would throughout the week, I felt incredibly grateful and slightly embarrassed by my Western whitewater privilege. The disparity in our equipment put the contrast between our two countries on sharp display.

From the riverbank, I nervously analyzed the steep, boulder-choked drop I saw before me. After a few minutes, I mentally pieced together a route through the chaos. In the constant assessment of risk, consequence, and uncertainty that is the essence of whitewater exploration, I determined that I could make the maneuvers required to navigate the rapid.

Having concluded my risk was acceptably low, I turned my attention to the Russians. I nudged Eric. "How in the world do you think they are going to get that plote down this thing?" I asked in a low voice.

The plote was obviously too heavy to portage, so the only options were to abandon it and hike out or run the rapid. The line I saw for my run would require some sharp turns and aggressive paddling but was a very reasonable challenge for an eleven-foot plastic kayak. Not so for the bulky plote. I could not imagine how it would make it through.

Eric shook his head. "I have no idea, but I think we should go ahead and run the rapid and then help set up safety for them. This could be a train wreck."

Risk (1989)

Our group quickly flashed through the rapid before the soggy and bedraggled audience of Russian rafters. We then set up safety positions at critical locations, both onshore and within the river. Eric managed to catch a very tight eddy near the most congested part of the drop, as he had planned. His yellow kayak was a bright spot of color bobbing amidst a dark jumble of sharp rocks, surrounded by white foaming hydraulics.

As anticipated, within seconds of entering the rapid, the plote crashed into the boulder pile in the middle of the river with a sickening crunch. The force of impact catapulted two Russians handling the sweep oar on the front of the plote into the river. When only one of them came to the surface a few yards downstream, everyone began scanning the rapid for signs of the other Russian paddler.

For long agonizing seconds, and then minutes, the missing Russian was nowhere to be seen. The most likely scenario is that his foot had become entrapped, or his torso pinned or wedged underwater against rocks. Finally, after several minutes, his body finally floated up to the surface in the frothy water below the rock pile.

A Russian plote waiting at the bottom of the rapid swooped up the unconscious rafter, hauling him out of the water before he could be swept farther downstream.

His comrades immediately began CPR; after a few minutes, they managed to revive a tentative pulse, accompanied by the shallowest of breaths.

Not far from the takeout, a multinational team quickly coalesced to help with the evacuation. Eric offered his kayak—the largest one available—to be used as a travois to carry the unconscious man out of the steep gorge. The Russians quickly agreed.

A runner was sent up the trail to radio out for an ambulance, while Eric furiously set to work ripping out the outfitting in his kayak.

RISK

A team of about ten paddlers embarked on a life-and-death relay, taking turns jogging the kayak travois up the trail, even pulling the boat up with ropes in the steeper sections, with periodic breaks to continue CPR as the Russian paddler's breathing and pulse flickered on and off. I scrambled to keep up as best I could, carrying my boat, the torn-out guts of Eric's kayak, and our paddles, but quickly fell behind.

I arrived gasping at the top of the canyon just in time to see a Russian Army ambulance peel out, whisking the victim to the closest civilization: a military outpost located about ten miles away.

The next morning, back at camp, we learned that the Russian paddler had passed away sometime during the night.

I wondered if the competition would be canceled altogether after this tragedy.

But an hour after convening, the organizers announced the competition would go on.

Fortunately, I was not scheduled to compete on this first day, so I had the space to spend the day walking in a daze, coming to grips with the sobering reality of how far we were from civilization.

As the day faded into night, I realized that although the Russians were bereaved to lose a comrade, they accepted a higher level of risk as a community.

Years later, I heard a quote on NPR in which a Russian interviewed for the program said, "Learning to live with tragedy is ingrained in the Russian soul." For decades, the Russians have lived with hardship, through the deprivations of two world wars, the upheaval of a cultural revolution, and the darker side of communism.

Apparently, the perils of whitewater rafting were part of this universal national acceptance. For these Russian paddlers, the rewards of freely chosen exploration, the spiritual escape of

Risk (1989)

wilderness adventure, the challenge of using their wits and brawn to face the hazards of whitewater, even more so because of their handicaps in technology and technique, was worth the risk.

The rally would go on.

In the few days I'd spent in Siberia, I had come to understand that whitewater boating was considered too dangerous for the "weaker" sex in the Soviet Union. Based on what I had recently witnessed in skill and equipment development, I could understand why.

In comparison, my teammates and I had come from a privileged background.

The rally consisted of various slalom and downriver races in two- and four-person paddle catarafts, five-person oar/paddle combination boats, and one-person kayaks. In event after event, our all-women's crew placed high within the field of forty-nine men's teams, often ranking in the top ten. There were also two American co-ed teams.

My kayak slalom event was held on the third day of the competition, and I was predictably nervous at the start. Julie and Kelley had already set the bar high for our team, achieving fifth place in the two-person cataraft slalom event. Not only was I going to be the only woman, a few of the men from Europe I was competing against were also former national slalom kayak team members, and two were former world champions.

Fortunately, the Russians had provided me with a relatively decent boat for the competition: an ancient fiberglass slalom racing kayak from the era of the '72 Olympics. Although the craft was a relic compared to modern slalom boats, the racing design gave me a distinct speed advantage against my competitors, all of whom were in recreational plastic kayaks.

As I burst out of the start, I was aware that I was racing in front of a crowd as large as any international or national competition

RISK

I had ever competed in. But unlike those competitions, where I had never been among the top paddlers drawing attention, here everyone was eagerly watching to see how the US Women's Team was going to represent.

Fortunately, my years of training kicked in as I stroked toward gate one. My brain tuned out everything but the three gates and the river in front of me. No thoughts of the spectators, no more pre-race jitters. I was on course, engaged in the singular focus of dynamic movement.

After clearing gate one, I shifted focus to gates two through four; clearing gate two, I moved attention to gates three through five, continuously linking the sequences, planning two gates ahead of each gate I approached.

Flying across the water, I was in the zone. No missed strokes or tapped gate poles to break my rhythm, my dance with the river flowed seamlessly from gate to gate. However, about halfway through the course, I could no longer tune out the roar from shore. As I forced myself to turn my attention away from the noise, I could not help but register a singular chant, which sounded like "AH MA ZOCKEE, AH MA ZOCKEE, AH MA ZOCKEE!"

Although I did not know what it meant, I knew it was for me, and an additional surge of adrenaline spiked through my body. I completed the run full of exhilaration.

I knew I'd had a great run with few penalties and expected to rank high in the results. As had been happening all week, several of our fans rushed up as I pulled up to shore, eager for the honor of carrying my boat and congratulating me in exuberant Russian; although I did not understand the words, the sentiment was clear. I still didn't know if this carrying-the-boat courtesy was because the Russians thought it unseemly for women to carry heavy things or only part of the package of being a groupie for our "rock star" team.

Risk (1989)

After all the runs were completed, my teammates and I crowded around the scoreboard, eagerly looking for my result. My heart fell when I did not see "USA Women" near the top. I desperately began to search down the list for our team's name, wondering if I had somehow been scored with a fifty-second penalty (a missed gate). To our dismay, our team wasn't even on the results list.

Seeing our consternation and confusion, one of our Russian friends came forward to show us where we were on the board. I was ranked fifth with my run, under the name "Amazonkis." Evidently, we had been given a nickname. And that was the cheer I had heard as I paddled down the course.

Later that evening, we got the whole story as to how we had earned this name. When the Russians heard the US was sending an all-women's team to the rally, representing some of our nation's best rafters, they had assumed we would look like the women athletes they were used to seeing in Olympic swimming and rowing competitions—so when they saw us file off the bus, they were surprised to observe that most of our team was average in size and bulk, and several of us were downright petite.

Their amazement had only grown as they witnessed our skills on the river. They named our team "Amazonkis," the Russian derivation of Amazons, because of the incongruity between our appearance and our capabilities on the water, and they treated us like celebrities.

For the rest of the Chuya River Rally, the Russians continued to carry our boats, feed us throughout the day, and serenade us at night with passionate songs. And every time our team competed or our placing was announced during the awards ceremonies, a huge cheer erupted from the crowd, closely followed by the now-familiar "AMAZONKI" chant.

RISK

Witnessing our team excel in a sport that they had previously considered only within the purview of men was eye-opening for the wives, sisters, and daughters present at the Chuya Rally. After seeing us compete, they immediately began to demand their place in the sport. Women-only river rafting exchange trips in Russia and the US started the following year. The impact of the Chuya Rally in the years to come included improvement in the collective skills of the Russian paddling community and the inclusion of Russian women in the sport. The Chuya Rally was also just the beginning of a long history of international rafting competitions that, to this day, continue to emphasize cross-cultural exchange in river conservation and paddle sport.

I will always be proud of our team for our small part in the dissolution of the Iron Curtain and our role in showing our female comrades that the perceived barriers to their participation in whitewater paddling were an illusion.

The US Women's Team's participation in the Chuya Rally also resulted in some long-lasting friendships with, and even marriages to, our Russian comrades. To me, this was a singular example of the power of the river and river sports to create a lasting and robust community across cultural and political differences.

Prior to this experience, I felt disappointed in where my competitive slalom kayak career, by this point already over, had landed—decidedly short of my original goals. But the Chuya Rally allowed me to see the bigger picture. In unimagined ways, a developed skill can keep providing success throughout a lifetime, beyond your original intent. I was grateful that all those years of slalom training had given me this belated opportunity to feel like a champion—expressed through the outpouring of support from hundreds of hearty people in the remote reaches of Siberia.

Chapter 19
Broken (2018)

Deep breath in. And then slowly out. I open the door of Seth's second-grade classroom.

"Oh, hi Sue, come on in," Mrs. Davis says over her shoulder as I walk into the bright, airy room.

The tiny chairs around low tables are empty, and Mrs. Davis's broad, tall frame is turned away from me as she continues with her task, writing in red marker on the whiteboard.

I am used to Mrs. Davis's class being quiet but have never been here when kids are not. Once a week, I help with reading as a parent volunteer. There is no chaos or fooling around in Mrs. Davis's classroom. After having watched her correct her students with her steely voice and iron maiden stare, I am in awe and a little afraid of this woman.

Mrs. Davis is also kind, even-tempered, and compassionate. But she suffers no fools.

And this is precisely why Seth was placed in her class, out of the four second-grade classrooms at Truckee Elementary. Based on the school's assessment of his performance in first grade, his support team decided he needed a teacher known for maintaining structure and discipline. Mrs. Davis, with over twenty years of teaching experience, knows how to keep order in a classroom of twenty-four unruly second graders.

RISK

I've been amazed during my parent volunteer sessions, observing Seth in this classroom. I have never seen him be so still and attentive. He still squirms on his seat and often works his squeezy ball furiously to keep his hands busy. But he doesn't indulge in his usual banging, singing, and gibberish noises. He knows the boundaries he needs to stay within.

Mrs. Davis points to a low semicircular kiddy conference table surrounded by bright green, blue, and red plastic chairs. "Go ahead and take a seat at the table while I finish this up."

I squat to perch on one of the tiny chairs and carefully slide my legs under the table. At five foot four, I just fit, my thighs pressed firmly against the bottom of the table. When Mrs. Davis takes a seat, I notice that she sits on her chair in a somehow elegant sidesaddle.

Just as I begin to worry that I may have to engage in small talk with Seth's imposing teacher, the door to the classroom opens. A young and energetic trio briskly enters the room: Sarah, the vice principal; Kelly, the school psychologist; and Daphne, Seth's special education teacher. Together these women comprise Seth's support team, working together in various roles to help him succeed at school. And he does need help.

After a brief exchange of greetings, Daphne begins the meeting.

"So Sue, as we discussed on the phone, the purpose of this meeting is to discuss how Seth is doing at school and go through the results of the assessments we've conducted over the past month. Then we'll go over the actions we are proposing to take to help him be more successful. Did you get a chance to read the assessment we sent?"

"Yes . . . I did," I say haltingly. The language they use is always kind, but after reviewing his midyear progress reports and assessment, my take is that Seth is basically flunking elementary school.

Broken (2018)

"Based on his first-grade performance and psychoeducational evaluation," Daphne says, "we have identified several areas where we believe he could benefit from additional support."

I nod. Reading through these documents, I tried to focus on the positives. But it was not easy.

"Based on the assessments, Seth has been identified with some learning disabilities that prevent him from learning at the same pace as his peers. He is smart. He exhibits strong skills related to spatial relationships and math. But his language arts skills are below grade level, and his processing speed is slow."

These statements are an oxymoron to me; I don't really understand. How can someone be smart and slow at the same time? But I just listen.

"Seth also has trouble focusing, is easily distracted, and suffers from impulse control, which affects his ability to interact positively with his peers. We don't make a formal diagnosis here, but he exhibits many of the metrics for ADHD. He really needs to be seen by a physician to get an official diagnosis. Have you by chance done that?"

"No . . . do you think I should?"

"Well, it is, of course, up to you, and we would never require or recommend any specific medical treatment. But there are medications that only a doctor can prescribe that can help manage ADHD behaviors. It's just something you might want to check out, as a tool."

At the mention of medications, I cringe. I have read articles critical of parents medicating their kids to make the parents' lives easier. On a gut level, I am averse to the idea of giving Seth medication at this young age. Medications to alter behaviors that could probably be managed with better parenting. I feel like putting him on drugs would be an admission that I just can't hack the job. I am not ready to go there. Yet.

"Anyway," Daphne continues, "here are copies of a draft IEP

RISK

and BIP we have prepared. These describe the deficiencies and behaviors we are trying to address, and goals to help him catch up with his peers."

Everyone takes a moment to get a copy of the two documents, each about four pages long.

The IEP (Individual Education Program) outlines deficiencies, goals, and strategies to improve Seth's academic performance in reading, writing, attention, and focus. It is hard for me to read the language explicitly describing Seth's inadequacies.

His BIP (Behavior Improvement Plan) is even harder to read but—based on the number of calls I get from the school—not a surprise. This document outlines goals and actions to improve his social and emotional coping skills. These are essentially goals and strategies to reduce how often he loses control and hits or curses at other kids.

As described in the document, Seth exhibits difficulty managing his impulses on the playground, standing in lines to get from one place to another, and in the lunchroom. Basically, anywhere where he does not have the close supervision of Mrs. Davis to keep him in line.

My reaction to these documents is visceral. I feel both intense brain fog, making it difficult to fully absorb what I am reading, and slight nausea.

A year or so ago, I remember saying to a friend that I did not care how intelligent Seth was as long as he turned out to be a good person. But I was lying to myself. I do care that Seth does well in school, not just socially but also academically.

I've always thought that David threw his life away because he never went to college or pursued any kind of advanced learning that could have propelled him into a satisfying and successful career, despite testing so well in high school.

Now I'm having a hard time not seeing Seth as a reflection of

Broken (2018)

David, doomed to make the same mistakes. And it's even worse. Seth is flunking elementary school, for Christ's sake.

I find I cannot seem to keep track of the acronyms . . . SELPA, ADD, ADHD, IEP, BIP. I know what they are when I hear them but find it almost impossible to remember them when speaking. Ironic, considering I work for a government agency. I sling hundreds of acronyms around each day at my job. But my reptilian brain rejects this shorthand of special education/learning disability concepts, which I simply don't want to accept.

Many of the phrases I see on the IEP and BIP plans, such as "below average in reading and writing," "processing weakness in the area of attention," and "struggles to cope when upset, resulting in hitting and tantrums," cause me alarm.

Fortunately, the words Seth's team uses during this meeting are much more optimistic.

"When Seth is given the space to work without distractions," Daphne says, "he does really well. In fact, I think Seth will stop needing an IEP before he leaves elementary school, with a year or two of support. He is a smart kid and just needs a little help to catch up."

Again, I struggle to be reassured. Can a kid that is behind catch up if he simply doesn't have what it takes?

Kelly, the school psychologist, says, "I have great conversations with him after incidents on the playground. He is a special kid. Seth understands and can articulate how he should be handling situations. He is just physically unable to stop himself in the heat of the moment. It's simply going to take time."

I can see why Seth adores Kelly so much. A pretty blond with a soft voice and big, compassionate blue eyes, she is obviously the good cop to Mrs. Davis's bad cop.

"Addressing Seth's behaviors is very important on two levels," Kelly continues. "First, so he can learn to develop positive

RISK

peer-to-peer relationships and have friends. Second, because we know that negative behaviors can inhibit learning."

This I can understand. The brain fog I am experiencing, Seth also shares in his own way. It's the result of anger and anxiety producing toxic chemicals that inhibit the brain's functions.

"ADHD is not a disability; it just is a brain that is wired differently, and I'm speaking from personal experience," Sarah, the vice principal, says with a laugh. She does not elaborate, but I take this to mean she may also have this diagnosis. With her long, bright red hair and runner's body, Sarah is a ball of energy. When she sits, it clearly takes her effort to stay still. She moves her hands when she talks, frequently shifts position, and darts her eyes around the room. She is also always the first to leave a meeting. Understandable, given her impossibly busy schedule—but also, I think, a relief for a woman who likes to be on the move.

Seth always needs to be in motion too. He can only concentrate when he is doing something with his hands. But when he's building things with his LEGOs, especially while listening to a story, he can remain focused and quiet for hours.

"As you know, we have been spending quite a bit of time together lately," Sarah continues with a chuckle.

"Yeah, I know," I say with chagrin. Sarah's office is where Seth gets sent when he has gone too far—which usually means hitting another kid during some dispute.

"He can be a really funny kid," she says, "and after he finishes writing his apology, he draws some really cool pictures."

Kelly jumps in again. "It will be important for us to work together on strategies to reward Seth for good behavior. We do need consequences, both at home and at school, but rewards have been shown to be more successful for modifying behavior."

"So . . . he gets dessert and screen time taken away if he gets in trouble at school," I say slowly. "But I'm not sure what you mean by rewards?"

Broken (2018)

"Well, it's how you frame it," Kelly responds. "Communicate that screen time and dessert are rewards for good behavior. When he has a bad day, he does not earn those rewards. But he can always gain it back, and maybe you can allow him to even earn some of it back on that same day if he can talk to you about what happened and identify a positive solution for next time."

I nod, pondering this common-sense change of perspective.

After a moment, Mrs. Davis pipes in, ready to get back to academics. "Also, Sue, be sure he reads for thirty minutes a day, and keep reading to him. He sometimes mixes up his letters, so he may have mild dyslexia. But with practice, this should get better."

"Yes, he hates reading," I say, "but he loves being read to. In fact, he is so into it, I got him an iPod. He listens to his stories for hours."

"That's great," Daphne says. "The reading will come eventually, as long as he loves stories."

After half an hour, the meeting ends; everyone has somewhere else they need to be in the fast-paced schedule of elementary school.

Driving home, I think how lucky I am to live in a place with a well-funded school district with such attentive and caring staff. If Seth had ended up in some other family in an impoverished school district, how much more difficult would it have been for him to overcome his challenges?

I know I can't avoid disappointment when Seth gets low marks for academic performance. But I can try to focus on his successes. And although it will be difficult, I have to try not to make assumptions about how his skills may evolve. His teachers are clear: in taking kids with atypical brains out of the traditional learning environment and providing them with time to learn in a format that works for them, the IEP process gives them a much better chance at academic success.

I just have to play my part.

RISK

After this meeting, I make appointments with a pediatrician to get Seth assessed for ADHD and with a counselor available through the County Family Services. The ADHD assessment, conducted by me and two of Seth's teachers, asks a series of questions regarding how Seth behaves and reacts in various situations.

The results are clear: Seth is classic ADHD. A condition he is unlikely to outgrow but could learn to manage.

After conducting an additional assessment, the county counselor also informs me that he feels Seth is probably slightly within the autism spectrum.

There are times it is hard to view Seth as anything but broken. He has been diagnosed with an atypical brain, is below grade level in all areas of language arts, and struggles with social engagement with his peers.

He is a kid that needs to be put in special education.

I am furious at David and Gesi, whom I blame for making him this way through either their weak genetics or failed parenting.

But I know this kind of thinking is not going to help Seth. How can he have a chance if I don't believe, like his support team does, that he can catch up? He can learn. He can grow. He can become.

But I also know that Seth is walking a thin line—one bordered by many potential pitfalls. If he can stay on the line, he might just grow up to be a happy person and to lead a rewarding and independent life. But if he falls off the line, he might very well spiral into a life of addiction, isolation, poverty, or mental illness.

I am clearly never going to be able to stop worrying about the line. But I need to believe Seth's current challenges do not necessarily mean he is going to end up like his dad. My challenge is to broaden my definition of success and to support this little boy

Broken (2018)

in finding his own unique path. To not be hampered by thinking that my own life experience, or his father's, will become his destiny.

I need to allow Seth to be himself—challenges, strengths, and all. Hopefully, if I can just support Seth in finding his joy, his path to resiliency, he can figure out the rest himself.

Chapter 20
US Women's Whitewater Team (1993)

"Hey, Sue!" Julie greeted me one afternoon on the phone. "What do you think about joining me on a team to compete in the Camel Whitewater Rafting Challenge on the Zambezi?"

"The Zambezi?" I repeated. "The river where Kelley worked a few years ago?"

My head filled with images I'd seen in Kelley's slides. Terrifying images of the most monstrous whitewater I had ever seen.

"Yeah. Glen from SOTAR Rafts wants to sponsor an all-women's team from the US because the race organizers are threatening to eliminate the women's class. They think the water is too hard for women to compete on."

"Well, that's bullshit." Immediately, my competitive spirit kicks in. "Would I be kayaking or rafting?"

"It's only a rafting competition, but we need your slalom experience."

"Oh," I say, disappointed. *You can't Eskimo roll a raft. What if we flip?*

During my early years of kayaking, a few memorably horrific whitewater swims had hardwired my instincts to do anything I could to stay in my boat. I was still terrified of swimming whitewater, and as a result I had developed a bombproof Eskimo roll

US Women's Whitewater Team (1993)

to keep me in my kayak over the years. Although I had kayaked Class V many times, I had no interest in being in a raft on rapids of that difficulty level. To me, whitewater rafts were ungainly beasts and left too much to chance.

It had been five years since Julie, Kelley, Beth, and I had competed in international whitewater competitions organized by Project RAFT. During those events in 1989 (Siberia), 1990 (North Carolina), and 1991 (Costa Rica), I had participated in both the rafting events and kayak events, but the difficulty had never exceeded Class IV. Though we had experienced a few unplanned hole surfs, tube stands, and high sides in the raft and some of my teammates had been pitched into the water on occasion, I had managed to never fall out. In a video clip of a classic hole surf during one of our races on the Reventazon River in Costa Rica, I looked like a frenetic squirrel as I skittered around, seeking the high side, while the raft spun and bucked in the hydraulic.

The Batoka Gorge of the Zambezi is famed for the number and size—arguably the biggest whitewater in the world—of Class V rapids it contains within one fourteen-mile stretch. I thought again of Kelley's slides: gigantic, watery mushrooms of foam, swirling vortexes, and exploding haystacks created from the force of an impossibly large volume of water.

Rafts flipped violently and often in the Batoka Gorge.

"Who else would be on the team?" I asked.

"So far, it would be you, me, Kelley, and Beth. We need to find two more strong paddlers for the middle seats."

It was a strong start. I couldn't imagine paddling with three more competent rafters in the world—men or women.

I had been friends with Julie and Kelley since our days working as raft guides and kayaking instructors on the South Fork of the American River in Coloma, starting in 1983.

Jules, with her deep-set, dark blue eyes, mane of untamed tawny blond hair, broad shoulders, and fearsome drive, had moved

RISK

on after Coloma to work regularly on a Class IV section of the Tuolumne River. She'd also become the first woman to work as a raft guide on the Class V section of the Upper Tuolumne, the iconic Cherry Creek run. An exceptionally technical boulder-strewn run with multiple small waterfalls, Cherry Creek was the most challenging river run guided commercially in California. Eventually, she'd begun guiding full time in the Grand Canyon. Jules pushed her limits in rafting faster and harder than anyone I'd ever met. Every horrendous flip and swim only hardened her resolve.

Kelley, with her striking sky-blue eyes, long, bright blond hair, and smoothly muscled limbs, was the most talented athlete I had ever met. Whether rowing an oar boat, pumping up a raft, or carrying gear bags, she performed every movement with powerful, supple grace. From her humble beginnings on the South Fork of the American River, she'd gone on to guide Class IV rivers throughout California, Idaho, and Alaska. As her reputation grew, she'd been hired by Mountain Travel Sobek, a premier pioneering adventure travel outfitter, and become the only woman on the first crew to run trips year-round through the Batoka Gorge of the Zambezi, taking passengers on astoundingly high water and exploring the edge at which the river became too dangerous to run safely. She had also worked in Hollywood, first as a member of a river safety team supporting explorations on Jim Fowler's *Wild Kingdom*, and then as a whitewater stunt double.

Kelley's most notable role was as the stand-in for Meryl Streep in the movie *The River Wild*. To her credit, Meryl did some of her own Class III rowing—but the Class V stuff, that was all Kelley. The makeup was so good, the only way you could tell the difference was by looking at their bare arms and legs. Kelley's were the sinewy ones.

I had known Beth Rypins for less time, but we shared a mutual passion for whitewater kayaking, and she was an imposing figure. She always walked with a swagger, leading each stride

US Women's Whitewater Team (1993)

with her broad shoulders, firmly planting her feet and muscular legs with every purposeful step. Her thick brown hair framed sharply sculpted facial features, dark brown eyes, and a wide, toothy smile. Her passion was exploring Class V rivers in California and South America. Like Jules and Kelley, she was driven to keep raising the bar on the difficulty of rivers women rowed, guided, and paddled.

These three were among the strongest women I had ever known, and by far the bravest. Because of the inherent level of risk they encountered as part of their jobs and explorations, they had by this point developed a robust set of skills to deal with situations when things went wrong. They knew how to swim out of Class V rapids, flip an upside-down raft back upright in the middle of whitewater chaos, and unwrap a raft pinned on rocks in almost any situation.

Their drive to keep pushing the boundaries of extreme whitewater rafting was inspiring, even though I had little desire to be part of it. My fear of physical harm kept me well within the boundaries of my skill level. The stories of whitewater carnage they had survived on their exploits sent shivers down my spine.

But I knew that if I was going to step outside my comfort zone and into a big, cumbersome tube of inflated rubber to drop into some of the world's biggest Class V whitewater, there was no better group with which to do it.

"Okay, I'm in," I said, with excitement as well as trepidation.

"Great!" Julie said. "Let's schedule some dates to train and hold tryouts for potential teammates."

Ready or not, it looked like I was going to the Zambezi.

Finding two more women to paddle with us in this competition was not easy. Although there were a fair number of women who were competent at guiding Class IV rivers, surprisingly few had rigorous athletic backgrounds. Many of the women who attended

RISK

our tryouts could not modify their guiding skills into an efficient race paddling technique or did not have the power and endurance needed for sprint and long-distance competitions.

And for the Zambezi, we also needed individuals who could manage Class V whitewater, whether the raft was right side up or upside down.

Eventually, we found them in two remarkable young women.

I had first met Brooke Winger ten years before, when I was in my thirties. I'd run into a group of young kids one day on the South Fork of the American River and immediately noticed Brooke, the only girl paddling with five boys. She'd flipped in a small rapid and had proceeded to attempt an Eskimo roll ten times—managing to get little gasps of air with each try—before finally making it up. I'd been flabbergasted. I'd never known an eleven-year-old girl with such tenacity. Remembering my temerity at that age, I'd known she was of a different mold.

Brooke's parents were not paddlers, so I'd joined a broader paddling community that had "adopted" Brooke and her younger brother, Ethan, over the next few years—coaching them on slalom gates, bringing them with me to races, and taking them on their first overnight river trip.

Brooke looked like the girl next door, with reddish-blond hair, a shy smile, and freckles sprinkled over a cute button nose and plump cheeks. She was short like me, and a tiny bit stocky, with the telltale broad, strong back and powerful shoulders of a serious paddler. By this point she was one of the top women in freestyle kayaking, with three world championship titles under her belt—and, like Beth, a bad-ass Class V kayaker. She brought with her a unique fearlessness, bolstered by the single-minded determination I had seen on that first day we met on the South Fork.

The last paddler to join our team was Juliet Wiscombe. Juliet had a big white smile like Beth, long golden blond hair and bright blue eyes like Kelley, a short, stocky build like Brooke,

US Women's Whitewater Team (1993)

and a focus and wit that were all her own. Juliet was a respectable Class IV raft guide, but more importantly, she had rowed crew at UC Berkeley. Although her guiding accomplishments at the time were not particularly remarkable, from the first workout we paddled together, it was clear she had "it." She quickly absorbed our coaching, adapted her paddling technique to suit our needs, and was both powerful and tireless. Juliet knew how to paddle in the pain room. Maybe more than any of us.

Brooke and Juliet proved their abilities on the water, but more importantly, they also could hold their own within our pack of alpha females.

One of the biggest challenges we faced on our team was learning how to work together. Everyone was comfortable with either paddling alone or, when guiding, being in sole charge of commanding a raft. Paddling on a competitive team with so many chiefs in the boat would require a special kind of communication.

Raft racing is entirely different from paddling a guided recreational or commercial boat, where typically just one guide, stationed in the back, calls all the shots. Rafts are momentum pigs. Once a fourteen-foot raft loaded with six paddlers moves in one direction, it takes considerable power to change that trajectory. Therefore, recreational and commercial rafting involves a lot of back paddling. This allows the guide to maneuver the boat in a backward ferry in one direction or another while slowing the downstream momentum. The guide also limits the amount of time the passengers in the boat paddle during the flat sections, saving their strength for when it's needed to make a move in a rapid.

In raft racing, all those techniques are thrown out the window.

"Raft racing" is almost an oxymoron, since there is nothing about the design of a whitewater raft that helps it go fast. Whitewater rafts are designed to carry a group of people through rapids without flipping. They are made of rubber. They are heavy and have absolutely no glide.

RISK

Getting a raft to go fast requires every paddler in the boat to paddle as hard as possible, in near-perfect unison, constantly, to drive the boat to the finish line.

Learning to paddle a raft quickly and precisely through whitewater was the most challenging communication scenario I have ever experienced. All four paddlers in the bow and stern of the raft need to help steer, and these four paddlers need to know at all times where the raft needs to go and what they individually need to do to get the raft to go there. Furthermore, when plan A goes into the shitter, the entire team needs to quickly get on the same page to implement plan B or C.

We spent hours on the shore next to slalom courses and challenging rapids debating the fastest lines and the safest lines and discussing who needed to do what and when to get where we needed to go, making sure we had all come to a consensus on plan A as well as plan B.

Plan C, we knew, would have to be formulated on the fly.

When plan A and B failed in the middle of whitewater chaos during our training runs, the many chiefs in our boat frantically tried to take command, with everyone executing split-second input and reactions until something clicked. Once we had survived whatever mess we had gotten ourselves into, we pulled the raft into the closest eddy to debrief, analyze our mistakes, air our grievances, and make whatever apologies were needed.

It was team building on steroids. Six alpha females, driven by our individually unique but mutual desire to survive and succeed, figuring out a way to achieve that together.

I tossed restlessly under the sheet, draping one leg out of bed to cool off, my brain feverishly replaying our discussions with Kelley about the river the night before.

Rapid five, rapid five, rapid five. Super steep drop, like dropping

US Women's Whitewater Team (1993)

off a two-story building. Huge holes on both sides of the tongue; gotta miss The Catcher's Mitt on the left and hit the monster raft-flipper wave at the bottom just right. Rapid five. Rapid six, no big deal, just two big waves, and then some flat water. We will have to paddle hard through that to put distance between the Brits and us. Rapid seven, rapid seven, rapid seven. Longest Class V rapids on the river. Gotta avoid The Crease at the top, then stay on line and keep digging to keep the boat upright through the Land of the Giants. DO NOT WANT TO SWIM HERE! Todd said he almost drowned; whirlpools held him under for so long, even with his lifejacket. He is planning on making some shorts out of foam and duct tape to increase his buoyancy. Rapid seven.

Christ! I need to stop thinking about the rapids and get some sleep; I'm exhausted.

I looked over at the red numbers of the digital clock in our open-air lodge outside Victoria Falls. Three in the morning. Of course my biorhythms were all screwed up; we'd just flown in from California the previous day. But tomorrow would be our first day on the river, and I needed to be rested.

I know, I will count my breaths—count of seven in, count of seven out. Relax, relax, relax. One . . . two . . . three . . . four . . . five . . . WHAT IS THAT!?

The screech of a wild beast cut through the night, but my untrained ear couldn't tell if it was lion, warthog, baboon, hyena, or God knew what else. Our lodge was located right next to a water hole. That evening, over cocktails on the deck, we'd watched wildebeest, cape buffalo, zebras, and elephants all amble in for their evening dip and drink.

Well . . . I just hope nothing is getting eaten. Gotta get to sleep. Relax, relax. Breath in for seven, out for seven, one . . . two . . . three . . . four . . . five . . . six . . . seven . . . Rapid eight, rapid eight, rapid eight . . .

RISK

~~~

The next morning, everyone looked tired.

"I didn't get any sleep at all last night," Brooke said. "A warthog woke me up, rustling around in my pack."

"Crap, he came in here?" Kelley asked. "Did you have any food in it? They told us to make sure everything was locked up in the kitchen cupboards before we went to sleep."

Brooke sighed. "I forgot about my energy bars."

"Well," I interjected, "I couldn't stop thinking about the beta Kelley gave us on the rapids. I was obsessing about it all night."

"Me too," Juliet exclaimed. "I can't wait to get on the river. No matter how bad it is, it can't be worse than my imagination."

"Yeah, I can't go through another night like last night," I said, "and I want to make sure we have plenty of time to learn the lines, so we don't flip."

Kelley and Jules both burst into laughter.

"Sue Norman!" Kelley scolded me. "We are definitely gonna flip!"

"Yeah," Jules added, "it's just a matter of where and how often. You are going to have to figure out how to deal!"

"The rafts we're using for the competition are small and light," Kelley said. "But fourteen-foot boats are going to be really squirrelly in this water. The commercial outfitters here use heavy sixteen- to eighteen-footers."

I looked at Brooke, and we exchanged a look of uneasy camaraderie. *And this is EXACTLY why we kayak instead of raft.*

Seeing the consternation on our faces, Kelley offered a piece of wisdom that changed my perspective in accepting the challenge of big Class V whitewater rafting: "You just have to remember one thing: if the raft goes over, hold on—and do not let go!"

US Women's Whitewater Team (1993)

≈

"Here we go, ladies." Kelley smiled cheerily as we began the 330-foot descent into the Zambezi Gorge.

Clad in flip-flops or cheap sneakers, three porters were already trotting ahead of Kelley with our raft rolled up like a fat yellow slug draped across their shoulders. Their lean brown muscles were already shiny with sweat as they glided swiftly down the path.

Looking down the trail, I saw now why we needed them.

Using my paddle as a walking stick, I began my much more tenuous descent over steep, shiny bedrock; loose dirt and gravel; and, in the really sketchy bits, cable-bound wooden ladders bolted into the rock.

Twenty minutes later, I was a hot, sweaty mess. I eagerly waded into the Zambezi's cool, opaque green waters in the surging launch eddy to give myself some relief.

The porters, meanwhile, had already passed us again, trotting back up the trail for another load. They got paid for each round trip and, competing with the other porters to get the next raft, were eager to get back to the top first.

The power of the river was immediately evident. The water surged over a foot up on the shore of our launch eddy, and there was a steep, whirling vortex where the eddy met the main flow of river current. Looking downstream, I could see only a smooth, flat horizon line above the first rapid—except for the small bursts of spray popping and fizzing above that line, sent up by the hidden hydraulics below.

Sipping water with electrolyte powder, we spent another thirty minutes blowing up our raft and securing grab lines. Seeing the intricate web of nylon straps Kelley and Jules expertly threaded around the raft and over the thwarts gave me some comfort that

RISK

I would have plenty of handholds for clinging to. We were rigged to flip.

Kelley pointed to a thin line of webbing she had tied down across the back thwart. "This is your line, Sue. Just hold on to this if we start to go over. Since you're so small, if you keep hanging on when we flip the raft upright, we can just pull you back in as the raft flips up. Then you can help pull all of us into the raft."

At least there was one advantage to being the smallest person on the team.

At last, we all boarded the raft, cramming our feet into the crevices available in our respective seats to lock ourselves in for the wild ride that was about to begin. I practiced grabbing the various safety lines around me, particularly the one across the thwart. I made sure my hand could easily slip under the line but there was not so much of a gap that I needed to worry about an arm or a leg getting trapped under it in a violent capsize.

Peeling out of the eddy, adrenaline pushed the pent-up anxiety from where it had been building inside my body for weeks. Following Kelley's lead, everyone quickly synced their stroke to hers, and our raft surged into the current.

Every fiber of my body and brain neurons was actively engaged as we paddled through the hydraulics of the Zambezi. We used precisely timed power strokes to punch through crashing walls of water, jumped off our seats and threw our bodies across the raft to weigh down the side being lifted into the air by welling mushrooms of foam, and thrust draw or rudder strokes to set boat angles. In every rapid, we fought to avoid exploding hydraulics larger than our raft and push through mountainous waves that, if we allowed our momentum or angle to fall off for even a second, would likely flip us.

Our first flip was in rapid six. Six was one of the easier rapids, only requiring us to power through a couple of gigantic but

US Women's Whitewater Team (1993)

relatively smooth waves—but we made the mistake of trying to rest while paddling through it. Just as we were climbing up the surface of the second impossibly tall wave, I felt the raft's momentum begin to bog. That was all the curling lip at the top of the fifteen-foot wave needed. The lip lifted the front left of the raft up and pushed our right stern down in a tube suck, under the current piling onto the back of the raft.

I had just enough time to grab my thwart line before we were upside down and I was getting swirled like a kite in the wind in the underwater currents of the Zambezi.

Holding my breath, I walked my hands along the thwart line to grab the side rope and pull my head above the water. Jules and Kelley were already on the upside-down raft, clipping the flip lines they carried around their waists onto the D rings on the boat's side. They both scrambled back to stand up on the opposite side of the raft from me, and when Kelley called it, leaned back and pulled with all their weight on their flip lines. Still holding onto the thwart line with my right hand and the side rope with my left, I pushed, then pulled my body up as high as I could out of the water as the raft flipped back upright. The momentum of the flip pulled my entire body out of the water and into the raft.

From the moment we'd turned over, I'd been in the water for all of fifteen seconds, tops.

I lunged over to grab paddles and lifejacket straps, assisting my teammates as they pulled themselves up out of the water. Within another ten seconds we were all back in the raft, scrambling to grab our paddles and lock ourselves back into our seats.

"That was great!" I exulted at the bottom of the rapid. "I didn't have to hold my breath for more than a couple of seconds."

"Yeah, but we were lucky we flipped there instead of rapid seven," Juliet said. "That's where Todd said he basically passed out."

"Yeah," Kelley jumped in, "rapid seven is the longest rapid on

RISK

the river and has some of the deepest whirlpools. It's the one rapid you definitely do not want to swim in."

"Man, we won't be able to let up at all!" Jules exclaimed. "It's going to be hard to sprint through all the pools and then keep pushing that hard in the rapids, too. We are going to have to figure out how to pace ourselves in the flats."

"I know," I said. "It's going to be tough to hold our breath underwater if we are already gassed before we go over."

We congratulated ourselves at the end of the run for having successfully navigated all twenty-five rapids of the Batoka Gorge with only one completely avoidable capsize. There would still be numerous opportunities to flip in the upcoming days, and we had a lot of work to do to memorize race lines, but we at least knew we could handle the river.

I felt a peaceful ooze of contentment, slowly seeping into the void left by the recent flood of endorphins and adrenaline. Day one on the Zambezi was in the bag.

That afternoon, during a quiet moment, I pondered the decisions that had led me to this moment.

Why was I driven to do this? I was turning forty in just a week. What did I have to prove? I already had a respectable paddling career. I had a master's degree and a prized position as a US Forest Service hydrologist in Lake Tahoe. Christ, I even owned a house now, situated next to a gorgeous meadow along a small stream.

What I didn't have was a partner. Or kids. Not having a partner was not by design, but not having children—that was. What I had was freedom, and in fact, one of the reasons my last relationship had ended was because I had felt trapped in an unhealthy dynamic that was increasingly putting limits on what I could do in life.

I wanted new experiences, I wanted challenges, I wanted to

US Women's Whitewater Team (1993)

explore. I did not want to compromise. And I wanted to sometimes be uncomfortable. To sometimes be pushed away from the smooth, soft planes of life to the hard, gritty edges. Granted, I tried to choose the circumstances for exploring those edges. But something in me craved not staying too comfortable for too long. I wanted to know that I could still face fear and uncertainty, as I had throughout my life, and grow stronger and more resilient from that experience. I wanted to know that whatever future challenges life might throw my way, I could handle them.

The week that lay ahead on the Zambezi River was going to give me what I craved—satisfy that something embedded deep in my psyche that made me push boundaries.

I would be lucky to maintain this fleeting feeling of contentment through dinner, much less through another long dark night.

But for now, it felt good.

The 1993 World Rafting Championships was a victory for all four of the women's teams that competed in the event. After three days of competition in sprint, slalom, and downriver races, we edged out a strong team from Britain to capture first place overall. Both of our teams outperformed a third to a half of the men's teams during the three events. By doing so, we firmly secured a place for women in the sport of Class V international whitewater raft competition.

Not every woman rafter could compete on Class V whitewater, of course, just like not every man could. But similar to women who competed in other adventure sports during the nineties, we proved success was primarily determined by training and skills, not XY chromosomes.

The day of the downriver race just so happened to fall on my fortieth birthday. The physical and mental challenges of the Camel Challenge were more demanding than any competition I had ever entered before. I was exhausted after six days of training

RISK

and competing on one of the most challenging sections of Class V whitewater in the world, including the grueling 330-foot descent and 590-foot climb out of the gorge every day. But at forty, I felt as strong as I ever had.

As the top three teams walked off the awards stage with our medals still around our necks, congratulating and hugging each other, I reveled in the glow of my personal accomplishments in preparing and performing in this event—as well as my team's.

The Camel Challenge marked a definite peak in my athletic life. I had pushed my physical limits to achieve ultimate success, and still had the energy to party like a maniac the night of the final award ceremony.

Now that the competition was over, most of our team would spend another week and a half in Africa to see the wildlife and to relax and savor our accomplishments. Afterward, I would return home to a secure foundation. To a thriving career at the Forest Service and a home I owned in a beautiful mountain town in the Sierras.

I was where I wanted to be, living the life I wanted, with little compromise. Like a healthy river, my life was moving in a harmonious flow, filled with pools, glides, riffles, and cascades.

I was leading a life in balance, and it felt incredible.

Chapter 21
Finding the Gifts
(2016–2018)

The ski team coach approaches me with a look I have come to recognize. It is a certain tension in the facial muscles, the eyes making brief contact but quickly cutting away. The body language of someone who is about to engage in a conversation that will be uncomfortable—and, depending on how I, the parent, might react, potentially confrontational.

"Hi, Sue, uh . . . I need to talk to you about Seth . . . some issues we are having," the coach starts awkwardly.

"Oh, I'm sorry," I say, bracing myself. "What's going on?"

"We're having trouble getting him to listen to his coaches. He's not following instructions."

I grit my teeth in frustration. This again.

"I'm sorry," I say again. "I'll have a talk with him."

"Don't get me wrong—he is a great kid, and he seems to really enjoy being here. But Seth is disrupting the class. He doesn't want to wait for the other kids and takes off down the run by himself. Also, when the coaches are talking, he messes around, trying to get attention from the other students. If he keeps this up, we're going to have to ask that he not come back."

With Seth's rudimentary skiing ability, he is in the lowest-level group. He still skis mainly in the pizza position, not carving parallel turns yet like others his age or younger in the more advanced levels. But he is more confident than a couple of the other kids in his group—and because he always wants to be moving, he quickly gets impatient with listening to instructions.

His skiing is improving some, but as the weeks go by, I can see that some kids who were initially more fearful have now become better skiers than Seth. Their willingness to listen and apply the technique drills to become more controlled and skilled skiers is paying off.

We make it through the season without getting kicked out of the program, but barely. We have not been so lucky with other sports. I have enrolled Seth in many organized athletic programs. I've found it challenging to find opportunities for Seth to engage in unstructured sports like I did when I was young. Now, there are teams, leagues, and programs for a dizzying array of sports.

At first, I was hopeful these activities would enable him to make connections with his peers and form friendships. Also, I felt athletics was a good way for him to release some of his energy. But structured sports programs typically involve a large number of kids, with commensurate expectations for performance and behavior.

Seth is not wired to succeed in these settings.

When Seth is five, I get him his first bike, a pedal-less bike called a strider.

On our first trip to the pump track, I take him over to the easiest course at the bike park. It is oval-shaped, with banked turns and carefully designed dips and rises so that little kids can learn to use the speed on the downhills to easily make it up the next hill.

Wanting to ease him into it, I walk him down halfway on the start ramp and hold the seat of his bike as he swings his leg over and settles on the saddle.

"Okay," I say, "just coast, and don't try to go too fast."

Finding the Gifts (2016–2018)

Without a word, he begins pushing his feet against the ground, trying to break free from my grasp. I reluctantly let go.

He whizzes down the ramp but fails to push with his legs at the right time to get up the next rise. As his bike coasts to a stop a few feet from the top, he screeches with rage and throws the bike to the ground.

I run down the track, embarrassed by this tantrum only minutes in.

"C'mon, it's no big deal," I encourage him. "Here, I'll help you push the bike to the top. This takes some time."

But when I reach for the bike, he grabs it away and stomps up to the crest.

"Now, when you start going up the next hill, be sure to push with your legs when you feel the bike start to slow down."

I cheer when I see him make it up the rise. But descending the next down ramp, he gets going too fast into the first turn. His handlebars wobble back and forth, and boom, he's down. This time he wails as he lies sprawled in the dust, tears streaming down his cheeks.

Again, I run over to him, helping him untangle his pretzeled body from around the bike frame and checking for injuries—all while three-year-olds confidently and gracefully whiz by us.

"Okay, honey," I say. "We can go if you want. If you've had enough."

But Seth grabs the bike from me and pushes off again. For the next twenty minutes, I decide to stay out of it. Letting him fall. Letting him cry and pick himself back up.

By the time he decides he is done, he has learned to get around the track without crashing. He's not the fastest kid, or the most graceful. But he's better.

Before he came to live with me, Seth was rarely taken to a playground. He was not shown how to kick or throw a ball. Never

RISK

taken sledding or for a walk on a trail to climb on logs and rocks.

Living in a community of overachieving Tahoe wunderkinds is a tough place for him to play catch-up. Many of the kids who live in our small mountain town exhibit precocious athletic skills. I'm amazed by how talented many of Seth's peers are. I guess it's not a surprise, since many parents who have made their home in Tahoe are also excellent, and sometimes even famous, athletes. These kids have inherited strong athletic genes, and they were put on bikes, skis, and hiking trails as soon as they could walk.

Thinking I'm motivated by purely noble goals, I keep trying different sports, hoping to find something that will suit his personality, maybe capture his interest enough so he'll thrive. Involvement in sports would help build his self-esteem and confidence, I tell myself. He could make friends, and coaches could become positive male role models.

But eventually I have to face the fact that I'm also hoping for something that has more to do with *me* than him. I want Seth to be successful at sports so I can feel proud. So I can claim some of the credit and capture some of the glory of my kid's athletic success. Maybe to make up for the fact that I miss no longer receiving that kind of social currency from my own athletic endeavors.

I understand why I've fallen into this trap. I cannot help feeling envious of parents I know with high-achieving athletic children. But I also recognize how unhealthy my expectations for achievement are for Seth. I can't force him to be someone he's not.

After Seth is expelled from his soccer league, ju-jitsu class, and sailing camp, and after I watch him struggle to master even the most basic skills in hockey and basketball, I have to refocus my goals for Seth as a parent. What do I want to achieve by encouraging Seth's involvement in sports? What is necessary for his quality of life and development as a human being?

Finding the Gifts (2016–2018)

Because of Seth's challenges, organized sports are not meeting enough of those goals. I, therefore, must shift my focus to noncompetitive lifestyle activities and sports. I will have to provide him unstructured space where he can find his joy, hopefully in a like-minded community.

I also want him to find the connection to nature that I did as a child. I want him to experience the calming and grounding aspects of immersion in natural settings.

Maybe in that environment, his ADHD will become a superpower rather than a disability—as it did for his hero, Percy Jackson, the half-blood son of Neptune from the Rick Riordan stories he's listened to repeatedly on his iPod, and the many famous neurodiverse musicians, artists, and athletes I've discovered in my online research.

The trick will be finding the setting where Seth's transformation will best evolve.

Even before I became Seth's guardian, I was aware of the benefits of nature-based sport to young developing minds. Over the years, I have coached several kids in whitewater kayak slalom, which has also included mentoring river playtime, planning overnight river trips, hanging out at surf waves, and just generally messing around in boats. I've witnessed how powerful the unstructured and non-competitive element of whitewater paddling can be; I've seen that unstructured play on rivers and in other outdoor settings is what really engages kids in outdoor sports, which they may or may not turn into competitive athletic goals, and that this lifelong engagement will likely be more meaningful to their lives than will competitive endeavors.

Starting with Seth's first day in Tahoe, the day Lisa and I taught him it was okay to pee outside, we've primarily built a foundation of playing in nature for him during our daily dog walks.

RISK

Not that Seth doesn't frequently complain about going on a dog walk. It's too hot, too cold, it will be boring, he's not done playing with his LEGOs, yada, yada, yada.

But once he's out of the car, Seth is quick to switch gears.

One of our favorite places to go for dog walks is Donner Lake State Park. Located on the outskirts of Truckee, less than a ten-minute drive from Lisa's house, the park features easy hiking trails along a stunning blue alpine lake. Wandering through the pines, the paths also offer majestic views of the granite peaks of Donner Summit and lead to several beaches formed from decomposed granite.

Often the best time of the year for walking at Donner Lake is in the fall, after the lake levels have quickly dropped from supplying late-season water for Truckee River water rights. The low lake levels create large swaths of shoreline beach to walk along next to the water.

Today, as soon as we leave the car and start down the trail, Seth begins to skip. He is listening to a story on his iPod—either Harry Potter or Percy Jackson. I know he is intermingling the characters and stories in these books into our environment as he picks up a stick and begins wielding it like a sword (or a wand) to attack a threatening bush.

"I will NOT surrender," he exclaims. "Take that, you git!" He gives a branch a sharp whack, then runs after Maddie into a copse of trees, jumping over fallen logs while continuing his exhortations in an imaginary battle.

After about fifteen minutes, we reach a large rock the size of a house, a frequent stopping point on our walks.

On cue, Seth whines, "Can we take a break now? I'm tired!"

I have learned that this is code for "I'm bored." I have read that people with ADHD get bored more easily than others. Their antsiness and lack of focus simply come from not being interested in a particular activity. The trick is, keep it interesting.

Finding the Gifts (2016–2018)

It is time to change it up.

This time I notice a hollowed-out tree stump located about fifty feet from the rock, and observe that it is just big enough for a small child to sit in. "Sure," I reply. "How about we make a little fort out of this stump? We can make a floor out of rocks and use branches for a roof."

Seth's face lights up immediately. He *loves* building forts. He can spend hours creating elaborate structures around chairs and coffee tables—dragging out every pillow, blanket, and top sheet he can find in the house—and then filling them with his toys and books. Although I can intellectually see how this is satisfying and essential creative play for Seth, all Lisa and I can physically see is chaos. It drives both of us absolutely bonkers at home. But here in the wild, forts are cool. Using nature's gifts to create a bit of temporary human order out of the environment's ordered chaos.

Humming a tune, Seth scampers around the beach, looking for flat rocks and fat pieces of driftwood.

Despite his ADHD, Seth exhibits hyper-focus when he is building things, whether forts or fantastical and intricate LEGO creations of his own imagination. He also demonstrates tremendous creativity and a high level of spatial awareness in these efforts. His counselors say he has a brain wired for engineering. If you ask what he wants to be when he grows up, he will declare, "An inventor."

Lisa says, as usual, "I'm going a little farther with the dogs, okay?"

"Yeah, you know where we'll be," I say.

Twenty minutes later, the dogs come running back up. Seth and I have just finished carefully placing and matching rocks to create a flat granite floor in the stump, but only have about half the roof complete. It's getting late, though.

RISK

I stand and brush the dirt from my knees. "Okay, Seth, it's time to go."

"No! We just got started," he wails. "I don't want to go back."

"I know, I know," I say, "but we have to get back and start dinner. We can come to finish this on our next walk out here."

He resists a little longer, but after I promise again that we can come back soon, he finally acquiesces and scampers after the dogs along the trail toward the car.

During our hour at Donner Lake, Seth has exercised and engaged in creative play. He has not gotten into trouble for using inappropriate language or use of his body. He has been happy. Our fort building won't lead to any future sports medals, but it has met two of my goals for outdoor activity with Seth: health and fun. It has also strengthened bonds within our family, both furred and unfurred, and with the natural world. Foundations for both community and resiliency.

It is in this unstructured play in the outdoors that I feel like I know how to be. How to be a friend, a partner. A parent.

When Seth is six, I discover that he has a solid affinity for an activity that's not part of my world.

A friend of mine gives Seth a guitar at his sixth birthday party, which we hold on a paddlewheel boat on Lake Tahoe. When the acoustic duo performing on the boat this evening begins playing, Seth picks up the guitar and walks to the front of the stage. I can't hear his strumming—it is, thankfully, overwhelmed by the band's sound system—but I can tell he is on the beat. He displays the same intense focus I've observed during his building projects, swaying and strumming to the music, for almost half an hour.

In addition to exhibiting a natural sense of rhythm, it also becomes apparent over the ensuing months that he has a musical ear and a beautiful singing voice. I am surprised by how many

Finding the Gifts (2016–2018)

lyrics he memorizes, and how he sings on key to songs he hears on the radio. His singing voice is also different from his speaking voice, devoid of stammer and hesitation.

I sign him up for choir and a small musical theater program through school, but he is painfully shy and basically lip-syncs during these early performances. So, wanting to nurture this possible gift in a less stressful setting, I decide to sign him up for voice lessons.

His teacher confirms what I have observed. He has talent—he displays a mastery of pitch, harmony, and rhythm. And unlike in his sports programs, he is calmer and better at listening to instructions during his voice lessons.

After three months of lessons, his teacher says he is ready to perform with her at the next music school performance showcase at a local pub.

Seth and I go early with a friend and her two sons to get a bite to eat and listen to some of the other performances before Seth's. But Seth, again gripped by stage fright, can't eat.

Some of the younger students in the showcase are horrible from a musical standpoint. But the kids are cute and eager, seemingly unperturbed by their flaws or the audience. Most of the older kids, who clearly have put in the work on top of the talent they were born with, are really good. After a solid performance by a high school duo, it's Seth's turn.

Sitting there, feeling anxiety on his behalf, I wish he could have performed earlier, with the younger kids.

Seth's three songs all include harmonies with his music teacher. The teacher is a pro and aware of his stage fright, so she sets him up on a stool with a music stand placed in front of him like a shield. We can still see him, but he can hide behind his music sheets to block the scary eyes staring at him from the audience.

RISK

When Seth begins their first song, "Puff the Magic Dragon," my eyes instantly start to tear. My fears of him whispering his lyrics, of losing his place, disappear.

His voice is strong and pure, without a quaver. His teacher has turned down her microphone to a slightly lower volume than Seth's, letting his voice dominate. Their harmonies are perfect. Her voice is soft and sweet; his is a tad lower, a distinct, soulful tenor. By the last song in their set, "California Dreamin'," everyone in the audience has gone quiet and is smiling at the stage. Several are singing along to the words they know.

At the end of the song, Seth's eyes lift from his sheet music, and he looks up at the audience as they hoot and cheer. A small, delighted smile plays over his lips. Then he grabs his sheets and scampers back to our table.

When he sits down in his chair, he lets out a big exhale and picks up his fork.

"Well, I'm not going to do *that* again for a really, really long time," he announces before filling his mouth with a massive mouthful of spaghetti.

My friend Emily exclaims, "Seth, you were so great. That was awesome!"

"You don't need to perform again right away," I chime in. "But hopefully you will when you're ready. I'm very proud of you."

He does not look up from his plate, but I can see him trying to suppress another smile. I probably do not say that enough.

Although I will always keep Seth involved in an active outdoor lifestyle, I think his unique gifts are more likely to evolve in the world of music. In an environment where he will find his own expressions of joy, grounding, and community.

Music is a landscape foreign to me. But as Seth's parent, my job is to do my best to introduce him to new worlds, both familiar and unfamiliar to me, to enter and explore.

To introduce him to spaces where he can fit in.

Chapter 22
Strength through Vulnerability (1999)

"Well, I hate to have to admit it, but I think Sue was right," Beth said.

Finally, I thought, looking around at my teammates as we crouched onshore underneath our upside-down raft.

Rain and hail pounded relentlessly on the underside of the raft, and half-inch-diameter balls of ice bounced on the ground around our makeshift shelter. Looking downstream, I saw black thunderclouds and jagged lightning continue to march upriver.

"Well, it's going to suck, but since we haven't entered the gorge yet, we can paddle back upstream to the put-in once the hail stops," Kelley said. "At least we will get a workout and can practice our timing."

Shivering in neoprene shorts and our short-sleeve paddle jackets, everyone nodded in agreement.

Our original rafting team from Africa—Beth, Brooke, Juliet, Kelley, Jules, and me—had reunited to compete at the US Whitewater Rafting Team trials in Colorado. My teammates had only gotten stronger in the past six years.

Still, Gore Canyon was one of the most formidable Class V sections of river run for either kayaks or rafts in North America. So, when the rest of the team had insisted that we run our

RISK

first practice run solo, late in the afternoon, just after arriving in Colorado, I had pleaded with them to reconsider. Having lived in Colorado for several years as an undergrad, I knew how fast and fierce late-afternoon summer thunderstorms could hit in the Rockies, and I was worried about the looming dark clouds visible in the distance.

I'd also kayaked Gore Canyon before and had vivid memories of portaging around several sharp rock–choked Class V rapids, and over equally heinously jagged boulder piles along the shore. On that same run, a member of my party had been sucked out of her boat, flushed beneath an undercut rock, and had her cheek pierced by a stick. She had to walk out that day.

My team hadn't been willing to listen to reason before we got in the water, but luckily, they were listening now.

After the hail stopped, we got in the raft and started paddling upstream.

We'd try again tomorrow.

Gore Rapid, the crux point on the Gore Canyon run, was a long, steep drop. The entrance was narrow, a barely raft-wide slot on the far left shore. To get into the slot, we had to steer with a left angle past some guard rocks and then turn a sharp right to drop into a narrow torrent of water that shot all the way back to the right shore.

Right after we made the first turn at the entrance of the rapid and dropped into the steep chute, it all went to crap.

The front of the raft ground into a rock on the right side of the chute. This spun the back of the boat so the rear slammed onto another rock, pinning us in the middle of the chute. The force of impact tipped the raft up on its side, and I saw Beth falling backward over the downstream edge of the raft. I reached down to grab her life jacket, but my feet slipped on the steep pitch of the raft's floor. I pivoted at the last second and lunged for the

Strength through Vulnerability (1999)

grab line to avoid going over the side after her, into the steep rock garden of jagged boulders and hydraulics.

Pitched sideways at a 30-degree angle, the raft was firmly and precariously stuck between two rocks at the worst possible location in the rapid as Beth was swept downstream.

The five of us still left in the raft tried to delicately bounce the raft off the rocks. We clutched desperately onto the grab lines to keep from sliding out of the boat while simultaneously balancing our weight to not tip the boat even more downstream, causing it to flip.

After about thirty seconds of this, Kelley yelled, "The only way to get unstuck is for us to get out of the boat."

"Out of the boat?" Brooke exclaimed. "Where exactly do you think we can go?"

"We just have to get as many of us as we can on this rock," Jules replied, clutching a small knob on the pyramid-shaped boulder the back of the boat was stuck on. "I'll get out first and hold on to the stern line."

"Jesus Christ, you better hold on tight," I said. "I don't want to be stranded in the middle of this shit."

"Everybody, just stay calm," Kelley commanded. "And be ready to jump back in as soon as the boat starts to move."

One by one, we gingerly made our way out of the raft and gathered on the rock like fairies on the head of a pin. As each person got out, we pressed more tightly together, clutching onto each other while precariously balancing on micro edges and cracks on the steep sides of the boulder. Kelley was the last person in the boat, and as she put one foot out onto the boulder, the front of the raft suddenly swung free.

Cursing and shouting, we desperately scrambled to get back in the raft before it was swept downstream.

I launched myself from the rock into the middle of the boat behind Kelly's feet as she lunged up to the front of the boat. I

RISK

landed on my knees and was desperately scrambling to my feet when I was suddenly body-slammed back to the floor by one of my teammates. I pushed up with herculean strength, lifting the body on my back into the air, frantic to get into a paddling position as the boat started picking up speed.

As I pulled myself up on the tube, I heard Juliet screaming, "Sue, pull me in, pull me in!"

I had flung Juliet off my back and into the river. She was now desperately clinging to the grab line on the side of the raft, her eyes bulging in terror. As our raft careened into the screaming left turn, I grabbed the shoulder straps of Juliet's life jacket and yanked her in—just before the side of the raft slammed into the rocks along the right bank.

At almost the same instant, I saw Beth leap into the raft from the shore, holding her paddle like Wonder Woman with a spear as the raft ricocheted off the rocks. I had a brief moment to marvel—*Beth !?! Where the f . . . ?*—before we all scrambled into our seats and paddled as if our lives depended on it. Powerful and in sync, we clawed our way back to the center of the rapid, narrowly avoiding the rock garden of death.

After catching an eddy at the bottom of the rapid, we burst into exultant high-fiving, cussing, and hysterical laughter.

Brooke jumped out of the raft onshore and held the bowline. I gazed upriver, awed by the gradient of the frothing, toothy whitewater we had just, miraculously, survived completely unscathed.

After we had calmed down some, Kelly said, "Well, I don't think we could possibly have had a worse run. It can only get better."

"I hope so." Beth shook her head. "I don't want to go through that again."

"Hey, just where in the hell did you come from, Beth?" I exclaimed. "That was some kind of goddamn miracle!"

"No shit," she said. "I thought I was fucked. But one of the

Strength through Vulnerability (1999)

Oregon boys was right there when I came by the right bank, and he hit me dead-on with the throw bag. When I got out, I watched the whole thing. When you guys crawled out on the rock to get the raft loose, I thought for sure someone was going to get stranded."

"There was no friggin' way I was going to get left behind," Brooke said. "I just jumped."

Juliet laughed. "Yeah, we all did, but then Sue threw me back out!"

"Jeez, I'm really sorry," I said, chagrined. "But shit, you hit me like a ton of bricks. I was terrified about going through the rest of the rapid splatted on the floor of the raft. At least I got you in before you got crushed."

She rubbed the back of her neck and cast a look back up the rapids. "Yeah, but that was too damn close."

"I'm just glad you ladies are fit," Jules exclaimed. "It was amazing that we made that move to avoid the rock garden at the end."

"Well, I think that was our one fuck-up for this river," Kelley said. "If we got ourselves out of that mess, we can get out of anything."

For the rest of the run, we rode the wave of our endorphin adrenaline high, totally pumped up.

After recovering from such a disastrous situation, we were confident we could take whatever the river had to throw at us.

The team trials on Gore would determine which US teams would compete in the following year's world championships, to be held in February on the Futaleufú River in the Patagonia region of Chile. Over the next three days of competition, we would be competing against only three other women's teams. But we knew one of them was going to be tough. The Colorado women's team consisted of a group of uber-fit Colorado raft guides. They had

RISK

the added advantage of having several team members who guided Gore Canyon regularly.

Even so, in the first race, the head-to-head sprint, we quickly leaped out ahead of the Colorado team right off the start and never looked back.

After the sprint race was over, we paddled down the river to practice on the rapid where the slalom race was to be held the next day.

That is where the conflict began.

We had practiced slalom in the raft over the summer, but not nearly as much as I would have liked. After trying several seating configurations, we'd decided to keep me in the back of the boat with Jules for this race instead of moving me to the front like we had in previous competitions.

But this arrangement put Jules and me in a difficult position. With her superior raft guiding experience, Jules was the obvious person to lead when we were running challenging rapids. But because of her lack of slalom experience, she did not have as good a sense as I did for how and when to set boat angles to negotiate gates.

About two gates in on our first practice run, I started taking over, calling out the commands and initiating steering strokes to turn the raft.

By the time we pulled into an eddy at the bottom of the course, Jules was furious.

She turned to me, eyes blazing. "I can't paddle with you if you aren't going to trust me!"

She jumped out of the boat, slammed her paddle on the ground, and stomped off.

Shit, this is not good.

Jules was coming into this race in an emotionally fragile state. We'd had several conversations over the past year about some weighty issues that had recently emerged in her family. I knew

Strength through Vulnerability (1999)

she was dealing with a lot of delayed emotional fallout that had left her feeling ungrounded.

That's a tough enough place to be even in less intense circumstances. Being in a high-stakes competition in a high-stakes environment only upped the ante.

I looked around at my teammates and knew what they were thinking: I had to fix this, and quickly. We needed to be a team to safely make it down the river. We had yet to complete all the Class V rapids on this river, and we needed to do that before the day was over.

I got out of the raft, walked across a small strip of sandy beach, and began carefully stepping from rock to rock, navigating my way to the large flat-topped boulder where Jules sat a hundred feet away, her back to the river.

Jesus, how did she get so far so fast? She was fearless and nimble at rock hopping and had easily covered the ground to her chosen spot at twice my pace. *Well*, I thought, *this will give her time to calm down, I guess.*

I stopped a few yards from where she was sitting. "Jules, are you ready to talk to me yet?" I asked softly.

As she turned to look at me, I could see the glisten of tears in her eyes. "Yes. But what is it going to take for you to trust me?" Her voice was shaky. "You totally undermined me out there."

"I wasn't even thinking," I said. "I just started reacting. It has nothing to do with trust. There is no one I would rather have guiding this raft than you."

"But you need to communicate with me," she said, sliding off the rock to face me. "You can't just take over."

I thought about this for a moment. Kayak slalom was so much easier. Just one brain in one small, light, fast boat, solving the infinitely dynamic puzzle of the river. Integrating time to communicate with another person in the midst of all that was so much more challenging.

RISK

But she was right. I needed to communicate better with everyone on my team during slalom. Especially Jules, since we needed to work together in the back of the raft.

"You're right, and I'm sorry," I said. "I think the first thing we need to do is take more time onshore and really talk through our strategy so we are on the same page before we get on the water."

"Yes. Then we can figure out who will initiate turns for which gates." She squinted her eyes, thinking. "I guess you need to set the angles for left-hand turns, and I will control the right turns."

"Yeah, that makes sense . . . but are you okay with me saying something if I think you're missing the angle?"

"Yes, I just need you to talk to me."

"Okay, I can do that." I smiled. "We're just going to have to tell the rest of the crew not to pay attention while we work it out in the back of the boat."

She nodded her agreement.

"This is not going to be easy," I said, looking directly into her eyes. "Slalom is hard, and paddling on a team makes it even harder. But I literally trust you with my life. Please don't doubt that, even when we have disagreements."

In response, Jules reached out for a hug. Our lifejackets and helmets clashed together like armor as we squeezed each other tight.

"Okay," she said, "let's go tell everyone we're okay."

Our team broke out in smiles when they saw Jules and me approaching the boat with our arms slung around one another's shoulders.

"All right," Kelley said with relief, "you guys got that course figured out yet?"

"Not yet," I replied, "but let's all walk up and do it together. Jules and I have a plan."

Anything could happen on a river as brutal as Gore Canyon, but our confidence was high, based on our runs and races the previous

Strength through Vulnerability (1999)

couple of days. Working out our leadership dynamics resulted in another win for us in the slalom race. And our last run through the canyon, the downriver event, was almost perfect. After cutting a clean, precise line through Gore Rapid, we continued our dance with the river. We glided around the big hole in Scissors, plunged over Pyrite Falls, and then Tunnel Falls. We bobbed and weaved through Toilet Bowl and Kirshbaum, as well as the many unnamed Class IV rapids in between these Class V drops.

Julie's steering was not flawless, but it was close. She was confident in her commands. Her precise steering strokes set our angles without slowing the raft's momentum through oversteering or corrections.

And at the end of Kirshbaum, where the two-and-a-half-mile flatwater section began, we gave it everything we had. Reaching forward together, rotating our shoulders to plant our catch as far forward as possible, we strained to drive the raft forward. Engaging our abs, lats, and glutes to push off our wedged feet and pull the boat up to our paddle blades. Using every muscle to paddle as one organism—twelve arms, twelve legs, six bodies, working in unison.

The men's teams that had started and finished ahead of us cheered as we came across the finish line. Once the results were tabulated, we discovered our time was fast enough to beat over half the men's teams.

Climbing out of the boat, reality set in. I'd never have to run Gore Canyon again, thank God. And in February, six months from now, we would compete in the World Rafting Championship on the wild and beautiful Futaleufú River.

Settling into the trailer for our long drive home, every muscle in my body ached with fatigue. The lactic acid and adrenal overload from the past five days could no longer be ignored. It would take weeks to recover fully.

RISK

Beth was taking the first shift driving, and the rest of us secured various nooks in the trailer to cozy up in. Not for the first time, I was thankful for our slow but cushy ride as I fluffed up a pillow on the couch I'd made on one of the kitchen bench seats.

As I lay back with a book on my chest, I looked over at Jules on the bench seat across from me. "Well, I'm glad that's over with."

"Yeah, me too," she said with a wry grin.

"Are you okay? You know, with everything that's going on. At home, I mean."

"Yeah, yeah, it'll be okay." She sighed. "It's just something I need to work through."

"Just let me know, you know . . . if you need anyone to talk to about it."

"Yeah, I will. And . . . Thanks, Sue, for supporting me. It means a lot."

"Me too, Jules. We couldn't do any of this without you . . . without all of us."

This race had put stress on our team that was more than physical. This was not the first time we had to face danger as a team. But for me, at least, the emotional stress had been higher than ever before in this competition. Partly because the nature of the river, with its sharp rocks and steep hydraulics, was more threatening than most rivers. But also because my awareness of Jules's emotional fragility had heightened my sense of danger. Jules was dealing with a severe breach of trust within her family—so trust, right now, was her vulnerability with everyone she was close to. Paddling in such a threatening environment, we were deeply dependent on each other. If one of us was compromised, the whole team was compromised.

Ultimately, our team had successfully met the river's physical challenges, and Jules and I had overcome our personal conflict. I was grateful she had shared enough of what was going on in her

Strength through Vulnerability (1999)

life so that I'd been able to understand what was really behind her anger that day on the river—knowing that it was at least partially fueled by pain she was feeling outside of our relationship.

As strong as our friendships and teamwork were, it was hard for us to show each other our vulnerabilities on the river, a time and place where it felt like there was no room for weakness. There was tremendous pressure to be strong, both physically and mentally, and not let the team down when we were paddling together. And at the time, none of us were evolved enough to fully understand that sharing our vulnerabilities could make us even stronger.

But I don't blame myself, or my team, or expect that we could have been different. We were products of the society and culture we'd been brought up in, taught to associate vulnerability with shame and weakness.

It would take greater challenges than racing a raft in Class V whitewater to show me the power of embracing vulnerability. It would never come easy for me. To this day, in fact, it's a thing I still often fight against tooth and nail.

But it's also a skill I've found essential for survival.

Chapter 23
Building Resiliency (2018)

When my phone rings at 12:30 p.m. on a school day, my chest constricts as soon as I see the number on my phone. Damn it. Truckee Elementary School, again.

I pick up the phone, gritting my teeth.

"Hi, Sue, this Sarah D. First let me tell you Seth is okay..."

The conversations with the vice principal always start out like this. This is not going to be a good call.

"... but he was involved in a little incident on the playground."

"Oh no. What happened?"

"Well, there was a disagreement about the rules for four square, and Seth got angry."

I pinch the bridge of my nose. "I'm so sorry. What did he do this time?"

"Well . . . words were exchanged, and Seth punched a kid in the chest and used some inappropriate language."

"Oh." My face flushes. Whatever words he used, he most likely heard from me.

"So, Seth is going to spend some time with me this afternoon instead of going back to class. Kelly, the school psychologist, is also going to check in with him. She has been working really hard with Seth on tools he can use to ask for help when he needs it."

Building Resiliency (2018)

"Okay, thanks for letting me know, Sarah. I will follow up at home."

For Seth's third-grade Behavior Improvement Plan (BIP), the school staff and I have agreed to work together to follow up on incidents like these.

Sarah and Kelly talk to Seth about better choices he can make when he gets frustrated or angry—for example, while playing the four square game he loves so much, but which so frequently leads to him losing his mind.

My job is to follow up at home, reinforcing the "better choices" messaging and enforcing the consequences for his actions. The severity of these consequences depends on the degree of physical violence and cussing he's employed, but always involves some combination of loss of electronic time and dessert.

I spend the rest of the day mired in low-level anxiety and irritability, dreading the confrontation that will come when Seth steps off the bus. At this point, he has even been put on a special bus with other kids afflicted with various forms of disability that prevent them from riding the regular school bus. In Seth's case, his disability is the frequency with which he gets in fights with other kids on the fifteen-minute bus ride between home and school.

When Seth walks into the house, I am ready with a snack on the counter—crackers and cheese and baby carrots with ranch dressing. He begins snarfing immediately. Since the ADHD medication he is on suppresses his appetite, he usually does not eat much for lunch and is ravenous by the time he gets home.

I hate giving him the medication, but his behavior at school is even more disruptive when he is not on it. Today's altercation occurred during morning recess, just after taking his meds at ten thirty. The meds are supposed to stimulate frontal lobe brain activity, the place where better choices live. Possibly the incident

RISK

occurred because the medication had not kicked in yet. Or, just as likely, the perceived grievance simply overpowered any benefit the meds are supposed to provide.

Once he is done with his snack, I begin in a voice I hope conveys calm, "So, Seth, we need to talk about what happened at morning recess today. Can you tell me what happened?"

Immediately his big brown eyes widen, and his voice rises in volume and tenor. "Well, it wasn't my fault. They were being mean to me!"

"Okay . . . " I'm still trying to keep my voice neutral. "How were they being mean?"

"Well, they said the ball went over the line and I had to leave, but I had just gotten in."

"Uh-huh . . . so Seth, did the ball go over the line?"

My question to Seth just enrages him even more. I am clearly not on his side in this.

"I don't know! It just isn't fair!" he screeches. "I didn't even get a chance to play! Everyone should get a second chance."

I have never played four square, and my understanding of the rules is shaky. I know a box with four equal squares is chalked on the pavement. The four kids in play bounce a rubber ball into each other's squares, trying to hit it hard enough so the receiving kid either misses the ball or hits it in a way that sends the ball soaring out of the box without bouncing into another square first. When this happens, that kid must leave the game and go back to the end of the line of children waiting to play.

Because Seth's hand-eye coordination and reaction time are not on par with that of many of his peers, he probably could not engage in a more frustrating activity. But he loves four square, and every recess, he races to get in line to play.

Part of me agrees with Seth, and I wish the school could segregate kids into playgroups based on ability. But not only do they not have the resources to do this, it also isn't going to help Seth

Building Resiliency (2018)

navigate the real world. A world in which the less talented, the weaker, are destined to lose.

As we engage in minutes of circular conversation regarding who did what and how it would be hard to play a game if the rules were not consistent, Seth becomes increasingly irritated by my lack of sympathy for how unfairly he was treated.

And now, without clearly laying down a foundation of empathy for the injustice he has endured, I make the mistake of moving on to the subject of consequences.

"Well, Seth, you know if you had just cussed and walked away, you would have only lost dessert," I say. "But since you hit Santi, you cannot have your hour of tablet time today, or your iPod."

At this, Seth's face crumples into a rictus of outrage. "That isn't fair!" he screams. "It was their fault they made me mad!"

He leaps off his stool, stomps over to an intricate castle he made from magnet tiles in front of the gas stove last night, and kicks it, sending the colorful geometric squares and triangles of plastic tile clattering and skittering across the hardwood floor.

Maddie leaps up from her bed and scuttles into the bedroom.

At this, my reptilian brain takes over and my body surges with adrenaline and rage. Even though some dim part of me knows I have now officially lost control of the situation and nothing positive will come from this, I cannot stop myself. I stride over to Seth, lean into his face, and bellow, "Pick that up, you little jerk!"

"No, *you're* the jerk, and what you say is what you are!" Seth screams back, shoving me in the stomach with his hands.

I reach over and grab him by the shoulders, implementing my form of the Vulcan death grip. Squeezing as hard as I can, my thumbs pressing into the soft tissue of his shoulders, I screech, "GO TO YOUR ROOM, GODDAMN IT!"

When I release his shoulders, he runs downstairs, wailing and slamming doors.

RISK

I stand there for a moment, shaking, knowing I have once again messed up a learning opportunity.

Why does he get so angry? Why do I get so angry? Where is this all coming from? Adrenaline courses through my body; my brain whirls from its intensity.

I do not consider myself by nature to be an angry person, and I would define myself as a conflict-averse personality. There was very little yelling in our family growing up. My dad was not a shouter. Although I pouted for sure and did more than my share of whining, I never raised my voice to my father. I also did not yell at my brother in that way, although I often verbally bullied him in an unattractive passive-aggressive manner.

This rage between me and Seth is a dynamic I have never experienced with another human being before. I hate it.

And yet the physical feeling pumping through my body is not entirely unfamiliar. It's the same way I used to feel above a Class V rapid or behind the start line of a race. I often channeled that adrenaline-fueled energy into a form of rage, gritting my teeth and telling myself, *Attack, be strong, damn it, attack, attack, don't be afraid, you can do this.*

Peeling out of an eddy or bursting across a start line, I gladly let the reptilian brain take over, allowing my brain to use all my training and skill development to navigate the rapid and the racecourse. And regardless of what happened—whether I won or lost, whether I got through the rapid cleanly or survived whitewater carnage—there was a release at the end. The battle had been fought, and it was over. Sure, if the outcome was not good, there would be a lingering residue of disappointment. But that soon wore off, and the world could soon be brought back into perspective.

This interpersonal dynamic I am navigating with Seth feels different. It's like I'm running a Class V rapid with a boat and paddle that don't fit. And unlike on a river, where my understanding

Building Resiliency (2018)

of currents and hydraulics is primarily second nature, I do not recognize the obstacles in front of me. Consequently, I keep falling into a recirculating hydraulic of anger, thrashing and bouncing out of control.

Trying to parent Seth to address his lack of impulse control makes me feel weak. Without the knowledge and skills to channel it into something positive, the adrenaline I have used so often in my life to overcome challenges has become a toxic poison.

Fortunately, Seth usually comes down from his rages very quickly. His brain typically resets within five or ten minutes. When he comes back upstairs, he's calm and ready for a hug.

I'm still jittery, but his ability to reset helps me to calm down.

"I'm sorry I got so angry, Seth, and I'm sorry if I hurt you," I say gently. "Here, do you want me to help you build your castle again?"

"That's okay," he replies as he releases his hug and sits down in front of his tiles. "I can do it."

We have never gone to bed at night angry with each other.

But I often go to bed fearful that my inability to control my anger will continue to hold him back in learning how to control his. This is a fear I have never experienced before. Neither the internal fears and insecurities I experienced growing up nor the gut-churning challenges I faced in my sport ever resulted in this level of terror.

The terror of causing damage to another human being. An already damaged human that I am now responsible for.

This is a fear that will not subside at the end of the day or even a week. This challenge will last for the rest of my time as a parent. And that is going to be a very long time.

"This is the class I think might help you learn some tools we have been talking about," Tim says as he holds out a pamphlet.

RISK

I strain to lean forward from his soft, saggy couch to grasp the piece of paper and sink back into the cushions. Scanning the "Loving Solutions" brochure, I am dismayed to see the course involves five consecutive Mondays of two-hour classes—more precious time taken away from doing the things I really want to do.

"Oh, that's a lot of time," I said.

"Yes." Tim chuckles. "But after all, this is going to take time."

A soft-spoken man with rapidly thinning hair and a rumpled sense of style, Tim is the counselor I have been working with for over a year through Nevada County Family Services. I quickly learned after our first couple of meetings that Seth was not going to acquire the skills he needs from Tim's counseling. Instead, these sessions are to help me gain the skills *I* need to parent Seth.

I am also slowly realizing that this will involve fundamentally changing core habits and consciousness around conflict and confrontation. Skills I will need for the rest of my life as Seth's parent.

Before Seth came along, I thought I had strong communication skills, especially under conditions of stress. Skills I initially developed with my often fiery-tempered raft team. Over the past fifteen years, my communication skills have also been refined as I've moved up a chain of supervisory positions at work.

When Seth moved in with me, I was the first line supervisor of almost fifteen employees in our Physical Sciences Group—a mix of hydrologists, soil scientists, and civil engineers. Over the years, I'd learned many techniques to manage their individual strengths and challenges and address my own communication style deficiencies when establishing expectations. I had successfully worked through several hairy conflict resolutions with and between some of my employees. Situations that required me to engage in some of the most challenging conversations I had experienced in my life.

I thought I had grown so much, become so much wiser about human interactions.

Building Resiliency (2018)

But I am finding those skills amount to diddly-squat when it comes to parenting Seth.

On the first day of class, the instructor hands out the course workbook, *Loving Solutions: A Parent's Guide to Raising Tough Kids (Special Applications to ADD/ADHD Kids)*. The title seems promising, at least.

The role-playing I participate in with two other couples and the course instructor is awkward and sometimes ridiculous. It is hard to embrace the six-step—for the love of God, *six-step*—process to communicate with our "tough" children through episodes of unwanted behavior.

The steps of the "I Love Messages" communication process are:

> I LOVE – tell the child how much you love them.
> I SEE – describe specific observable unwanted behavior.
> I FEEL – tell the child how you feel about their behavior.
> LISTEN – listen to your child's response (no matter how freaking awful it is, just listen).
> I WANT – restate the family rule regarding the behavior.
> I WILL – tell what you will do to support their success, including both consequences and incentives.

Christ. How in the world am I ever going to get through all that whenever Seth is throwing a fit?

I realize a significant character flaw I have in parenting Seth is my impatience. I have never been a patient person. In fact, attempting to be patient makes me *very* irritated. Through my job as a supervisor, I discovered that I tended to be judgmental about colleagues that I perceived as inefficient, frequently wrong, or lazy. I prided myself on my ability to figure out ways to cut through the bullshit and get tasks done faster and better—at least in my opinion.

My almost competitive approach to work was fine when the task I was knocking out was an individual task; in fact, I received plenty of accolades for those efforts. But over time, I had to learn to slow down my impatient, competitive tendencies to work more productively in a team environment.

However, this in no way prepared me for the level of patience I need in applying the six-step Loving Solutions process when Seth refuses to learn how to tie his shoes, doesn't want to do his schoolwork, or gets in peer-to-peer conflicts.

I realize I've been interpreting much of Seth's behavior as laziness and a "bad" attitude—an overly severe reaction, and one deeply rooted in my judgments regarding David's lack of success in life. This is why I get so triggered into anger when I feel Seth is failing to learn how to do a task, complete a job, or make better choices.

Although David has never been formally assessed or diagnosed, his inability to communicate effectively with others has me convinced that he's on the autism spectrum. And between his hoarding tendencies and his chronic pattern of starting projects he never finishes, he may also have ADHD. But he has never received professional counseling on understanding or managing an atypical brain. The counselors David has seen have treated him for depression and alcoholism, advised him to take anti-depressants and go to AA. But I don't believe he's ever gotten any support to address the underlying conditions that have likely contributed to his depression and alcoholism.

I also understand from my conversations with Seth's birth mom, Gesi, that she has been diagnosed with bipolar disorder and that her mother was institutionalized because of mental illness and severe addiction.

Building Resiliency (2018)

Who knows what genetic soup Seth's brain might be developing in?

The thought that he might be tripping down the same path to adulthood his dad or his birth mom traveled terrifies me, and I am projecting upon everything he does through that negative lens. *Loving Solutions* says that although much is unknown about ADHD, research indicates a strong genetic component. So it is likely that, regarding how Seth's brain is wired, he was born this way. The book also says that ADHD is not a condition people can outgrow; it's a condition they have to learn to manage. But it also provided an impressive list of past famous and successful figures that appeared to have behavioral characteristics associated with ADHD/ADD, including Beethoven, Leonardo da Vinci, John F. Kennedy, Winston Churchill, Jules Verne, and Charles Schwab, to name just a few.

The crushing weight of my responsibility is bearing down on me. Although there is nothing I can do about the state of Seth's brain development before he came to live with me, I am certainly in a position to do more harm. In fact, I am likely to be the most influential person in his young life. I can provide him with a chance to adapt to and learn to control his behavior. Or I can make it much, much worse.

I need a basic understanding regarding his lack of impulse control, oppositional defiance behavior, anger related to ADHD, and other lurking atypical brain functions yet to be fully understood. I need to provide the support and structure he needs to manage and redirect his behaviors toward positive rather than destructive outcomes.

I am hopeful that exposing Seth to my passions—spending time in nature engaged in a variety of outdoor adventures—can be a solid foundation to provide that support. But I also know this might not have the same positive impact on him that it did on me. It certainly didn't work for David.

RISK

Seth is his own person, unlike either David, his birth mom, or me. As this strong-willed, joyful, and tempestuous creature continues to grow, we are going to need to keep exploring—discovering the passions that will provide him with his personal foundation of resiliency.

I also am not going to figure this out on my own. Through counseling, classes, and books, I will need to learn how to manage Seth's unique and potentially destructive superpower. I am now retired, no longer responsible for supervising a large and complex staff. My only job now is to figure out how to communicate effectively with one "tough" kid.

My most challenging job yet.

Chapter 24
Fragility (2018–2019)

Our small room in a rustic lodge in Argentina has just enough floor space for two people to do mobility exercises, so we're taking turns. I relax on one of the three single beds while Juliet smashes her glutes on the lacrosse ball and Beth works her back on a foam roller. We are all in our jammies. Jules is sharing the room next door with her partner, Abi. She is so damn tough; she probably doesn't have to do any of the daily physical therapy the rest of us require.

After almost two decades, our California-based US women's team has been coaxed out of retirement by the International Rafting Federation to fill out a master's women's category in the 2018 World Whitewater Rafting Championships in Patagonia. It is November, and the weather and water have been cold. At the end of every day, we are tired and sore in ways we did not experience twenty years ago. Worn joints and past soft tissue injuries require daily management.

No one has any visible gray hair yet, although two of us are using hair dye for that. Juliet of course is not, since she is ten to fifteen years younger than the rest of us. But she has had one hip surgery already and a bout with thyroid cancer. Beth has not had a knee replacement surgery yet but is scheduled for one soon after

RISK

we return. Her shoulder is better than it was twenty years ago but still requires constant maintenance, and she has a new injury, too—a fractured sacrum, incurred by a nasty fall.

At sixty-two, I am holding up well but am very aware that my recovery time from physical efforts is dramatically slower than it used to be. I need more rest in between hard physical efforts and know the demands of the six days of continuous racing and practicing is going to be tough. I also just don't have the raw physical power I had in my forties.

The invite to the 2018 Worlds appealed to us partly because of the location, a beautiful and remote nascent resort area in the Patagonia region of Argentina. We also looked forward to having an adventure together again after two decades of pursuing careers, child-rearing, body-part failures and rehab, periods of marital struggles and breakups, and other emotional and physical travails. We thought it would be fun to compete here, in a relatively non-competitive master's division and on less extreme whitewater than the Class V rivers we used to take on.

It is a great feeling to be paddling together again, and we all feel good about how strong we are, considering.

But we also feel the dark space surrounding who is not here: Kelley.

I stayed closely connected to Kelley after we stopped racing rafts, mostly because we had both jumped, all-in, to outrigger canoeing. We shared a mutual passion for the ocean and were part of the same Northern California outrigger canoeing community. Kelley was equally as impressive at outrigger as she was at rafting, and she quickly became one of the strongest women within the circuit. We paddled on many crews together at races throughout California and Hawaii, and sometimes on crews racing against each other. For many years she showed up in my life, whether it was setting the pace in the canoe from seat one, swapping stories and drinking beer together after races, helping me install Pergo

Fragility (2018–2019)

flooring in my house, or leading my dream trip down the Grand Canyon. Kelley was simply one of those friends who participated in so many aspects of my life—a sister.

But on my fiftieth birthday in 2007, my friend who was always there for me called to say she couldn't make it to the big weekend-long celebration. She was experiencing debilitating pain in her upper legs and abdomen, and the doctor who initially examined her had diagnosed the likely problem as an ovarian cyst. She was going in for emergency surgery.

But two days later, when she came out of the surgery, Kelley was paralyzed.

They started doing more tests. Within days we learned that, in a bizarre coincidence, Kelley had developed a rare condition called transverse myelitis: a sudden inflammation of the spinal cord, usually caused by an unknown virus. Two months later we discovered that in her case the TM inflammation had resulted from an even more rare cause, schistosomiasis. The schisto parasite had likely entered her body six years earlier while she was rowing support for a source-to-sea rafting expedition on the Blue Nile River and lain dormant all that time.

Kelley, one of the most adventurous and athletically gifted women I have ever known, has been paralyzed from the waist down since 2007, and she suffers daily from the most debilitating nerve pain imaginable.

Here in Argentina, missing her, I continue to grieve her suffering and all that she has lost. And also what I have lost.

Kelley is still a close friend, and we talk and visit regularly. But the images of what could have been if she had not gotten sick never leave my imagination. Especially when I am on the water.

The river and locale in Argentina are just as beautiful as we imagined, but we soon find out we've underestimated the river's challenge, and the competition.

RISK

Although the rapids are only rated Class III–IV difficulty, the downriver course is located just below the outlet of a vast alpine lake very much like Lake Tahoe, and the gradient and rapids never let up. The five-mile course is basically one continuous rapid, and we find it virtually impossible to memorize lines. Our few practice runs are hectic, requiring last-minute decisions on where next to direct our boat at every turn. Swimming in the swift, rocky, icy cold water is hazardous in such continuous whitewater.

None of us expected to feel so challenged at this event. Although I know I'm in good shape compared to many women my age, I am also realistic about my diminished physical capabilities. I do not trust that I have the strength and endurance to swim to shore or pull myself on top of our raft if we flip, and Jules is very concerned about the new race rules that do not allow us to rig some of the safety lines we're used to using to pull ourselves into or on top of our boat.

After our first practice run, we all agree that if we had known the river was going to be this difficult, we wouldn't have chosen to come. Although we all are still very active and work out regularly, we also have significantly lowered the level of risk in our sports in recent years—a natural and healthy progression in the life of the aging athlete, as our own injuries and illnesses, as well as those of our peers, increase our awareness of the fragility of our bodies.

Also, our master's class (age forty and over) is way more competitive than we expected. The master's team from Norway, in particular, is formidable. The average age of their crew is about ten years younger than ours, and their average height is about four inches taller. They've come to this race searching for their first gold medal, not in the open division but in the master's class.

Having such intense competition in our master's class makes me question what I'm doing here. At age sixty-two, I am pretty sure I am the oldest competitor at this event.

Fragility (2018–2019)

After coming in second behind the Norwegian team in both the time trial and head-to-head sprints, suddenly, the race nerves come back as much as they ever did in my youth. No one on our team wants to settle for second place. This competition is no longer only about having a good time. It's about trying to win.

The slalom rapid is only Class II in difficulty, but there is a nasty four-foot drop into a powerful, river-wide hydraulic near the top of the course. And when we arrive on race morning, I discover that the final positions of the gates require moves that would not be easy in a slalom kayak. It is hard to imagine how we will make the maneuvers in a fourteen-foot raft.

Fortunately, our class is positioned after all the younger teams, so we have many opportunities to go to school on the boats competing ahead of us. We watch as crew after crew misses one or more gates on their first runs.

Our first run is also crap. Although we place second, behind the master's team from Slovenia, it is a miserable run with three missed gates. If we're going to do better on our second run, I know we must try something drastically different.

Standing by a difficult sequence of offset downstream gates before second runs, I say, "You know what, guys? I think we are going to intentionally skip one of these gates."

"Really?" Beth asks. "What about the penalty?"

"Well, I haven't seen more than a handful of the top men's teams make this sequence yet, and maybe only two women's open teams," I say. "And I have timed some of the boats. Even the teams making all these downstream gates are taking thirty seconds to ferry back and forth. And everyone going back for a missed gate is spending more than the fifty-second penalty to get there."

After watching several more teams and timing boats on my watch, everyone eventually agrees with my strategy. We will intentionally skip a gate in the hard-offset downstream sequence,

RISK

hopefully using the time gained and energy saved to our advantage for the remainder of the fifteen-gate course.

We just may have a shot at winning this thing.

Waiting at the top of the course for our second and final run, my race nerves are as fierce as they have ever been. After almost twenty years of hibernation, it all comes flooding back—the electricity running through my body, the sense of being in a time warp.

This is ridiculous, I chide myself, *why do you care? You are sixty-two years old; you are raising a child. You have nothing to prove in this arena, for God's sake.*

But old habits die hard, I guess. Sitting in the eddy above the start wand, my reptilian brain has taken over, and it is not going to listen to any reasoning on the matter.

We decided that because of the tight moves on this course, I can best lead our four-person raft from the front; that will allow for the extreme maneuvering required to negotiate the course. From this position, I can call out commands and set the boat angle with sweep-and-draw strokes in and out of the gates.

This strategy works great up to gate five, an upstream gate located just below the steep four-foot drop. But pulling out of five, I realize we've come through the gate too fast and are not going to be able to avoid getting sucked back into the hydraulic at the bottom of the drop as we try to ferry to gate six on the other side of the river.

We've seen many boats flip upstream and/or lose paddlers in this hydraulic after making the same mistake.

Sitting front left, I am on the upstream side of the raft for this maneuver, so there is nothing I can do except get my ass off the tube and throw my body across the thwart to try to move weight to the downstream side.

Beth is doing the same in the back left, while Jules and Juliet

Fragility (2018–2019)

are on their own on the right side to surf us across the hydraulic and somehow pull us out. I watch helplessly from my position straddled over the thwart as Juliet furiously pulls us across the seething hydraulic. Climbing up over the edge at the end seems impossible, but I watch her kick into yet another gear—and inch by inch, with her truly herculean paddling, aided by an equal effort from Jules right behind her, we slowly eke out of the hydraulic.

Once we're finally clear of the hydraulic, Beth and I jump back into our seats and sprint with our teammates for all we're worth. If we miss the eddy below gate six like we've seen many other teams do, we'll blow by three gates in a few seconds' time, and our race will be over.

We barely make it into the eddy, but we do it.

Pulling up through gate six, I know this is our frickin' chance!

By skipping gate eight, as planned, we easily negotiate the following two downstream gates, seven and nine. With surging adrenaline, we power over to the next upstream gate, gate ten, and enter it fast and clean, passing the raft under the inside pole just in front of my chest. It is a sweet move, and my confidence surges. We are paddling like a team, and we can all feel it.

Crossing the finish line, we know we've nailed it—know this is the best we were capable of—and the feeling is as delicious as it has ever been.

We win the race in the master's category, and our score is the fifth best time out of all twenty-four women's teams competing at the event. But more importantly, the Norwegians come in last in our category. Although they have substantially more strength and endurance than we do, they did not practice slalom at home and no one on their team has a kayak slalom background—and it shows.

Although the Norwegians beat us in the two races before this, our slalom win is huge. With the weighted points per event in the overall scoring system, we now at least have a shot at staying in the competition against this more powerful team.

RISK

Today, in the downriver event, the Norwegian team quickly reestablishes itself as the superior force in our class. This is the final event in our four days of competition, and it is worth the most points.

Within minutes of the start, they quickly pull ahead, their paddle strokes in perfect unison. In the lead before even entering the first rapid, they never look back. We are simply outgunned.

Crossing the finish line of the downriver race in second place, we resign ourselves to having lost the competition to the better team and paddle over to congratulate the Norwegian ladies.

The weather is bitterly cold today; there were even some snow flurries while we were waiting at the start. I've just pulled off my frigid neoprene pants and booties in the ladies' tent when I hear the loudspeakers announcing something about our team in Spanish.

I turn to Beth, a proficient Spanish speaker, and ask, "What did they say?"

Her forehead wrinkles. "Well, I don't understand, but they just said that we won."

A minute later, the message is repeated in English, and I hear the excited chatter from the booth across from ours, where the Norwegians are all changing, go silent.

After changing, we stand around the posted scoring sheets, which display the cumulative scores over the four events. They show that the Norwegians and our team are in a dead tie, each team scoring precisely 930 points.

I am confused. The Norwegians beat us in three out of four events, and they won the downriver race, which has traditionally been used to determine tiebreakers. There has to be some sort of mix-up here.

Fragility (2018–2019)

We finally find a race official to confirm what's happened. They explain that the scoring rules have changed since we last competed in an international rafting competition. According to the new regulations, in the case of a tie after adding up total points from the four events, because the slalom is considered the most technically challenging event in the competition, the winner is decided by who's placed best in that event.

It doesn't feel quite right, and I feel terrible for the Norwegian ladies. They put in so much work preparing for this race, and they soundly outpaddled us in three out of four events. But they are a class act and graciously share heartfelt hugs with us on the podium that night.

I embrace our unexpected win and pose for many photos holding the US flag, my medal around my neck. But I am glad it's over.

Throughout this event, I haven't been able to shake the feeling that as much as I'm enjoying spending time with my teammates and seeing a new part of the world on a beautiful river again, this is no longer where I belong.

I feel physically vulnerable in a way I did not when I was younger, even during our most challenging races. In addition to the stresses on the water, enduring the long waits for shuttle buses, standing around in the cold, eating dinners too late, and not getting enough sleep all make me anxious about my ability to manage the next day.

It feels a little ridiculous to put myself through so much discomfort, and this is a level of risk I no longer want to engage in. My old competitive instincts still kick in, yes, but now it all feels a little foolish. What does it really matter how we place?

Watching the younger teams, especially the U19 teams, I feel this is who the competition experience is really for. The next generation. The skill and heart displayed by these young teams has been thrilling to watch.

But why, I wonder, *is there no U19 team from the USA?*

On the flight home, I continue to reflect on how much the sport has evolved since I actively competed twenty years ago and how cool it would be to develop a team of young paddlers from my community.

I have become acquainted with several paddling families in the Truckee area through a watershed education program called the Truckee River Source to Sea Educational Paddling Adventure that I organized last year and this year. I led a group of middle school kids on paddles through different sections of the Truckee River, from its source above Lake Tahoe to its terminus at Pyramid Lake, Nevada, teaching the kids paddling skills and about the various uses of water and river ecology in their backyard watershed.

Many of the kids who participated in the program are second-generation paddlers who have grown up river rafting with their families. Would any of these bright, engaged budding river advocates like to see what raft racing is all about?

The answer, I'll soon discover, is yes.

In the spring of 2019, I begin coaching an evolving group of young paddlers between fourteen and eighteen years old in raft racing.

It feels good to give back, to pass on what was given to me when I was young. To provide support and encouragement to new generations pursuing a passion for this unique and dynamic sport.

An extreme adventure sport, whitewater rafting competition is still on the fringes. For many reasons, it will never be mainstream, even though the International Rafting Federation (IRF) membership includes national rafting organizations from fifty-four countries, and the connections and cultural exchange

Fragility (2018–2019)

from IRF programs and international rafting competitions have resulted in the growth of commercial rafting operations, youth paddler development, and river advocacy around the globe.

I see the young people I coach, especially the young women, find and grow into their power on the river—experiencing both power within themselves and power with others when paddling with their teammates. The same way I did.

Sometimes, when there is no one else to watch him, Seth, now nine, accompanies me during my coaching sessions. I doubt that he will ever want to compete or be coached by me, as he never expresses interest in it. But I think he respects what I do.

He is shy around these older kids, but he enjoys tagging along on the river and watching the head-to-head training.

Standing on the shore next to me while I am taking video, he cheers, "Go girls! GO, GO, GO!" as he watches the girls race the boys' team in a head-to-head sprint.

When they are on their line, as they are today, they sometimes win.

They do today, and Seth hoots and cheers, "YEAH GIRLS! GIRLS RULE! BOYS DROOL!" Then he turns to me. "Can I take the video next time?"

"Sure," I say, handing him my phone. "Just try and get some of the boys' team too."

I am not sure why he is cheering for the girls, exactly. It may be because he understands they are the underdogs in terms of physical strength, as I have explained to him that women often have to learn better technique and skills in order to keep up with the men.

I also believe he has crushes on almost all of them. I hope that what he sees when he looks at them is strong young women to be admired and respected.

As a facilitator for an evolving relationship with the river and paddle sport to a new generation, including my son, my current

RISK

role provides me the joy and grounding that I have always found in my sport. I don't pretend to know exactly where it will lead, but I am confident that my connection to the river will continue to provide.

Chapter 25
Bad Risk and Good Risk
(2018–2020)

Seth lines up his kayak above Old Scary and paddles the way I have shown him. His arms are straight, and he drives his paddle firmly into the water with each stroke. His little orange kayak bobs over the waves like a cork.

I hold my breath as he enters the hole. The mass of whitewater looks big framed against his eight-year-old body, and for a moment I can only see the top of his helmet.

He pops out the other side, a big grin on his face.

Whew, he didn't flip. Although Old Scary is only a Class II rapid on our backyard beginner run on the South Fork of the American River, rescue is problematic because it is a long rapid, and the big hydraulic Seth just navigated is located on the upper third.

One of the other kids is not so lucky. Following close behind Seth, Hazel's green kayak flips upside down in the hydraulic.

"Seth, paddle over to the eddy on the right!" I yell over my shoulder as I paddle toward Hazel.

Seth turns upstream and angles his boat toward the shore, executing what is known as a ferry. By successfully navigating into the eddy, he has kept himself from going downstream through the rest of the rapid.

RISK

We have one adult for each child in our six-person flotilla. Shauna, Hazel's mom, and I focus on rescuing Hazel and her gear while John hangs with Seth and Adam in the eddy.

After pulling Hazel and her paddle to shore, I paddle back upriver to Seth and the others to help escort him back into the current.

"Can we go now? I'm tired of waiting," Seth whines.

"Can't you see Shauna is still emptying Hazel's kayak?" I reply.

"Yeah, but why can't *we* go?"

"Seth, that's not safe," I say firmly. "We aren't going until everyone is ready. Just hold on."

I know what he is thinking about. It's not that he is eager to keep kayaking. He wants his ice cream.

Seth's paddling skills are decent, better than most his age. Since he never seems to respond directly to my instructions, I credit this ability to his watching me over the last four years. But he's not really very interested in kayaking. The only way I can get him to go is with bribes of ice cream afterward.

I tend to think it's because he's afraid. Totally understandable, although I have been conscientious about not pushing him too hard and he has never taken a bad swim. I hope that, over time, he will grow more confident and start enjoying the sport.

It takes a couple more years for him to make his position clear.

"Hey Seth," I say one day to my now ten-year-old son, "Stacy and her kids are coming up to paddle with us this weekend. Do you want to kayak or riverboard tomorrow?"

"Mom!" he replies, his tone frustrated. "I'm not a kayaker. I'm a riverboarder."

"Oh," I say. "So, you don't want to kayak again?"

"No, not really."

"Okay . . . Can you tell me why?" I prod. "Is it too scary?

Bad Risk and Good Risk (2018–2020)

Because once you learn how to do an Eskimo roll, it gets a lot less difficult."

"No, no, that's not it," he says. "I just like being *in* the water instead of on it. I like how it feels."

Suddenly, I get it. It's not fear or rebellion. It's sensory. My ADHD, sometimes hypersensitive-to-stimuli kid loves riverboarding and swimming, jumping in the waves in the ocean for hours on end, simply because he loves the feel of the water on his body.

Riverboarding is similar to ocean boogie boarding. The swim fins are the same. A riverboard is just a bit longer and thicker and has handles attached to its surface for hanging on to.

Seth was introduced to this fringe sport through my former rafting teammate, Jules Munger, a pioneer in riverboarding.

Jules and two of our other teammates, Kelley Kalafatich and Rebecca Rusch, made the first self-supported riverboard descent of the Grand Canyon, captured in an award-winning documentary called *Three Women, Three Hundred Miles*. This incredible feat was even more remarkable because they did it in December, when the days were short and cold.

Riverboarding can be challenging in rocky technical rivers in terms of bashing knees and ankles. But on many rivers, if you have a strong kick, it's easier to learn than kayaking. You can't really flip, and you always have flotation to keep you from getting sucked under by river currents if you keep a hold on at least one of the handles. Because I am not a good swimmer, I've never been drawn to it. My couple of attempts at it confirmed that I pretty much sucked, and I gave up on it.

But Jules has introduced riverboarding to all the children raised by our former raft team, and many of them love it.

I am not sure how Seth became a strong swimmer, since he never seemed to listen to the instructor during his swim classes. In fact, he got kicked out of his last course for being so distracting

RISK

to the other students. But any chance he gets, he is in the water—whether it is in the pool, our pond, or any section of a river that allows for swimming.

When Jules introduced Seth to riverboarding, I was amazed by how strong he was in the water. I had brought an inflatable kayak with me because we were running a more challenging section of the river, with numerous Class III rapids, and although Seth had rafted that section with me many times, he couldn't have kayaked it on his own. I assumed I would need to put him in the inflatable with me for most of the way.

I was wrong.

Although he was the youngest and smallest of the kids, he moved his board across the currents and around every obstacle like a pro. From our other river exploits, he had developed a strong ability to read the water. He also knew how to edge his board in the currents, and his swim kick was powerful. Although I made him come in the inflatable kayak for a few of the more demanding Class III rapids, he did most of the twelve miles of river that day on his own.

And he loved it.

I marvel at his comfort in the water, so different from me. From my earliest memories of capsizing in rivers, I have never been comfortable in the water without a watercraft. I am better now, in the ocean and in lakes. But in the river? Forget it. I want to be in a boat—any kind of boat.

I realize now, having this conversation with Seth, that his preference for riverboarding is a clear message: he is different from me, with other skills and likes. And I need to pay attention.

The truth is, for me, this is the best scenario. I certainly do not want to get back into whitewater kayaking again in a big way. That part of my life is behind me. If Seth did decide to become a kayaker, I would have to quickly farm him off to other people. But with him being a more freewheeling water kid, I can spend

Bad Risk and Good Risk (2018–2020)

more of my time as a parent with him pursuing the ocean-based sports I'm now into. And when we do go on the river, especially during the multiday river trips we do at least once a year, he can either raft or riverboard. As long as he can get in the water and swim, he will be happy.

And, with his evident passion for being in the water, riverboarding can be the medium I use to provide him with "good risk."

From my years of counseling with Seth, I have learned that kids with ADHD are more prone to addiction than other children. One of Seth's counselors explained that although on some level all kids can easily fall into addiction if left to their own devices, ADHD kids, because of delayed frontal lobe development, are even less able to modulate and moderate than other children.

The parental responsibility of helping children make good choices and control unhealthy behaviors begins when they are toddlers and never ends. Addictions in early childhood, such as electronics and sugar, have a firmer grip on ADHD kids, and are therefore more likely to evolve into drug or alcohol addictions as they get older.

When I learned of this particular challenge for a child with ADHD, I decided to try to offset this tendency by fostering a healthy addiction to "good risk."

Of course, I can also provide opportunities for healthy addictions that do not involve risk, like art and music or other creative endeavors. But based on my own childhood experience, I feel adventure sports, with the challenges they present, can offer something more. They help build confidence; they serve as an outlet for Seth's sometimes boundless energy; and they offer opportunities to find harmony with nature, even in its more formidable forms.

Canoeing, kayaking, and camping on rivers with my dad profoundly impacted me growing up. I am still learning and pondering the complexity with which immersion in nature can affect the psyche, how these experiences can build resiliency and

RISK

provide grounding. How time in the natural world can heal and restore. I want to introduce Seth to these same experiences, and at the same time discover *his* passions, those things in life that will help him thrive.

Seth first learns to riverboard during the COVID summer of 2020. The summer when all organized kid sports and camps are essentially canceled. The silver lining to that reality is that more families are out paddling with their kids on the South Fork of the American, our backyard river, than I have ever seen before.

This summer, the river is where many in the greater paddling family choose to escape their isolation, seeking both community and recreation. Paddling provides a relatively "normal" experience when many other aspects of American life have become inaccessible, overwhelming, surreal, and depressing.

We've spent almost every weekend this summer on the river.

Seth is usually the only kid on a riverboard, while the other kids obediently follow their parents' desires to introduce them to kayaking. Having Seth on his riverboard, a craft where he is almost entirely in control, means I am free to rescue the other kids when they capsize. I am the least stressed-out parent on the river. Besides never needing to be saved, Seth is so proficient in the water that he even helps with rescues, often snagging up loose paddles and bringing them to shore.

We had the fortune of being invited on a multiday river trip on the Main Salmon in Idaho this month. I've always wanted to float this classic section of wilderness river but have never been able to because of the competitive lottery permit system, so I'm thrilled to finally be here.

As a bonus, the trip leader is my old friend Dana, a two-time Olympic medalist and my best friend during my slalom racing days.

The Main Salmon is primarily a Class III section, and this year the water is high. This means not a lot of rocks but lots of

Bad Risk and Good Risk (2018–2020)

big waves, and a few monstrously large hydraulics to avoid. Since I am rowing one of the gear boats, I will have to rely on Dana or one of her family of world-class kayakers to help guide Seth into the rapids on his riverboard.

Dana is skeptical at first of taking on this role; she's cut from the same cloth as me and relies on paddles and high-performance kayaks to navigate whitewater. Above one of the biggest rapids, when I say I don't think Seth needs to go in the raft, she is clearly nervous for him.

I know from reading the guidebook that there are big holes on the right and left in this section, but the wave train in the center is clean. I go first, and from my perch in my fourteen-foot cataraft, I can easily see the line between the two holes. However, the rapid is located on a turn in the river, which means you have to enter it on the smooth tongue of current with a hard left-to-right angle in order to navigate through cleanly.

I yell to Lisa, my passenger, to point to the right, so Dana in her kayak and Seth on his riverboard know how to line up in the tongue.

Unfortunately, because Lisa is facing me in the raft, she points to her right—my left.

Dana and Seth begin paddling and kicking in completely the wrong direction, toward a monstrous hydraulic that could easily swallow a fourteen-foot raft, much less a little ten-year-old on a riverboard.

"No, no!" I scream at Lisa. "Point the other direction, to your left, your left!"

Lisa jumps up and waves her arm furiously, pointing to the correct line. Dana expertly pivots her slalom kayak and paddles with Olympic form to get back on course. To my relief, I see Seth also spin his board right behind her, kicking furiously, and effortlessly skim over the water behind Dana to enter the tongue right on course.

RISK

Entering the first wave, he disappears from view. But at the top of each exploding six-foot rooster tail wave, he and his board fly almost entirely out of the water toward the sky before disappearing again into the next trough. Listening to his hoots of joy, I can feel the adrenaline and endorphins that I know are coursing through his bloodstream. He is at one with the river, feeling the force and flow of the water all over his body.

Again, I marvel at his comfort in the wild water of the river. I still remember vividly the terrifying unplanned swims I experienced when I was his age, in conditions much less challenging than these.

This is what I wanted him to develop an addiction for: the pleasure of adventurous play. Focused on and immersed in the powerful elements within nature. Gathering the knowledge and skills to take good risk. To learn how to safely push his boundaries in nature, to experience the joy, the exhilaration.

Throughout the week, I watch Seth absorb the magic of the river while building sandcastles on the beach, riverboarding through waves, and sleeping on a tarp under a cool blanket of stars on the sandy beach, still warm from the day's sun. In a time when the world is in the grips of a global pandemic, this blissful week of adventure and peace is grounding for us. Here, we get to be separate from that reality for at least a little while, albeit with more rigorous hand washing and hand sanitizing than usual.

I don't know yet how Seth will one day use his time on the river, oceans, and mountains with me to navigate life on his own. But I hope that the cumulative experience of having engaged in good risk all his life will provide a solid foundation for him—one that will keep him from becoming "at risk."

In a world where the perils of climate change, social media and technology overload, and a global pandemic seem to be making life riskier every day, our wilderness adventures in the natural world feel like a relatively safe place to be.

Epilogue

In 2017, a few months before I retired from the US Forest Service, I presented Lisa with an ultimatum. Again on a dog walk, our best forum for difficult communications, I told her that I thought Seth and I should move in with her, and if she did not want to do that, we should break off our relationship.

If that sounds crazy and desperate, that pretty much describes the state of mind I was in after having parented Seth mainly on my own for the previous two years.

Logistically, it would have been easy for Lisa to say no. Even though we were married, it had always been important to both of us to maintain our independence and individuality in our relationship. We owned separate homes, kept most of our finances apart, and had always given each other the freedom to pursue passions the other was not interested in without guilt.

I would not have blamed Lisa if she had said no. She was terrified of the chaos Seth and I would bring into her home, and there would be nowhere to escape to. Photographing wild horses galloping around her in the desert wasn't nearly so scary.

But by the end of that conversation, we'd agreed upon a compromise. I'd rent out my house, and we would try it for a year.

Seth and I lived in Lisa's home north of Lake Tahoe for six years. In 2022, when Seth entered the seventh grade, he and I moved back to my house in South Lake Tahoe—but the three of us are still a family.

RISK

I'm not sure how I would have survived motherhood during Seth's elementary school years without Lisa's support.

I still constantly battle my impatient and controlling tendencies to avoid unhealthy and unproductive battles with my son. As he has exploded into puberty (he is now fifteen), our conflicts have become more intense because now he is a crazy man-child. Testosterone is a potent and occasionally toxic substance.

Fortunately, our conflicts are also much rarer these days, and we have more productive conversations afterward when we have both calmed down.

Seth and I will have to work for the rest of our lives to control our edgy natures. We continue to get easily frustrated, impatient, or angry, especially when tired. But we also want to resolve our conflicts just as quickly, and we still always hug each other before saying good night.

Seth is also discovering his own grounding path through his passion for music and martial arts. He continues to enjoy our time on the river and has become a notably competent oar raft and paddle rafting captain. But it is clear he will also be traveling other avenues toward joy and resiliency.

Childhood trauma cannot be swept under the table, and it often takes a lifetime of intention to not let it adversely affect the quality of your life or those around you. Although I have examined this stuff closely through the perspective of my family's personal history, as I've gotten older I have also become ever more aware of how world events disrupt the lives of thousands of children worldwide every day. The damage is real and will require collective awareness for individual and societal healing.

The next time you are around a child who is not easy, I encourage you to take a moment to consider why this might be and how you can help guide them away from their undesirable behavior. I am incredibly grateful for the adults in my life who

Epilogue

"get it" and have helped support my son and me in our less attractive moments.

I have provided suggested resources on this topic at the end of this page. There is a wealth of information on the internet, and many schools and local government family services agencies provide helpful resources for free. However, I must also acknowledge that for many underserved populations, these resources are overwhelmed. So, please support state and local bonds that pay for these programs. I promise you that we will all be better off if they are available.

A long time ago, I accepted that success in life, whether at work, in sports, or in personal relationships, requires good hard work, and that it is best to embrace the process and then savor the resulting joy. Lisa, Seth, and I continually struggle to overcome the molehills. But so far, we are still climbing the mountain together, one step at a time.

Helpful Resources

https://parentproject.com/loving-solutions

https://www.nctsn.org/what-is-child-trauma/trauma-types/complex-trauma/effects

https://childmind.org/article/how-trauma-affects-kids-school

https://www.verywellmind.com/what-are-the-effects-of-childhood-trauma-4147640

Acknowledgements

I started writing this memoir the first year after I retired from the US Forest Service, in a revisionist writing workshop led by Karen Terrey of Tangled Roots Writing in Truckee, California. In our first session, one of the women best articulated the group's feedback on my first 3,000-word submission: "Your story is fascinating, but . . . it kinda reads like a scientific paper." Which is what I was very good at writing after working as a hydrologist for 27 years.

Over the course of almost five years, slowly and caringly, this group of women helped me learn the art and craft of creative writing. Thank you, Karen, Elise, Meghan, Peggy, Melissa, Shannon, and Priya, for sharing your work, talent, and insights. Working with other writers to collectively improve our craft has been one of my life's most rewarding and energizing experiences.

As almost every author would agree, my book was significantly enhanced by the talent of my editors, Brooke Warner and Krissa Lagos. Their guidance and expertise have been instrumental in helping me tell the story that truly matters.

Thanks to Caroline and Colleen for believing in me as a writer and a human and sharing quality time outdoors and in conversation. I also want to thank my sisters by water, too many to name, who, throughout various points of our lives, have shared our common love of rivers, oceans, and paddle sport. You know who you are and what I am talking about.

RISK

And finally, I would like to thank my son Seth, who, although he thinks I would make a lot more money if I wrote a children's book, said it's okay if I write about him, as long as it's true and I say I am proud of him. Which I am, big man, I am.

Author Biography

At age two, I was introduced to whitewater while canoeing in the Ozarks with my family. Thus began a lifelong journey with the river, working, exploring, competing worldwide, and winning National and World Championship titles as a member of the U.S. Slalom Kayak Team and the U.S. Women's Whitewater Rafting Team.

I began writing my memoir soon after retiring from a hydrology career with the US Forest Service in Lake Tahoe and while learning how to be a first-time parent after becoming the legal guardian of my four-year-old nephew at age 57.

RISK is not just a memoir, it's a testament to resilience. It is the story of how I used the lessons learned from the river to confront the effects of childhood trauma, both for myself and my nephew.

My future writing will continue to focus on the joy and power of immersion in wild sport in wild environments to build the resiliency, strength, and grounding for facing life's inevitable losses and challenges.

I live in Lake Tahoe with my son/nephew Seth, my partner Lisa, and our two dogs.

Looking for your next great read?

We can help!

Visit www.shewritespress.com/next-read
or scan the QR code below for a list
of our recommended titles.

She Writes Press is an award-winning
independent publishing company founded to
serve women writers everywhere.